# NOT LESS THAN
# EVERYTHING

# NOT LESS THAN EVERYTHING

*Catholic Writers on*
*Heroes of Conscience from*
*Joan of Arc to Oscar Romero*

EDITED BY

## Catherine Wolff

HarperOne
*An Imprint of* HarperCollins*Publishers*

HarperOne

HarperCollins books may be purchased for educational, business, or sales promotional use. For information, please e-mail the Special Markets Department at SPsales@harpercollins.com.

HarperCollins website: http://www.harpercollins.com

HarperCollins®, ♦®, and HarperOne™ are trademarks of HarperCollins Publishers

FIRST EDITION

Library of Congress Cataloging-in-Publication Data
Not less than everything : Catholic writers on heroes of conscience from Joan of Arc to Oscar Romero / edited by Catherine Wolff. — 1st ed.
p. cm.
ISBN 978–0–06–222373–9
1. Catholics—Biography. 2. Catholic authors. I. Wolff, Catherine, 1952–editor of compilation.
BX4651.3.N68     2013
282.092'2—dc21     2012033660

13  14  15  16  17     RRD(C)     10  9  8  7  6  5  4  3  2  1

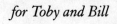

*for Toby and Bill*

*Cor ad cor loquitur—Heart speaks to heart.*

—JOHN HENRY NEWMAN

# CONTENTS

# Contents

## Contents

# Contents

# INTRODUCTION

This book has been a long time coming. I grew up in a Catholic family in San Francisco during the 1950s and '60s, when it seemed like everybody was Catholic: Irish or Filipino or Italian or Mexican. Catholicism was the medium in which my five siblings and I thrived.

Our family was well educated, staffed by Jesuits, devout. But we were not unquestioning. We had books by Teilhard de Chardin and John Courtney Murray in the house along with *The Imitation of Christ*. We were never told we had to believe in something "just because." We were brought up to explore ideas freely. There was no contradiction between questioning and faith; indeed questioning was how we made sense of faith, how we made it our own.

It was also the time of Vatican II, the great council called by Pope John XXIII to throw open the windows of the Church, to read the signs of the times, in effect to come to terms with modernity. There was a tangible sense of hope that things were changing—the Church that seemed increasingly rigid and authoritarian even to faithful Catholics was reaching out to us and to the wider world. That optimism sustained us through many changes both in the Church and in society. But we have come to a time when the promise of Vatican II is being subverted by those who would nullify or thwart many of its reforms. Catholics today harbor grave concerns about the state of our Church.

It's a long list. Most discouraging are the twin scandals of clergy sex abuse and malfeasance on the part of bishops covering it up. A lack of transparency and accountability in financial matters has led to a fresh series of scandals, reaching into the Vatican itself. In the United States, bishops are intervening in politics and public policy in ways that violate prudent boundaries while refusing to welcome women into full membership and leadership in the Church or to address the retrograde, even ignorant teachings on human sexuality. Church leaders show no interest in making changes in Church governance that would bring about more participation by the laity and a greater sense of collegiality representative of the magnificent diversity of the global Church. The hierarchy, in some cases inept or corrupt, is increasingly isolated from those it claims to lead.

These problems undermine the ability of the Church to mediate faith for its members, with all that entails: preaching the gospel, fostering a community of faith, establishing moral guidelines in response to the legitimate demands of the society in which we live.

The task of remaining within the Church today is a difficult one for me. I'm not speaking of having doubts about the essential tenets of the gospel—for some reason I have never experienced those, and I am truly thankful for that. However, I am continuously appalled by the behavior of many of those who claim authority over me and over the practice of my faith. To what extent is anyone required to submit to those in authority who have seriously compromised themselves and others? To what extent do such figures even hold legitimate authority? I yearn for other spiritual leaders.

———

Where better to look than the communion of saints? The Catholic cosmos is crowded not only by those present but also by those who have gone before. As Saint Augustine said, it should not seem a small thing to us that we are members of the same body as these. Theologian Elizabeth Johnson, who has explored for contemporary Catholics our communion with the "friends of God and prophets," writes that "their adventure of faith opens a way for us," that we together form "an ongoing river of companions seeking God."

In the early days of Christianity, people felt closely connected to others who had paid a great price, even death, for professing their faith. They experienced sustaining companionship with those beyond the grave. Later, as the Church took on characteristics of the Roman system, saints became patrons and intercessors.

In the paintings of the nativity and other biblical scenes, starting in the early Renaissance, you'll see saints in prayerful attendance. They are engaged in *sacra conversazione*— sacred conversation. Sometimes you'll see a little donor or two as well, but the saints possess power to put in a good word for us, dramatizing a relationship that transcends time and space, that requires a leap of faith into the unknowable.

Many Catholics think of saints as companions and hold a much broader sense of who a saint is than those who have been formally canonized. Since the twelfth century, canonization has been carried out exclusively under papal authority, resulting in a group that is lopsidedly male, celibate, clerical, or aristocratic. Most of us have our own unofficial list of saints: people whose unusual courage and grace we have witnessed; people whose stories have been reverently handed down, like that of Hildegard von Bingen. (Wonderfully enough, as we were working on this collection, which includes an essay on Hildegard by her sister Benedictine Joan Chittister, Pope Benedict XVI inscribed Hildegard into the catalog of saints.)

Many of these official or unofficial saints have been in situations similar to our own in Church history. They have spoken or acted in ways that challenged the prevailing authorities, knowing they risked reputation, livelihood, sometimes their heads—all while remaining faithful. How did they do it? Why did they not just leave the Church or go on to another calling? What disposed them to dissent while remaining faithful to principles, to community? What was the source of their strength? What were the predicaments they found themselves in, what records do we have of their responses? And most important, what can they teach us?

---

I wondered if I could write a book on such people and sought advice from Father Jim Martin, S.J., author *of My Life with the Saints*. He thought it was a great idea but said it would take me the rest of my life! So I asked writers I know through my husband, Tobias Wolff, and theologians I know through my late brother, William Spohn, to write essays about individuals whose experience spoke to them, whose witness they valued. They in turn led me to others who might contribute to the collection.

I had no program of my own about which figures to include. I sought the engagement of writers whose intelligence and wisdom I trusted with heroes of conscience whose experience had touched them. In fact, most of the authors already had such models, such companions, and they responded warmly to the chance to write about them.

Our hope is that this collection will appeal not only to Catholics troubled about their Church but to a wider audience. The essays deal with near-universal themes of the conflict between conscience and authority, of how we learn from others, of what it means to be a member of a community while in tension with that community. We believe that these accounts will resonate in many areas of human endeavor: science, art, politics.

As I gathered these essays, their authors mentored and inspired me. Along with their subjects they form a small band in that communion of saints on which I increasingly rely for my sense of belonging in the Church today.

The authors are contemporary journalists, novelists, scholars, poets. The women and men they celebrate are to be found throughout the course of Christian history, from Jesus's time to our own. The interplay between writer and subject yields a distinctive tone in each essay—from the scholarly to the poetic, the historical to the personal. Indeed, several authors found that their essays took an unexpected turn under the influence of the person they chose to encounter.

Some write of friends and mentors: Charles Curran on Bernard Häring, Ann Patchett on Charles Strobel. Some recount profound personal experiences, such as Tom Beaudoin's faith journey conducted through Ignatius's *Spiritual Exercises*. Some let the subject's story speak for itself, as in Bo Caldwell's lyrical narrative of the life of Henry Bartel.

In a deft twist on the theme of faithful dissent, Lisa Cahill demonstrates that the traditional image of Mary Magdalene represents a subversion of the strong, independent, faithful woman who has emerged through modern scholarship. Mary Magdalene as seductress was more useful to those who manipulated her reputation than Mary Magdalene, Apostle to the Apostles.

The saints have always been used as projections for political or personal purposes. In thinking about my own patron saint, Catherine of Siena, I looked at several accounts of her life.

One is a chapter in *Heroines of Christ,* published in 1949 by a group of Jesuits (one of them an uncle of mine, Joe Costelloe, S.J.). Catherine is portrayed there in cloying, saccharine terms: not just her piety and visions, but her habits of extreme fasting, self-mortification, her rejection of married life, her campaign to persuade Pope Gregory XI to move the papal court back to Rome from Avignon. In this version it all goes quite smoothly, and then she dies surrounded by her friends.

The author clearly makes the case for a particular kind of asceticism—there is no hint that some of this behavior might be pathological—and also emphasizes the primacy of Rome in Church politics.

Another account, from the 1990s, is by Mary Ann Sullivan of the Blue Army of Our Lady of Fatima, a pious, traditionalist organization. She describes Catherine's letters as "shocking the reader into reality." Indeed, "she sometimes broke with polite convention," as when she rebuked three cardinals as "flowers who shed no perfume, but stench that makes the whole world reek."

However, we are cautioned not to imitate Catherine in her strong words, for Catherine's calling was unique to her, one described by Pope Paul VI as her "charism of exhortation."

Finally, there is a moving, indeed disturbing chapter on Catherine by Kathryn Harrison in *Tremors of Bliss,* published in the mid–1990s. It's intensely personal, weaving into the saint's story an account of the author's emotionally starved childhood and the scrupulosity and anorexia that nearly ruined her health. Harrison does not downplay Catherine's pathology; she enables us to understand it through the drama that played out in her own life.

But she does not dismiss Catherine's experience nor her sanctity. Harrison says that she has tried to distance herself from faith, but has found that she cannot *not believe.* She has healed to the point where she understands her behavior, but recognizes that she will never understand the mysterious working of her faith.

These different accounts of Catherine demonstrate how a saint's story can be told through very different perspectives to very different effect. Nevertheless, what comes through clearly in all of them is that Catherine could be a difficult person to deal with.

And truth to tell, many saints, and those figures chosen for their inspiration by the writers in the book, would make us downright uncomfortable—not only because their worldviews and their readings of the faith might be different from our own, not because the expressions of their faith, the things their faith led them to do, might seem odd or foolhardy, but because they seem to feel no obligation to observe the social conventions the rest of us rely on.

At best they have what Elizabeth Johnson calls "uncanny integrity." They see through a lens of great moral clarity, and their passionate motivation serves as leaven to the rest of us.

We love to tell their stories. There are times when it is a comfort to rely on them to light for us a path they have already traveled. Indeed, when a Protestant friend once wished me a Happy All Saints' Day, he said he knew he wasn't supposed to believe in talking to dead people "like you Catholics," but he found himself doing it anyway.

---

We are social beings, living in community, and we learn from others. We use patterns of behavior that we observe and internalize to figure out what to do when faced with a new situation. This is very different from learning to behave according to rules, useful as they may be.

Think of the parable of the Good Samaritan from Luke. In answer to the question from an expert in law about who his neighbor is, Jesus recounts the story of a man beaten and abandoned. He is ignored by priest and Levite but rescued and restored by the Samaritan. The lawyer acknowledges the Samaritan, the one who had mercy, as the model neighbor, and Jesus then says simply, "Go and do likewise."

In his book *Go and Do Likewise,* William Spohn emphasizes that the mandate is not "Go and do exactly the same" as the Samaritan. The term *likewise* implies that Christians should be faithful to the story yet creative in applying it to their contexts.

There are certainly times when Jesus lays down a rule. We are never to harm children; we are ever to care for the poor. But most of the time Jesus teaches in parables and by example. Both require thought and imagination. We must learn to *spot the rhyme* between the teaching and our own circumstances and act accordingly.

The concept of discipleship is helpful here: obedience to external commands is never enough. Our behavior, our motivation, our identity should reflect the teachings and the example of the one we are following. The writers in this book may not be disciples of their subjects, but each demonstrates a fascination and a deep identification with her or his subject that goes beyond historical account or scholarly critique. They spot the rhyme between their subjects' lives and their own.

———————

Max Weber's definition of authority is useful here: ". . . the probability that certain specific commands from a given source will be obeyed by a given group of persons." The legitimacy of a leader's commands depends on the voluntary obedience of his followers. This principle has been sorely tested in today's Church.

In the fourth century, the alliance of the spiritual power of the Church with the temporal power of Rome developed into a partnership that dominated—some would say formed—Western European civilization. For centuries, prominent Italian families vied for power in the Church, with the aim of attaining the great wealth and influence that went with it. During the Inquisition, religious and civil authorities operated hand in glove to root out their perceived enemies. In those days you could lose your life for speaking up, or for just being different in the wrong way.

There have been efforts to establish a different kind of Church governance than that of the papacy as a sacred monarchy, which was well established by the twelfth century. In the early 1400s, the Council of Constance called for conciliarism, but the reforms were never carried out. Catholics today are still subject to a monarchical authority that continues to oppose democratic principles in Church governance. Those of us who live in modern democracies, flawed as they may be, cherish our ideals of individual freedom, human rights, and self-government. Indeed, these were affirmed in the documents of the Second Vatican Council. Yet papal power has been strengthened through centralization, the influence of the worldwide body of bishops has waned, and the laity has almost no power to effect doctrine, policy, or change.

There persists within the Church hierarchy a tendency to command and control rather than to teach and inspire, as we have seen with the removal of progressive bishops and the censure of theologians and American women religious. It is tragic that a faithful Christian is forced to live in fear rather than in hope.

If members of the Church hierarchy wish to reestablish their authority, I would suggest that they lead exemplary lives: adopt simplicity in dress and language, cultivate humility, listen to members of the Church in ways that enable them to imagine themselves in the other person's shoes, and demonstrate loving justice in what they say and in what they do.

---

Conscience takes precedence over authority, not the other way around. Thomas Aquinas said that it is better to perish in excommunication than to violate one's conscience. And Joseph Ratzinger, in his commentary on the documents of Vatican II, wrote that "one's own conscience . . . must be obeyed before all else, even if necessary against the requirement of ecclesiastical authority." Yet this exercise of individual conscience has long been a source of vexation for Church authorities, who tend to insist that their doctrinal and moral insights are to be given primacy by the faithful over those that may arise in their own minds and hearts.

And yet we hold dear our right to think for ourselves. In matters of faith and morals, we no longer obey teachings without understanding them, and we can't be scared into obedience.

The philosopher Charles Taylor writes that the Church must recognize the right of every Christian to exercise his or her judgment in applying the gospel to moral or political circumstances, and the right to be included in the great conversation from which the authoritative sense of the faithful emerges.

This great conversation has not yet come to pass, but it is my hope that the writers in this book may serve as an inspiration. Their celebration of saints official and unofficial is eloquent testimony to their appreciation for all that is good in the Church. We hold out hope, and that very hope is our pathway toward those who go before.

# CURATED FREE FALL

## IGNATIUS OF LOYOLA

*Tom Beaudoin*

SOME TWENTY YEARS AGO, in Kansas City, Missouri, I was on a religious quest in young adulthood, trying to reconnect with the Catholicism of my youth while tasting other religious fruits. The beginning of my attempt to reconstruct my faith was playing in a Christian rock band sponsored by a Pentecostal church. In that band, the women outnumbered the men, and as I look back, women were crucial traveling companions on my quest, although I never dated Catholics. Protestants, Jews, agnostics, atheists, yes. A Jewish girlfriend challenged me that I knew nothing about Jesus if I had not been to Israel and studied the Torah. So I traveled to Israel, hoping that getting close to the monotheistic "source" would help me figure out what was true about religion as much as which religion was true. Two other girlfriends took me to two different Southern Baptist churches (this was Missouri, remember), and I started to learn about the Bible and a personal Jesus. Just for good measure, my most influential professors in college were robust atheists. For a suburban Catholic, this was a lot of resorting in just a few years. A new stage of my religious education was underway, but I was confused about where this left my Catholicism.

The religious part of my life has for a long time been complemented by the rock-and-roll part. The conclusion of my childhood years as an altar boy was the commencement of my adolescent membership in mail-order tape clubs that shipped me cassettes and music posters every month. Hard rock and pop was the common language of my middle-class white suburban friends. I took up the electric bass in high school and began living with an identity strung between Church and boom box. A fellow altar boy gave me my first rock album in grade school, by Kiss (rumored to be a Satanic band). Catholic boys seemed to have a particular weakness for rock and roll. By the time we had grown up and were testing our Catholic roots, I was getting much more deeply into rock culture: attending concerts, collecting music, dressing rockishly. After getting hassled for playing "worldly" music in my Christian band, I left that group and turned toward "secular" rock and roll with increasing energy.

Religion and music were becoming my dual obsessions. A few weeks before I was to start graduate theological studies, I went to the Woodstock '94 festival in New York, along with three hundred thousand other people, to endure torrential rain, dozens of bands, and overpriced everything. The preparation for my intensive study of sacred theology was a profane weekend of casual drug use and disinhibited living, caked in mud. Not long after, freshly showered, ready to rediscover my

Catholicism, pulled along by restless and searching desires for women, music, and God, I met Ignatius of Loyola.

I was enrolled at Harvard Divinity School in Cambridge, Massachusetts, but immediately started taking classes at the nearby Weston Jesuit School of Theology. The Jesuits, a Catholic religious order founded by Ignatius, were among my first teachers in graduate school. A Jesuit professor began my first ethics class by posing three questions that Ignatius raised in his *Spiritual Exercises:* "What have I done for Christ?" "What am I doing for Christ?" "What ought I to do for Christ?" This Catholic priest sounded like the Pentecostals and Baptists with whom I had prayed and played! I was ready, eager, to find the paradox compelling: a highly educated Jesuit placing our studies in the context of an almost childlike devotion and personal service to Christ.

This was the beginning of a series of references to Ignatius in my theological education (which later continued at the Jesuit-sponsored Boston College), and I soon picked up his famous retreat handbook, *The Spiritual Exercises,* and later read his *Autobiography* and other writings from his many letters, as well as notes on some of his mystical experiences in the *Spiritual Diary.*

I learned that he, too, had been on a (considerably more dramatic) quest. Ignatius had been born into a relatively well-off Basque family in the late fifteenth century and was brought up to excel in matters of the royal court, arms, and women. While recovering from a war wound that left him with a permanently disabled leg, he began to redefine his life in imitation of the saints, in the service no longer of a worldly but a heavenly king. This turn caused him to thoroughly reassess himself, and he spent the rest of his life sculpting himself through struggles with his own desires for authority and for the company of women, among other things. He doggedly pursued God's will, which he believed could be apprehended with the help of ascetic practices, through proper attention to God's influence on the individual. He did not think of the spiritual life as the exploratory and open-ended personal quest that I had undertaken; for Ignatius, Church authority was worthy of deference (although he sought many times to sidestep it, and he felt the capricious, fearsome hand of the Inquisition on several occasions).

Feeling little compulsion to repeat the half-millennium-old contents of his life, it was the restless, reckless, and inventive style of his search that captivated me. I could identify with his calling himself "pilgrim." He was on the move throughout his life, on the trail of the next step in a deepening vocation to serve God, willing to redefine his next move when plans did not pan out. Even when he founded the Jesuits, he tried to get out of leading them. I also identified with the importance of women in his life. His mother died when he was young, and he was sent to a foster mother for a time. His young adulthood was apparently replete with erotic adventures, perhaps providing material for the many confessions he later felt compelled to give. His recovery from war was helped along by his lovely sister-in-law. It was her religious books that he found so engrossing. He had many women patrons over the years and a particular dedication to the dignity and propriety of women, with a special interest in the care of prostitutes. He was even persuaded by some influential women to let them take Jesuit vows. What did these important relationships with women mean for this famous saint? The riddle I sensed emerging in his own life could, I hope, help me unriddle my own existence.

I turned to read his *Spiritual Exercises* and discovered that they were not meant to be "read" but to be lived through, ideally on retreat, in order to foster closeness to God and to encourage wise life decisions. Still, I could not help myself. Plunging in, I was compelled by the graphic psychedelia of his imaginative meditations, interspersed with intensely earnest prescriptions for self-examination. The basic idea of his spiritual program is to do whatever helps to overcome your "inordinate attachments"—crazy-making cravings—so that you are more free to serve the "king." To do this requires a curated free fall into our own soul by way of meditations that are vivid, imaginative adventures, like: Picture hell, imagine what the souls there are going through, and think about all the reasons you deserve to be there; imagine Christ on the cross and strike up a conversation with him on "whatever comes to your mind"; imagine scenes from the Bible and insert yourself into them. Do you want to take the part of Mary, the disciples, of Jesus, of a bystander, or of an animal, rock, or tree? Fill in the missing dialogue and feelings. He treats the scriptures as a Montessori space: What draws you in? Take time with that until your savor is sated, he counsels. Through this indirect approach to your own depths, which you should only undertake with a trusted spiritual guide, your superficial desires for yourself will not prove satisfying, and your deeper desires for your life will surface. Through such spiritual exercises, Ignatius believed, God is drawing you forward toward greater conformity to the divine will.

You can only go down this road with Ignatius if you think that what is natural about our human desires is permanently suspended in some untamed and untamable sacred beyond. We can then press through every experience to find God excluded from no experience. And this is so in a way that is radically particular to the individual: God and the person have to deal directly with each other. I embraced this about his Catholicism: a man learning to befriend his fantasies, dreams, wishes, imaginings, and feelings. It was as if retreat time, or even the time spent reading Ignatius's work, which for attentive readers could be a retreat of its own, was a liminal space in which one's rococo inner world of delights and disgusts could be acknowledged, and maybe welcomed, as a weaker or stronger part of the "yes" that we are accumulating over the course of our lives in our journey to God.

Both Ignatius and rock and roll were giving me a menu for self-examination, were using their own techniques to teach me spiritual exercises, making me ask, What am I and what could I become? What is real in my life? What are my desires? What is the space between my desires and my reality? How do I conform myself more fully to what is real? What does that imply for my desires?

To live with these questions is the meaning of the ancient term *asceticism*. Ignatius helped me connect the *askesis* I had found in rock culture—the peculiar way that identity and desires are worked over, indirectly, through sensory-rich musical experience—to the *askesis* of Catholic culture, where identity and desires could be worked over, indirectly, through sensory-rich meditations.

For Ignatius, the way to make progress is to come to terms

with "inordinate desire," overinvestment in things that keep you from living with and for what is ultimately real. The good "spiritual exerciser" lives with the hope of being indifferent, where indifference means a lack of debilitating grasping at what one needs to be the case. And this indifference is not only toward the world, but to one's own life, so that one can learn to live more and more in transition, in translation. This is what Ignatius commends in his famous "Suscipe" prayer, in which he surrenders to God "all my liberty, my memory, my understanding, and my entire will." Everything about oneself can be handed over as transient material—not because our lives do not matter, but because their mattering is not restricted to our own awareness alone.

Do I need to add that this way of finding Ignatius was also my own projection? I do not know how to come to a saint or any other revered figure apart from the process of discovering why I am drawn toward or away from her or him. And it seems that the investment we make in saints is always a matter of our need for new ways of both sealing off and opening up our lives. In fact, saints were never an important part of my life. Even after meeting Ignatius, he remained a friendly resource rather than a constant companion. To indulge much more than that seemed to risk superstition or a naive reliance on childhood wishes for magical beings. But I was warm enough on Ignatius, and my attraction to him helped me imagine myself as his postmodern avatar, allowing me to keep my Catholic background and my Dionysian tendencies corralled in this man I could admire.

Ignatius's *Autobiography* and his *Spiritual Diary* are both records of his experiences of sensing God and are replete with accounts of what he took to be God's direct and consoling intervention in his life. This often made him cry. Sometimes it made him see visions or learn something so deep he could not articulate it. Occasionally he heard a specific message. But he also knew that not every experience that felt like a revelation from God was to be trusted. This led him to develop ways of probing his experience. He would consult trusted mentors. He would pay attention to the effect of the experience: Did it issue in states and behaviors that were too small for him? Did it result in increased faith, hope, and love, or "consolation"? Did it attune him more firmly toward service of God? Did it cohere with how God had dealt with him before? Was his conscience clear enough to be able to discern in the first place? This kind of deep attention to self, which many now associate more with the therapy hour than with religion, is one of the great contributions of Ignatius's life that has stood the test of time.

Such ways of discernment, which I was learning from Ignatius, sat alongside the art and science of interpretation, called "hermeneutics," that was a large part of my theological education. Hermeneutics arose in almost every class in graduate school, and its embrace has been one hallmark of Catholic theology since the Second Vatican Council. Hermeneutics, in theology, means the practice of making sense of complicated texts, like the Bible, official teachings, or the writings of theologians. Most of the Catholic theological battles in the past several decades have been over which hermeneutic—which interpretive lens—is most faithfully Catholic. Because it is widely accepted in theology today that we do not know anything apart from interpreting it—that there is no direct, unbiased access to the truth—the question then becomes which way of interpreting is most adequate. This is especially urgent because almost everything of interest to theology—doctrines, scripture verses, key theological phrases—is subject to debate. No theological claim enjoys universal agreement. So we work on our hermeneutics, arguing about how to make sense of texts.

There are many approaches to hermeneutics, but they boil down to three: holding texts and contemporary life and experience in a mutual dialogue; making certain texts (doctrines, scriptures) more important than contemporary experience; and making the tradition's texts answer to the pressing issues of our lives today. The debates go around and around, with each camp arguing that the others are not honoring something important, whether classical religious orthodoxy, urgent human concerns, or the notion of dialogue itself. The debates allow so many positions that it is easy to get caught up in them, to think that they explain a great deal about Catholicism, and thus to see Catholic theology today as caught up in a tremendous hermeneutical crisis.

As I made my way through these hermeneutical positions in graduate school and as a young professor, I was delighted to see the congruence between theological hermeneutics and Ignatian discernment. Both agreed that you have to interpret your way through the world in search of God and Truth. Nothing is directly as it seems. Reality is there, and you just have to make critical sense of "what is" in order to get to it. This convergence between Ignatius and academic theology was another reason for me to be held secure in the progressive Catholic identity into which Ignatius had helped me grow.

That identity worked for me until I sat a few feet away from a white-haired man who described being raped by a priest when he was an altar boy. This was in 2002, in Boston, at a meeting of a lay Catholic group called Voice of the Faithful, formed in response to the emerging round of sexual abuse revelations about to shock the United States anew and shake the Church profoundly. I read the daily accounts in the newspapers describing widespread, heartbreaking breaches of trust. Slowly, the details of the cover-up by bishops came out: priests shuffled around and victims silenced, with maintaining the appearance of sacred clerical power and holiness more important than children's lives. The children and teens abused were often my age-mates, kids from the 1970s and 1980s.

This was around the time I had begun teaching theology at the first of several Jesuit universities. As the scandal unfolded globally over the next several years, I came to question the overwhelmingly male, celibate governance structure of not only the Church but of Jesuit universities as well. University life helped me understand better the sexual abuse scandal. Jesuit (and other Catholic) universities often provide a relatively safe space for gay clerical culture. Safe—but furtive. Bounded by practiced circumspection, the gay priesthood is an open secret among most priests and faculty. The costs are profound: a double life for most gay priests who cannot officially be who they are, and all those who keep their secrets, who learn to associate protecting a holy institution with not telling the truth. The Catholic clerical closet has also made gay priests the scapegoats for the abuse crisis, despite the established absence of a link between homosexuality and child sexual abuse; few gay priests can speak out in their own defense without risking their priesthood by violating the Catholic Church's version of "Don't ask, don't tell."

I kept on my Catholic path, reading Jesuit theology and spirituality, zealously working in lay ministry with young adults, taking on a Jesuit spiritual director, and exploring deeper into Ignatius's life, even as I felt less certain where the Catholic Church was headed.

Meanwhile, over the years, I learned what studies confirm: that gay and straight priests sometimes are sexually active. However much sympathy one might be able to muster for individual priests or their partners, keeping this reality under wraps requires another layer of forced quiet. I started to see the connection between the silence, secrecy, and shame in the clerical culture and the Catholic Church's capacity to shut up and close ranks when priests abused children. I confess that it felt like a Catholic privilege for me, as a married layman, to be drawn into these tangles of clerical secret-keeping. I took my initiation into these secrets to mean that I was getting closer to the center of how Catholicism really worked. By blithely setting aside these confusing truths about my Church, I told myself that I was witnessing—and furthering—true pastoral concern for complex moral predicaments. But over time, protecting secrets seemed too often the paramount virtue. The preoccupation with secrecy validated that the dynamics of the abuse crisis are also there in Catholic university life, including an absence of women in power over men, a clinging to a sense of the priesthood as spiritually "special" and privileged, and a lack of understanding of the dynamics of family life with children.

Theologians find ways to endure these realities by falling back on hermeneutics. Whatever is going wrong in the Church must, it is thought, be an aberration from an otherwise pure Christian essence—an essence to be defended through a particular model of interpretation. We can interpret away whatever seems outmoded or benighted and interpret our way to what is liberating and modern. In these ways, many people who disagree with Catholic teachings are able to stay in the Church and even claim that they are closer to the essence of the Church than are Church leaders. I too was able to live like this until the tensions got so strong that I began to see hermeneutics as a potentially decadent way of Catholic intellectual life. By coming up with so many interpretations that were at such odds with how the Catholic Church functioned in most people's lives, I had been able to preserve the privileges of being thought of as a Catholic—even though I disagreed with such a substantial amount of what most people would take Catholicism to be.

I realized that hermeneutics was a way of keeping thinking Catholics inside the Catholic game. While interpretation will always have its place in any theology, the importance of hermeneutics in Catholic theology today is a sign that the Church cannot tell the truth about itself, that the Church draws far too much of its energy from its silences.

I realized that by publicly identifying as a Catholic, I received "benefits" (a religious status, access, connections) that were possible only through a remarkably widespread nexus of male secrecy, grounded in the sexual shame involved in mandatory celibacy and premodern claims to sacred power. Did I want to benefit any longer from being thought of as a member of this religious community? Did I want to claim a religious identity predicated on long-expired and still destructive treatment toward women, toward out gay men and lesbians, toward children?

The answer was already there and had been building for years: to keep growing, I had to leave, to twist away from the Catholic Church. Ignatius had taught me to be honest about my own discernment and to consent to the uncontrollable spiritual future announced by my own intimate pilgrimage toward God or some better reality. Beginning to imagine a "yes" bigger than Catholicism gave me hope and seemed to fit as a next step. It would require overcoming my "inordinate desire" to be affiliated with Catholicism, to be known and respected as a Catholic. By trusting what I had learned from Ignatius, I had effectively graduated from the Catholic Church.

I then found myself back at the desk with Ignatius. If I could not interpret my way toward staying Catholic, I could still sift carefully through Ignatius's life and teachings in light of my own pilgrimage. From the far side of my forty years as a Catholic, the greater part of his wisdom, for me, has been his dedication to placing the creative and discerning exercise of imagination among the chief spiritual works. Perhaps because I am a musician, I respect the beauty of form, and I take the form of Ignatius's insights to be of deep consequence. By that, I mean that the shape of Ignatius's dynamism for chasing down what God might be about, by way of spiritual exercises, remains of incomparable value for our post–Catholic era. In this form of radical spirituality—exercises of the imagination that render one more available to consenting to an essentially uncontrollable future—I take Ignatius to be teaching about the importance of permanent transition as essential to the spiritual life. This transition is perpetual discernment, regular disorientation by a call from beyond.

Ignatius was trying to inculcate a radical freedom for God. But for me, the radical freedom that he began to dream through his exercises pitches itself beyond Christianity, not disposing with Jesus Christ, but placing Christ in the pantheon of teachers who can give life today. Indeed, my priority now, with and beyond Ignatius, is being converted to life. I am just one of millions of Catholics—I mean post-Catholics—who found a way through and beyond Catholicism with the help of Catholicism itself. While this might have been deeply disappointing to Ignatius, I have come to see my Catholic exit as a generous legacy of his powerful life and writings.

# APOSTLE TO
# THE APOSTLES

## MARY MAGDALENE

⬿⬿⬿⬿

*Lisa Sowle Cahill*

N OT LESS THAN EVERYTHING" brilliantly characterizes Mary Magdalene, one of Jesus's first apostles, whose life has come down to us through a distorted vision in which she is depicted as a repentant prostitute. Who was Mary Magdalene, really? What do we know of her life? Can she serve as a model of Christian witness today?

Let us begin with the better-known if less authentic Mary. A seventeenth-century oil painting, *The Penitent Magdalene* (by Giovanni Gioseffo dal Sole), is a typical portrait. Mary Magdalene gazes at a crucifix, representing Jesus suffering for our sins. From her dolorous expression, she appears mindful of her own misdeeds, and as if to recall for us what these were, she is bare breasted, with nothing but a cloth and her long flowing hair to cover her. The edge of one breast is visible. She wears the halo of a saint, but what is most striking is the implied sexual excess Mary has evidently left behind.

The flowing hair is a reminder that Mary Magdalene is often connected with another woman, who weeps over Jesus in the Gospel of Luke. During a dinner to which Jesus and friends have been invited at a Pharisee's house, a woman comes into the room, pours a jar of perfume on Jesus's feet, bathes them with her tears, kisses them, and dries them with her hair (Luke 7: 36–50). The evangelist Luke does not give the woman a name, saying only that she was from "the city" and was "a sinner." Parallel narratives appear in the other Gospels, varying in details. According to Matthew and Mark, an unidentified woman (not described as a sinner) pours a jar of "costly ointment" on Jesus's head while he is dining at the home of "Simon the leper" (Mark 14:1–9; Matt. 26:6–13). John's Gospel identifies this woman as Mary of Bethany and places the dinner at the house of her brother Lazarus, whom Jesus raised from the dead (12:1–8).

Despite any lack of explicit connection, the popular imagination has tied this vivid story with Mary Magdalene, naming her sin as prostitution and envisioning the loosened hair of Luke's version as a symbol of her sensuality and seductiveness. When I visited Israel and Palestine a few years ago, I went into a local crafts and souvenir shop in Bethlehem. One of the items for sale was a vial of perfume labeled "Spikenard Magdalena." On the attached card, the "woman and ointment" stories of Matthew, Mark, and Luke were quoted verbatim (in Latin), never noting that none of these mentions Mary Magdalene.

One contributing factor to the confusion surrounding Mary's identity is that Luke follows the ointment story with a new chapter, which he begins by noting that as Jesus traveled around Galilee proclaiming the good news of God's kingdom, his companions, along with "the twelve," were "some women who had been cured of evil spirits and some infirmities." Among these was "Mary, called Magdalene, from whom seven demons had gone out" (8:2). These women "provided for them [Jesus and disciples] out of their resources" (8:3).

Luke thus does identify "the real Mary" as a woman from whom Jesus had cast out seven demons. Yet, in the New Testament, demonic possession does not necessarily connote sin. There are accounts of Jesus casting demons out of people who seem clearly to have been mentally ill—for example, the man who lived and ran naked among the tombs; Jesus cast out his demons and restored him to normal behavior (Luke 8:26–27). Mary may have been suffering from some kind of mental or spiritual illness or undergoing some other kind of malady or trauma. We don't know for sure what demons represent, but there is no biblical basis for equating them with prostitution, adultery, promiscuity, or any behavior of a specifically sexual sort.

Some critics hypothesize that to call Mary demon-possessed might already have been a way to discredit her in the early Church rather than a historically accurate description. Yet more important than her possible history of demon possession is the fact that Mary was a dedicated patron of Jesus's mission and message. Women and men were traveling together in Jesus's entourage—the women apparently unaccompanied by male family members. This was highly unusual in first-century Mediterranean culture, whether Jewish, Greek, or Roman. It is an indication of changed relations among men and women in the community that formed around Jesus, a context that is important for understanding Mary's role as disciple and apostle. Feminist biblical scholar Elisabeth Schüssler Fiorenza hypothesizes that Jesus held out an ideal of a "discipleship of equals," as reflected in the early baptismal formula of Galatians 3:28: "There is no longer Jew or Greek, there is no longer slave or free, there is no longer male and female; for all of you are one in Christ Jesus." Mary exemplifies women's new status as partners with men in Jesus's eyes.

A related detail is that Mary was from Magdala (Migdal), a town on the western coast of the Sea of Galilee, known for its export of salted fish. Mary was an independent woman with disposable economic assets—possibly because she was involved in the fish trade, or because she was a widow. In any event, she, along with other women of some means, was a financial supporter of Jesus's mission to reform the people of Israel. She gave her resources to support Jesus and his message of solidarity and forgiveness for rich and poor, righteous and sinner, insider and outsider.

Another crucial mark of Mary's biblical identity is that she and other women were faithful to Jesus to the end, even after the male disciples had fled. The men no doubt feared meeting Jesus's fate, imprisoned or put to death as part of the Roman sweep of "dangerous" elements in the crowds swelling Jerusalem in the days leading up to Passover. The Passover feast attracted many Jews from the countryside to the Jerusalem Temple. Roman officials were on the lookout for disruptive and revolutionary elements who in the holy day rush and fervor might successfully foment an uprising. John's Gospel places Mary Magdalene at the foot of the cross, along with Jesus's mother and aunt (19:25). In Mark, Matthew, and Luke, Mary Magdalene, along with a few other women, watch from a short distance away. As Matthew reminds us, "They had followed Jesus from Galilee and had provided for him" (Matt. 27:55).

We know, according to the New Testament witness, that Mary Magdalene went with other women to perform for Jesus a religious ritual respecting the dead, a duty within the purview of women's customary responsibilities. The women went to the tomb on the third day after Jesus's death, when the sabbath had passed, to anoint his body with oils and spices. This leads to the most important fact about Mary Magdalene. All four Gospels portray her as one of the first witnesses to the resurrection. In at least two Gospels—Matthew and John—she sees Jesus before the male disciples John and Peter do.

John's Gospel has the most personal and striking account of Mary's interaction with the risen Jesus. As Mary weeps outside the tomb, Jesus appears, but she does not recognize him. When Jesus calls her by name—"Mary!"—his identity is clear. Yet Jesus instructs Mary not to cling to him; she has a mission. She is to go and tell his "brothers" the good news of the resurrection. John's Gospel uses the specific word *announced*: "Mary Magdalene went and announced to the disciples, 'I have seen the Lord'" (John 20:18). This word, in Greek, is of special significance; it is used of the apostles' mission to preach the gospel. Hence Mary Magdalene is an apostle by the same criteria as "the apostle Paul"—neither of them were one of "the twelve," but they both saw the risen Jesus and were sent by him to preach the gospel. Bernard of Clairvaux, a medieval theologian, called Mary Magdalene the Apostle to the Apostles. John Paul II in his letter on the dignity and vocation of women, *Mulieris Dignitatem,* calls her by the same title.

The tradition as a whole, however, has refused to concede to Mary her true role of exemplary faithfulness, commissioning, and leadership. A fateful source—though not the sole cause—of Mary's misinterpretation is a sixth-century sermon of Pope Gregory the Great. Gregory identifies the sinful woman in Mark and Luke with the Mary from whom devils were exorcised on the basis that the seven demons symbolize the seven capital vices; and, moreover, he infers egregiously that Mary had previously used the ointment she poured on Jesus "to perfume her flesh in forbidden acts"! Rather than a model apostle, Mary here becomes a reminder to women to repent of their wanton sexuality, "immolating" themselves in lives of penance and self-abnegation.

Of course, this portrait of Mary works very effectively to exclude women from positions of apostolic leadership in the Church, relegating women to traditional "feminine" roles and constraining women behind boundaries and barriers meant to contain their supposed unruliness, including the presumed threat they pose to male sexual self-control. In the case of Mary Magdalene (a case that is far from unique), female seductiveness is in reality a projection of male desires, fears, and denials, in truth symptomatic of a very un-Christlike desire to blame, dominate, and control.

There have been several modern attempts to elevate the

status of Mary Magdalene by making her Jesus's lover or wife instead of a temptress. In the 1970s, there was the rock opera *Jesus Christ Superstar*. And in 2003, Dan Brown's novel *The Da Vinci Code* declared Mary to be Jesus's wife and the mother of his children, a more positive role, to be sure, but one still stereotypically sexual. The Mary Magdalene of the New Testament is not described in sexual terms at all—whether promiscuous or chaste—but is simply the exemplary disciple of Jesus and even an apostle.

The "real biblical Mary" helps bring home a crucial aspect of the New Testament depiction of a holy life: it is not defined according to gender roles. Discipleship does not depend on family relationships (or rank or wealth), however significant those may be at a human level. A woman's status does not depend on being a "good wife" or "good mother." It depends, as for men, on faith and on following the will of God as proclaimed by Jesus. Here is where Mary excels.

Mary's status as a leader in the Christian community, as one who was especially close to and beloved of Jesus, comes through in some of the so-called apocryphal Christian literature dating from the first couple of centuries of Christian history. The literature that we now know as the New Testament was in the process of composition until the beginning of the second century C.E. What we know as the biblical "canon" consists of early Christian writings that were among the most widely used and were eventually deemed most authoritative, a process that continued into the fourth century. However, these were not the only writings. Lacking one definitive work or collection of works around which to remember Jesus, various local churches preserved and retold available versions of the Christian story that suited their own experiences, beliefs, and needs. While the majority of early noncanonical literature is now lost, several of the surviving documents mention Mary Magdalene.

Perhaps most significant among these is the early second century Gospel of Mary, of which only fragments survive. This is an interesting case, because it both presents Mary Magdalene in a unique apostolic role and is a "Gnostic" gospel. The world *gnostic* comes from the Greek *gnosis* or "knowledge." Christian Gnostics (there were also Greek Gnostic cults) believed that Jesus brings salvation by imparting a secret knowledge to a select few, an elite who by following him are able to transcend the world, the body, and humanity's lower nature, entering into a higher spiritual realm.

The Gospels, in contrast, portray a Jesus who brings good news to the lowly; who is dedicated to every poor person, sinner, lost sheep, and social reject; and who is so immersed in the world and its suffering that he is willing to go all the way to death on a cross in order to bring new life to all. So we must ask whether the Gospel of Mary was repressed, suppressed, or otherwise excluded from the canon because it promotes the primacy of women's leadership . . . or because the message Mary is depicted to convey is not the real message of the Jesus as remembered, we trust accurately, by Matthew, Mark, Luke, and John.

In the Gospel of Mary, Mary Magdalene has a vision of Jesus and receives secret teaching from him about how to achieve the freedom of the soul from entrapment in the material world. The apostle Andrew objects that this is "strange" teaching, while Peter accuses Mary of lying to gain status among the disciples! Shocked, Mary begins to cry. Levi defends Mary, reminding Peter of his notorious hot temper and advising everyone to quit quarreling and go out to preach the gospel.

While we may agree with Andrew that the content of the Gnostic Mary's teaching is decidedly off base, her Gospel is still a signal that Mary may have had more significance, and been accorded a greater leadership role, in this and other Christian circles whose literature is no longer known to us.

This suggests the possibility that Mary might have sisters among Christians seeking today to be "no less than everything" in their dedication to the gospel. In her 2011 presidential address to the Catholic Theological Society of America, Mary Ann Hinsdale, I.H.M., suggests that we imagine a "Magdalene function" in today's Church. She offers that Mary Magdalene, an exemplary disciple yet a real and fallible woman in a specific historical context, reminds the Church of the need for continual reflection on its concrete reality and the need for self-criticism. Mary Magdalene models the value of collaboration and dialogue among disciples in discerning the will of Christ and the contemporary demands of the gospel. Both charismatic witness and official oversight structures need to be collegial and communal, inclusive of men and of women, of clergy and of lay Christians.

As I write this in the summer of 2012, some recent incidents involving U.S. Roman Catholic nuns remind me of the importance of a "Magdalene function" in contemporary ecclesiology. In 2009, the Vatican launched an investigation of all U.S. women's religious congregations on suspicion of a post–Vatican II erosion of commitment to traditional doctrine and traditional forms of religious life. Most Catholics reacted with incredulity, aware that it has been the nuns who have been the bearers of Catholic identity "in the trenches" of health care, education, and social service.

Yet in 2012, the Leadership Conference of Women Religious (LCWR) was targeted by Rome with accusations of "radical feminism" and failure to promote vociferously enough the preferred political priorities of the U.S. Catholic bishops: militancy against abortion, contraception, gay marriage, and even national health care reform. The Vatican granted an American archbishop oversight over the LCWR's statutes, programs, liturgies, and affiliations, particularly those involving advocacy for social justice.

One of the most visible and outspoken advocates of women religious and the LCWR during this period has been Simone Campbell, S.S.S., director of NETWORK, a Catholic social justice lobby. According to Sister Campbell, "The truth is that those suffering at the margins of society are the ones Jesus cares about," and U.S. national policies on taxes, poverty, health care, and immigration should reflect that but fail. She calls all Catholics and the U.S. bishops to a more active solidarity with the poor. To publicize these priorities, thereby serving a "Magdalene function" in relation to institutional authorities, Sister Campbell and dozens of other women religious completed a "Nuns on the Bus" tour of nine states, speaking out in local communities, with plenty of national media coverage—virtually all of it favorable to the nuns and their message.

Magdalenes today are still carrying the good news of Jesus to his "brothers," some of whom are timid, some of whom are hot tempered, some of whom are control obsessed, and many of whom are still caught up in the patriarchal power systems Jesus came to disrupt. Some, in line with Gregory the Great, see the nuns' message as just another "radical feminist" symptom of women's out-of-control refusal to stay in their subjugated place. Yet most Christians and Catholics recognize the authentic gospel embodied in the witness of Magdalenes close to and in solidarity with the poor, giving and risking "not less than everything" for the gospel.

# FARTHER ON

HENRY BARTEL

*Bo Caldwell*

H E IS BORN IN RUSSIAN POLAND on February 9, 1873, to Mennonite parents who, three years later, bring their small family to America. From New York they travel west and settle on a farm near Hillsboro, Kansas, where they keep the language they have brought with them—Low German—and live in a stone house that his father builds.

As Henry grows, he feels a battle inside. He knows he is not right with God, but he tells himself the problem can wait. For now he is occupied with school, where he is a good mimic and the defender of the weak, and with the farm, his passion. He loves watching all things grow, and when he thinks of his future, he imagines his own farm, and himself as successful, even wealthy.

As the years pass he begins to despair that he will ever have enough faith to answer the invitation he feels inside, but when he is nineteen, something happens. It is June, and as he is working in the cornfield, his soul is filled with God's peace, and he says yes to God. At church the following Sunday he stands in the balcony and tells what has happened to him, and two months later he is baptized.

He comes to believe that God has a task for him to do, and he wants to obey. His talents are small and few; surely God will leave him here, where he belongs. But, he thinks, What if God doesn't? What if God asks him to leave home? The spiritual books he reads discuss the necessity of one's absolute surrender, and he knows that to truly yield himself to God, he must be willing to give up both his occupation and his home. One morning when he is alone in the field, he begins to weep. He kneels and tells God what is in his heart: *Anything else. Anything.* And instead of what he hoped for—the reassurance that God will not ask him to leave home—he knows he will follow wherever his Lord calls, and he is filled with peace.

———

A man named John Sprunger visits his family's church, Gnadenau—Meadow of Grace—of the Krimmer Mennonite Brethren. Rev. Sprunger is the founder of a large mission in Berne, Indiana, and his words stir Henry. When the girls' dormitory at the mission burns down soon after and Sprunger asks for help in rebuilding it, Henry knows this is his calling. He dreads telling his father, but when he does, his father embraces him and kisses him. "My child," he says, "let nothing keep you. I shall not hinder you in the least."

And so, on August 21, 1899, he leaves home. He is twenty-six years old, tall, with a somber face and dark hair and blue eyes. At Berne he does whatever is asked of him, and the work gives him joy, as does a young coworker named Nellie Schmidt; he is smitten with her from the start. Like him, her Mennonite family came from Russian Poland and she is committed to her work. But their similarities end there, for she has no interest in Henry Bartel. Everything about him grates on her: his mannerisms, his sense of humor, his big nose, big hands, big feet. Although she refuses his advances, he does not give up, and one day he works up the nerve to tell her what is in his heart: that he believes it is God's will for them to marry. She turns him down but he is undaunted, and his cheerful certainty makes her question herself: What if he's right? God's will is dear to her, and the thought of not following him grieves her. She prays, *If this is what You want, let him propose again,* and Henry does so that evening. She tells him "Yes," and although she feels relieved and dutiful, she is not happy, or in love.

They marry on November 4, 1900. Not long afterward, Nellie comes upon Henry unexpectedly and sees that he is sobbing. Alarmed, she asks him what has happened, and when he answers, "You don't love me," she has no response. The sight of him fills her with compassion; she feels that she has been proud, and she asks him to forgive her. From that time on, she loves him deeply, with all of his flaws and quirks and, she sees, his nobility and grace.

Four months later, a missionary from the South Chihli Mission in northern China visits Berne. The missionary's name is Horace Houlding, and he has returned to America to gather new recruits for the work in China. Henry's heart is pounding as Rev. Houlding speaks. He can feel this man's passion, and he is certain that he and Nellie are being called to China. He worries that she will disagree, but late that evening when he tells her what is in his heart, she says she feels the same. They both believe that when God calls, he intends for his children to obey, and from that time forward, China becomes their goal.

-------

In late 1901, Houlding and his seventeen recruits arrive in the northern city of Paoting, China, where only a year earlier seventeen foreign missionaries were killed during the Boxer Troubles. A year later Henry and Nellie and three other mission workers open the new mission's headquarters in Tamingfu, and the young endeavor grows. A few years later there are twelve mission stations and hundreds of converts.

Henry's church at home has refused to support the mission. They say they don't know anything about this man Houlding, and although Nellie is Mennonite, she is from a different denomination. It is a thorn in Henry's flesh; he longs for the support of his church and he dreams of an independent Mennonite mission in China. In the fall of 1905, he thinks he sees a way forward: perhaps if the church at home were financially responsible for one mission station, it would awaken their evangelical spirit. That station could remain part of the South Chihli Mission; he knows he owes that to Houlding. He decides to wait a year before broaching the matter with Houlding and asks a few fellow missionaries to pray about it. But Houlding hears of it, and he is immediately angry. He tells Henry that he must decide then and there whether he can accept the authority of the mission without question, and if not, the Bartels will have to leave.

It is late fall. The mission compound's large gate opens and a mule cart carrying three adults and two children emerges: Henry and Nellie with their young sons, and a Mennonite woman who has chosen to go with them. They have only a few dollars, and Nellie is pregnant with her third child.

Henry has a destination in mind: there is a city to the south where there are no missionaries and where he believes they can start fresh. And so they go to Tsaohsien. Soon after arriving there they receive a check for fifty dollars from a couple in Kansas, enough to cover the next few months, and soon after that there are converts, their first fruits. In 1906 Henry travels to the United States to seek support from Mennonite communities, and he returns with seven new recruits.

When the famine of 1907 leaves scores of children without parents, the mission opens orphanages, and soon they are caring for more than two hundred children. They establish a home for widows, and they buy more land and build schools and industrial shops so that the boys can someday support themselves. "The Bartel mission," as it is popularly known, expands to include thirty pastors and evangelists and seven stations, each with outstations. It is the first Mennonite mission in China, and in 1913, it is incorporated as the China Mennonite Mission Society.

Tsaohsien becomes their home. In the late 1920s, when civil war breaks out and mission workers begin leaving the field in response to warnings from the U.S. consul, Henry and Nellie do not consider it. Tsaohsien changes hands ten times during the war, and the compound is occupied by one company of soldiers after another, all of whom take what they want and leave destruction in return. The fact that Henry and Nellie stay causes the people of the city to trust them in a way they never have before. And despite the trials of the war, Henry and Nellie do not allow themselves to be discouraged; they are doing the job assigned to them. Henry never tires of telling people of the God who loves them.

---

In the fall of 1941, he feels a longing inside: he wants to visit the west of China. Although much of the country is in the hands of the Japanese, the fighting has died down, and travel is possible. The timing seems right for the mission, too. It has fifty-six congregations and nearly seventeen hundred baptized church members in a field that includes eight counties and some 3 million souls, and he feels comfortable leaving it in the hands of the missionaries and national workers. When a check arrives from a supporter in the United States who asks that the money be used to spread the gospel in an area where Christ has never been preached, Henry sees it as a sign, and when he tells Nellie of his desire, he is happily surprised that she's willing to go. She has always trusted his guidance; if he is convinced that God is leading them, she believes him.

Early on the morning of October 16, 1941, they leave Tsaohsien, their home of thirty-six years, for a few months of vacation. They will first visit their son Paul, who is serving with another mission to the south. It is a beautiful time of year and they travel light, for they expect to return soon, and as they journey away from the fighting and to the west, the countryside grows peaceful. Henry is accustomed to traveling alone, and it is so good to have Nellie with him.

They make it safely through Japanese-occupied China to Free China and to Paul in Lungtan. And then everything changes: in December they learn of Pearl Harbor, and in January that the Japanese have taken Tsaohsien and sealed the compound. Although Paul invites them to stay with him, Henry's mind is already in the mountainous northwest. He thinks of a hymn he loves, "It Is Better Farther On," and that is what he believes. People try to dissuade him, warning of the danger of settling in a remote area in such uncertain times. But he is determined; the gospel is needed, he says; the Great Commission still stands.

The China Inland Mission and Christian and Missionary Alliance give him an area five hundred miles to the northwest, and he and Nellie set off, traveling on decrepit buses on rutted mountain roads, in riverboats on mountain streams. He is sixty-nine years old, she sixty-six. They work their way up the White Dragon River, and in June 1942 they rent a house in San Tui Pa in Szechwan Province, where Nellie can stay while Henry goes looking for a site for a permanent mission. He finds someone to travel with him, and when they reach the narrow mountain village of Pei Shui Kiang he leases a rundown house on the main street, despite the fact that he is met with distrust and that one of the walls of the house has caved in and is a heap of rubble.

He returns to San Tui Pa for Nellie and brings her to their new home, where they settle in with a brick oven, a bowl, two pairs of chopsticks, and a few boards for their bed. Rainwater runs down the mountainside and into the house through the rat holes in the walls and smoke fills the room when they cook, but Henry cheerfully begins planning renovations. The two of them do their own chores and Henry works outside, leveling the ground, building a chicken run, and planting walnut and peach trees while he dreams of a language school for new workers.

But the work is harder than he expected; they are lonely laborers in a difficult field, he says. The terrain is rugged, and most of those who show interest in their message are refugees who have heard the gospel elsewhere; the mountain people seem indifferent. Nevertheless, he feels the work is pleasing to God, and as long as he is able to climb mountains, he will continue. With the newness of the venture and the disruption in mail service, the support he and Nellie receive is scant, but they are causing more of a stir in the United States than they realize. People are touched by the story of this older couple pioneering a field that many younger workers would find daunting, and in 1945 it becomes the West China field of the Mennonite Brethren Church, the second Mennonite mission they have founded.

When new workers arrive in Pei Shui Kiang, Henry and Nellie push on once again, this time settling in Shuang Shih Pu in a house that is so small he says he must step outside to change his mind. He is growing deaf—much more so than he finds convenient, he says—but he still feels young, and he is in awe that he can still preach the gospel when so much of the country is closing. He hopes for another ten years, perhaps even twenty, but when he says this to Nellie, she quietly replies that she has no desire to live beyond the psalmist's three score and ten.

This pains him. He cannot ignore how frail she has become, and he knows she is failing. He wants to please her, so he hires carpenters and masons to improve their home. A visiting doctor examines her and says that her body is wearing out, and although there is talk of taking her to Sian for medical care, the journey is deemed too risky for her.

On March 3 she turns seventy, and there is no more talk of hospitals; she knows her time is drawing near. A month later, on the evening of Palm Sunday, she and Henry take a short walk together. She is worried about what he will do without her; he is so forgetful, and she has seen to his needs for so many years. She feels that her last task as his wife is to help him to face what is coming, and she speaks to him about it matter-of-factly; in a way, she says, she wishes he had gone first. She doesn't know how he will get along without her.

For the first time, he admits to himself that he will soon be without her, and that night he stays beside her, grateful that she is comfortable. When an hour passes and she does not stir, he calls out to her in alarm, but she has gone. The pain of her absence is so great that he doesn't know how he will endure it; she has been beside him for forty-five years. He helps to prepare her body, dressing her in Chinese clothes, and the carpenters he hired to work on the house build her coffin. On Monday when he walks through the village to the cemetery to choose a plot for her, he is in a daze; only yesterday she was walking beside him. Chinese neighbors crowd around him in sympathy, and he sees them as lost sheep; for an hour he forgets his grief and speaks to them of Christ's love. On Tuesday, as Nellie's coffin is carried through the streets, several hundred people gather, and he preaches to them again. He writes that he is cast down but not destroyed, and he prays for the grace to say yes.

His children visit, and their presence eases his grief. Soon he resumes his short treks in the mountains, and although he sorely misses his helpmate, he feels his work is unfinished; he wants only to keep preaching Christ. Time is short; once again, missionaries are being encouraged to leave China, but there is something else, something new. He is astonished to find that he has begun to feel old.

———————

By 1951 most of the missionaries still in China have left the country. His daughter, Agnes, and her family have joined him in the west and he tries to convince them to leave without him. But they will not hear of it, and he sees that he, too, may have to leave China, a thought that tears at his heart. But finally he agrees, and they apply for the required exit permits and are told they will arrive soon, but they don't. The country has fallen to the communists, and in the spring Henry, his son-in-law, and their Chinese coworkers are publicly tried, then taken 30 miles away and held under house arrest. They are released three weeks later, but the experience is a strain on them, particularly Henry, and on the long walk home, he falls and fractures his hip. The pain is excruciating, but once his companions have brought him home, he is certain he will be better soon; God has healed him many times in his life. The next morning when he is worse, he is truly bewildered; his daughter hears him murmur, "Surely God cannot have deserted me."

He recovers, slowly, and in November he celebrates fifty

years of service in China, less his few furloughs. On December 4, the family is suddenly told they are to leave for the county seat within three days, taking only what they can carry. They pack hurriedly, and in the midst of it when they sit down to eat a quick meal, the curtain separating them from the Chinese friends they live with is pushed aside. Their friends are weeping, but they are not allowed to say good-bye.

———

In March 1952, he leaves China for the last time. He flies from Hong Kong to Minneapolis, and when his son Paul meets him at the airport, the sight of his father brings him up short. The tall, vigorous man he remembers has grown old and frail. He is half a foot shorter and his eyes are blurred with cataracts. He leans on a cane to walk.

His children arrange for him to live at the Eventide Home in Mountain Lake, Minnesota, near his daughter and her family. For years he has slept on thin mats; now he has a soft bed in a lovely room with a heater he can turn on or off as he pleases and a wide window that looks out on the traffic outside. And he has time; he writes letters that are by turns cheerful, wistful, funny, and passionate, sometimes on scraps of paper one inch by three, the habit of a frugal life. He is homesick for his dear China and impatient with inactivity, but he prays and marvels at all that God entrusted him with. What could be sweeter than doing God's will?

A few years later he wants to return to his childhood home of Hillsboro, so he is moved to a home at nearby Inman, which his daughter Agnes and her husband manage, and where he is well cared for. He is eighty-nine years old and nearly blind and deaf, and his mind has begun to cloud. He repeatedly asks Agnes where her parents are, and when she finally answers, "Why, Papa, *you're* my father," he says, "Oh?" And then he leans forward, and there is urgency in his voice. "But you are a Christian, aren't you?"

---

On February 20, 1965, eleven days after his ninety-second birthday, Henry Bartel leaves this earth. He is buried in the Hillsboro cemetery, a few miles from the stone house his father built.

All five of his children serve as missionaries in Asia. During a visit to China in May 1987, his youngest son, Jonathan, travels to Tsaohsien, now Caoxian, hoping to see his childhood home. He stands out; there have been few, if any, westerners in the city for nearly forty years, and an elderly woman on the bus asks him, "Are you a Bartel?"

In the city, the police tell him that he is not allowed to attend church the next day, but that evening they bring three church members to see him. He is able to talk with them, and they tell him what they know. They tell him that there are Christians in every village in the county; they tell him there are more than forty churches and twenty thousand believers. They tell him that in the city they recently constructed a new church building—in seven days. They tell him that more than a thousand people attend the church in the city. And they tell him that the seed his father sowed is bearing much fruit. Still.

# THE AMERICANIST

## ISAAC HECKER

*James Carroll*

W HEN HAVE WE SEEN this picture before? The contest between a conservative Vatican intent on preserving the absolute timelessness of Roman Catholic doctrine and a liberal Catholicism assuming the need for timely adaptation; between a self-proclaimed infallible hierarchy and a broad laity quietly trusting its own experience; between truth conceived as unchanging and truth understood as unfolding in process; between political structures rooted in medieval monarchy and post-Enlightenment principles of liberal democracy. Such argument, so familiar to Catholics of the early twenty-first century, revisits the Church's great internal schism of the early twentieth century, defined most eloquently by the papal condemnation of the heresy known as "Americanism."

Americanism was named and anathematized by Pope Leo XIII in his 1898 apostolic letter *Testem Benevolentiae*

*Nostrae* (Witness Our Good Will). To be sure, there were aspects of American culture sorely in need of criticism just then—its triumphalism, imperialism, and nascent gangster capitalism. The genocide of Native peoples had just been completed, and the resubjugation of African Americans was fully under way. But the Church had other preoccupations. Among the pernicious ideas singled out for censure were basic notes of American polity, like the separation of church and state, the right to free expression, pluralism. Americanism was heretical, above all, for giving priority to individual experience over the authority of the hierarchy. Leo's rejection of the heresy stood between Pius IX's promulgation of the "Syllabus of Errors" (condemning, for example, that "the Roman Pontiff can, and ought to, reconcile himself, and come to terms with, progress, liberalism and modern civilization") and Pius X's rejection of "modernism," designated as the synthesis of all heresies.

That there are echoes of these disputes in the contemporary argument the Church is having with itself points to the relevance of the little known figure who, more than any other, was taken as the embodiment of Catholic liberalism by his critics and defenders alike—the American priest Isaac Hecker (1819–88). Indeed, the heresy condemned by Pope Leo was explicitly tied to ideas expressed in a French translation of *The Life of Father Hecker* by Walter Elliot, published in English in 1891 and in French in 1897. Hecker was the founder, in 1858, of the first American order of Roman Catholic priests, the Paulist Fathers, and he was associated with key members of the American Catholic establishment, like Cardinal James Gibbons, so there was a concerted effort to distance him from the anathemas. Deflecting the heresy charges, his defenders insisted (and still insist) Hecker was no Americanist. But when the Second Vatican Council (1963–65) attempted to call a truce in the Church's war against modernity, Hecker emerged as a prophetic figure, having indeed foreshadowed a reconciliation between the Catholic tradition and the American imagination, to the benefit of both.

Isaac Thomas Hecker was born in New York City to a family of German immigrants, loosely Protestant. The Heckers were bakers and manufacturers of flour, and, across the years of Isaac's life, the family business grew and eventually prospered. Young Isaac had little formal education, but his spiritual bent and intellectual curiosity inclined him to the life of the mind. The fervor of Great Awakening enthusiasm that marked public life in America drew him. In New York, he was enthralled by street orators, labor organizers, and reformers. Still a lad, he formed a first and enduring connection to Orestes A. Brownson.

Brownson was associated with the Transcendentalists, one of the defining movements of American thought, with its emphasis on self-reliance, its elevation of individual interiority, and its skepticism toward institutional structures of all kinds, including those of religion. Hecker was drawn into a New England circle that included Ralph Waldo Emerson, Bronson Alcott, Theodore Parker, Henry David Thoreau, Margaret Fuller, Elizabeth Peabody, and William Henry Channing. For a time, the Transcendentalists were centered at Brook Farm, a utopian commune near Boston, and in 1843 the twenty-four-year-old Isaac Hecker went there to live and work. Something essential to the American spirit crystallized at Brook Farm, and it is no surprise that the era's greatest novelist, Nathaniel Hawthorne, himself a Brook Farm member, should have memorialized it in *The Blithedale Romance*.

For all of Brook Farm's rebelliousness against the negativity of Calvinist religion and what Emerson called "corpse cold Unitarianism," the commune warmly emphasized the person and teachings of Jesus Christ, and young Hecker fell under his spell. Known by the sobriquet "Ernest the Seeker," Hecker found that his version of Transcendentalist "soul hunger" led, surprisingly, to the Roman Catholic Church. Penetrating to the heart of what would destroy the Transcendentalist experiment, Hecker intuited its main problem—how a radically democratic leveling of the hierarchy of being in the name of transcendence makes access to transcendence problematic, if not impossible. Setting himself apart from his peers, yet with a display of individualism worthy of Emerson, he declared at Brook Farm, "The Catholic Church alone seems to satisfy my wants. . . . I may be laboring under a delusion. . . . Yet my soul is Catholic, and that faith . . . responds to my soul in its religious aspirations and its longings. I have not wished to make myself Catholic, but it answers to the wants of my soul."

Perhaps Hecker's genius lay in his capacity to carry forward the competing strains of normally contradictory impulses. He left Brook Farm, soon becoming a Catholic, and then, in 1845, entering training for the Catholic priesthood. Yet all the while he attended to the trustworthy voice of his own "indwelling Supreme Spirit," in Emerson's phrase. Responsive to the native traditions of his own family, Hecker entered a German religious order, the Redemptorists, and, after ordination in 1849, only five years after leaving Brook Farm, he found himself preaching parish missions mainly to German immigrant communities. That he preached in English was an issue. The Catholic Church regarded the broadly Protestant—and Anglo—culture of the United States with suspicion and was erecting protective walls around a separatist Catholic subculture, with religious instruction usually carried out in the native languages of the newcomers—precisely to protect them from corrupting influences.

But Hecker saw things differently. Having come himself right out of an essentially American spiritual inquiry, and having found its fulfillment in the Catholic faith, he was convinced that the mutual hostility between the Church and America was shortchanging both. He began openly to argue for a compatibility between the American idea and the Catholic faith, an argument he brought eventually to Rome. The English language was a symbol of the skepticism Hecker encountered.

Rome had much to be suspicious of. Yes, American religious affiliation, given the free market of denominational coexistence, was supremely a matter of personal choice, but Hecker could argue that it enhanced devotedness. Yes, the American vision emphasized the future over the past, but that could amount to a secular affirmation of the theological virtue of hope. Yes, the ever-beckoning American frontier obliterated the purifying separations of Old World confessional boundaries, but that meant that a robustly preached Catholicism could come into its own. Concretely, Hecker was a strong advocate of preaching to immigrants in English—inviting their embrace of America, not their shunning of it.

Perhaps surprisingly, his vision caught the imaginations of powerful figures in Rome. In 1858, after breaking with the Redemptorists, he was authorized to establish a new religious order of priests expressly as a bridge between the Church and the American nation. He took Saint Paul as the order's patron, and it was called the Paulist Fathers. The four men who immediately joined Hecker in his enterprise were all converts to Catholicism, native-born Americans like him.

"We have contrasted the Church with the Soul," Ralph Waldo Emerson had preached, concluding, "In the Soul, then, let the redemption be sought." The contradiction between Church and Soul was assumed by anti-institutional Transcendentalists, yet, from an opposite point, so also had many in the hierarchy of the Catholic Church come to regard the dichotomy as absolute. It was Hecker's refusal to accept this bipolarity that marked his particular genius, his insistence that Church authority and the authority of individual conscience were complementary, not contradictory. The language he used to advance this notion lifted up the "Indwelling Holy Spirit." The Holy Spirit, as the tradition had always emphasized, lived in the magisterium of the Church, an emphasis that was redoubled when the First Vatican Council (1870) promulgated the doctrine of papal infallibility. Rigid authoritarianism trickled down through the structure of the hierarchy, which was making unprecedented claims for itself.

But Hecker was retrieving a note of the faith from the tradition, too: before Emerson used the word *indwelling,* Saint Augustine had. And before Saint Augustine, there was Jesus proclaiming, "For behold, the Kingdom of God is within you." Thus, Hecker naturally claimed connection with the great stream of mystical theology, insisting that the Holy Spirit was alive and a source of guidance not just in the magisterium, but within every individual member of the Church—lay as well as ordained. Indeed, the work of the Holy Spirit in the outer forms of Church authority was *for the sake* of the Holy Spirit's indwelling in each person. The Church and the Soul were not opposites. The Church was *for* the Soul. Or, as Hecker put it late in his life, "The Holy Spirit is thus the inspiration of the inner life of the regenerate man, and in that life is his Superior and Director. That his guidance may become more and more immediate in an interior life, and the soul's obedience more and more instinctive, is the object of the whole external order of the Church." The whole order, including doctrine, sacraments, and, for that matter, holy orders themselves—the ordained estates of priest, bishop, pope. All for the sake of the individual, not the other way around.

In an authoritarian age, this reversal could seem heterodox, and from a hill in Rome recently overrun by fiercely anti-papal secular armies, the shift could seem like an American slip into radical subjectivity. So could the inevitable corollary that came with this emphasis on the indwelling (as opposed to institutional) Holy Spirit, which was Hecker's intuitive trust in the primacy of individual conscience. Yes, conscience had to be shaped by and tested against the teaching authority of the Church, but finally conscience was the realm within which each person, autonomously applying the lessons of authority, had a direct encounter with the Holy Spirit. Freedom of conscience was the precondition of this spirituality. Tension between individual liberty and communal authority is built into the human condition, but for Hecker, when the tension became contradiction, his preference was clear. "As for me, I would rather suffer from the license of freedom," he wrote, "than from the oppression of authority."

This profoundly American grasp of freedom informed the way Hecker shaped the religious order he founded. For example, though the Paulist Fathers accept the traditional disciplines of poverty, chastity, and obedience, they do not bind themselves with vows. It may seem a small point, but Hecker insisted that Paulists would make promises, not vows—refusing to enclose the community in the scaffolding of "the whole external order of the Church." The vow, in fact, is a vestige of the feudal system by which vassals bound themselves to lords. The Paulist's word of honor, without the sanction of sin, or feudal submissiveness, was enough for Hecker. The promise meant the man was committed, but free. Similarly, following Hecker, the Paulists are governed not by a "rule," like that of Saint Benedict, but by a "constitution," like that of, well, Thomas Jefferson.

As the Paulists' structure reflected the character of Isaac Hecker, so did the work they undertook. Dubbing themselves "missionaries to Mainstreet," they set about as ardent advocates of the Catholic idea to Americans and as equally enthused sponsors within the Church of an American approach. Instead of shoring up the Catholic subculture, they left it. At a time when Catholic young people were supposed to attend Church-run institutions of higher learning, like those founded by the Jesuits, Paulists dispersed to "non-Catholic" colleges and universities as chaplains, the first Catholic priests to do so. In such places, they served young Catholics who, according to conservative bishops, weren't even supposed to be there. In the first decade of the twentieth century, Paulists founded America's first Catholic center of campus ministry at the University of California at Berkeley. They called it the Newman Club, and Paulists still serve there. The name is an explicit recognition of all that bound Hecker with his English counterpart, John Henry Newman, who had himself declared his identification with Hecker. Against the idea of a changeless "deposit of faith," Newman was famously the author of "the development of doctrine," and Hecker was its embodiment. When the heresy of modernism was condemned by Pius X, there was no surprise that several Paulists were implicated, and at least one was forced to leave the Church.

All such talk of heresy surrounding the figure and legacy of Isaac Hecker ceased with Vatican II, when even Hecker's most radical ideas were vindicated. *Testem Benevolentiae Nostrae* condemned the idea that "the Church ought to adapt herself somewhat to our advanced civilization, and, relaxing her ancient rigor, show some indulgence to modern popular theories and methods." Yet almost that exact formulation was reversed in Pope John XXIII's historic initiating of *aggiornamento,* the very "updating" of the Church that constituted Hecker's agenda. The council's affirmation of the equal dignity of the laity rests on a Hecker-like theology of the indwelling Holy Spirit—alive in the whole Church, not just the hierarchy. The council's ringing embrace of religious liberty echoes Hecker's insistence on freedom as essential to Christian life. The council's elevation of the primacy of "the dictates of conscience" as determinative of salvation shows

Hecker was right to trust the inner vision by which he moved through his entire life.

Isaac Hecker insisted that the Catholic Church had much to learn from America, and Vatican II spells out what the lessons have been. Hecker equally insisted that America had much to learn from the Church—and the blatantly unfinished projects of justice for all, and peace on earth, show with what this nation must yet reckon. The Catholic Church is no "perfect society," as the Americanism-condemning Pope Leo XIII once declared it was, but the gospel it upholds confronts the Church with principles of its own self-criticism, which can prove a pope to have been wrong. Responding to calls for change, the Church has shown itself capable of change.

In a similar way, America is not exceptional, as political rhetoric eternally asserts. It, too, with the U.S. Constitution serving as goad and guide, is continually called to more fully realize its own ideals. Isaac Hecker loved the Church and he loved America. He invited them to enter into a mutual compact of criticism and change, of influence and affirmation. They have done so, and, God willing, will continue to. That hope is Isaac Hecker's meaning, and his legacy. Isaac Hecker was the prophet of a renewed Catholic Church, a tribune of a more authentically religious America.

# THE WOMAN WHO WOULDN'T: WHEN VISION GIVES VOICE TO DISSENT

## HILDEGARD VON BINGEN

*Joan Chittister, O.S.B.*

In October 2012, Hildegard of Bingen, almost a thousand years after her birth, will finally have been elevated to the status of doctor of the church. And yet, until Pope Benedict XVI proclaimed her a saint by fiat, Hildegard was never canonized despite the fact that the process was begun fifty-four years after her death. In 1979, when the German bishops petitioned Rome for a second time to make her a doctor of the church, that petition, too, was overlooked. Thérèse of Lisieux, "The Little Flower," was chosen instead. The question is, What was there about this woman that took so long for such official recognition? And why did this name never really die in the memory of the universal Church? And what can she possibly mean to us in this day and age?

This is the story of a great woman: a mystic, a visionary, a reformer—a dissenter.

"Dissent" is one of the more difficult dimensions of public discourse to define. It's not the same as the political sparring that is expected of political parties—even required at some level—if a republic is to be a republic. And yet, dissent is easy to recognize. Dissent comes out of the depth of the heart and exists only in service to what both sides say they are each committed to preserving.

It comes out of a soul in anguish over life that must be bartered in the process of saving it.

Most of all, dissent always has a place and a time and a face we do not expect to see in this place at this time. It has the character of exactly what the institution wants most to produce: total loyalty and complete identification. The problem is that both sides define their one same loyalty differently. The establishment is always loyal to the very institutionalism of the institution in question. The dissenter is always most loyal instead to what the institution itself claims to be about.

As a result, loneliness is at the very heart of dissent. Loneliness is its character and isolation is its cost: it is one young man facing a row of tanks in Tiananmen Square. It is the pacifist Dorothy Day on a hunger strike in a Washington jail for having the temerity to protest in behalf of women's suffrage at the gates of the White House. It is the African American Rosa Parks refusing to get out of her seat on a public bus. It is the few who hold out against total dissolution of the highest ideals of any institution.

In which case, Hildegard of Bingen is indeed a dissenter.

## A CULTURE IN TURMOIL

The Europe into which Hildegard had been born fairly exploded with new life. It was an era of intellectual revival and international commerce. Vernacular literatures were emerging. Seafaring navigation equipment made exploration, trade, and human contact possible. Medieval universities made the spread of Arabic learning, Greek and Roman classics, and modern ideas possible. Failed Crusades weakened both Church and crown. And at the same time, the rise of scholasticism brought a new kind of learning that recognized the use of secular learning, reason, and logic as handmaids of the faith. It was a period of great tension, an unstable and feuding papacy, changing ideas, contrary theologies, and highly influential people—Bernard of Clairvaux, Anselm of Canterbury, and Peter Damian, among others—all bent on reforming a Church mired in corruption. It was a world rife with lax clergy and simmering with new ideas. It was, in other words, an era very much like our own.

And there, into the midst of it, came Hildegard of Bingen, one of the brightest thinkers of them all. The scene had the energy of a shooting star, on one hand, and signaled a world ripe for dissent on the other. "The Vita of Hildegard" hints of it: "In the eleven hundredth year after the Incarnation of Christ, the teaching and fiery justice of the Apostles, which Christ had established among the Christians and spiritual people, began to slow down and turn into hesitation, I was born in those times."

Born in 1098, Hildegard was the tenth child of minor nobility in Bermersheim, Germany, yes. But in 1106, she was given to the Church at the age of eight in gratitude for God's blessings to the rest of the family. It was a time-honored practice, one that became for her, however, a life commitment with an unlikely twist.

For most people, life is a kind of scavenger hunt. We move from one part of it to another looking for small, obscure objects along the way that can enable us to make the best of the helter-skelter world in which we live. Sometimes, though, as in Hildegard's case, life comes to us rather than our having to find it ourselves one uncertain, often painful, new step at a time. In that case, what can we possibly do? Our direction has been set for us already. A template into which we are meant to step, quietly and with predictable docility. The questions then are clear ones: Do we simply go along, passive participants in our own lives? Or are we left to carve our uniqueness out of it ourselves, one routine decision at a time.

One thing for certain: seventy-three years of life in a convent would not seem to be the place either to plunge through life with limitless zest, choosing this, discarding that, or to choose a life famous for its regularity and then pursue it irregularly. But as a matter of fact, for Hildegard it was. She made it so.

For Hildegard, as a woman, the convent was life changing. Her major dissent, it could even be said, is that she dared to be herself in such an age and place at all. As a result, for other women she has become a life-changing model of a different way to be.

## A LIFE OF REFLECTION

The historical skeleton of her life is ostensibly a simple one. At the age of eight she was entrusted to the spiritual tutelage of Jutta, an anchoress attached to the male Benedictine monastery of Disibodenberg. By the time Jutta died in 1136, some thirty years later, Hildegard, after years of instruction in monastic life, became the magister or prioress of the little group.

Perhaps even more important in that period, Hildegard, "instructed by the Living Light," "put her hand to writing" and began the first of her great works, *Scivias–To Know the Ways of God.* A major theological dissertation on the spiritual life, it would have been a classic under any conditions. But this was a theological study of all the major topics of Christianity—and it was written by a woman. It was a major display *of deep spiritual reflection,* of intellectual independence, and of personal spiritual development. Clearly, the dissent had already begun.

## A STRUGGLE TO BECOME INDEPENDENT

By 1147 the number of her disciples had grown. The living conditions at the male monastery became more and more inadequate for so large a group of women. The abbess Hildegard, then forty-nine years old, followed her vision and left the confines of Disibodenberg to set up her own independent women's community. She moved the then-eighteen members of the community and their dowries into the new monastery that she herself had designed, this time with running water and ample facilities. And despite the disapproval of the abbot.

The loss of the public attention and gifts that Hildegard's work and presence brought to Disibodenberg surely gave the abbot pause. But the loss of the women's dowries and the financial well-being they signaled for the abbey made the move totally unacceptable. Abbot Kuno's demands, entreaties, and castigations counted for nothing. Hildegard would not return to Disibodenberg. Instead, she opened her own monastery in Rupertsberg and wrote back to him, "And you, O man, who have been placed as a visible shepherd, rise up and hasten quickly to justice, so that you will not be criticized by the great doctor for not having cleansed your flock from dirt, for not having anointed them with oil."

Clearly, Disibodenberg was not a good place for women. But to leave it without the abbot's consent asserted the kind of independence unheard of in women in that era.

More than that, once settled in her new community in Rupertsberg, Hildegard prevailed on the archbishop of Mainz to confirm the act. Then, she also prevailed on Emperor Frederick Barbarossa, whom she had also upbraided—in one instance, it appears, for dismissing an archbishop friend of hers and in another for supporting a rival pope during one of the frequent papal schisms of the time. Barbarossa went so far as to commit to a secret document in which he promised his full protection in the event that anyone—anyone at all in either Church or crown—attempt to suppress it. The boldness of it all simply takes the breath away.

And yet, the bare bones of Hildegard's monastic life do not begin to describe the scope and depth of her dissent.

No doubt about it: Hildegard, the woman, had a sense of herself and her own moral agency that women in the twentieth century are still in the process of learning. She knew herself to be an intelligent human being. She made major personal and social decisions, not only beyond the limits set for women in her time but even in the face of male disapproval. She simply refused to live within norms that made her less than the creature of God she knew herself to be.

A dissenter? Indeed. In full bloom.

## A WOMAN WITH A MIND OF HER OWN

She was a thinker—both theologian and ethicist, in fact. Her major books, *Scivias* and *The Book of the Rewards of Life,* defined the entire spiritual life when her world could not imagine women moralists and her Church definitely did not want women theologians.

She was a woman who operated under what she knew to be the impulse of the God within. She had lived in a world of inner visions since the age of six and grew more and more in tune with them as she grew. She wrote:

> *When I was forty-two years and seven months old, a burning light of tremendous brightness coming from heaven poured into my entire mind. . . . All of a sudden, I was able to taste of the understanding of the narration of books. I saw the psalter clearly and the evangelists and other Catholic books of the Old and New Testament.*

Clearly, her visions were not sensual. Her visions were intellectual. She did not "see"; she simply "knew." She intuited; she did not "hear." She goes on:

*The visions which I saw I did not perceive in dreams nor when asleep nor in a delirium nor with the eyes or ears of the body. I received them when I was awake and looking around with a clear mind, with the inner eyes and ears, in open places according to the will of God.*

Led by those internal insights, prodded by that sense of the will of God, Hildegard became the feminine voice of God for women—"God's little trumpet," she called herself. She was a fully functioning moral agent, a model of female agency when women were considered the dependents of men, more children than adults, the lesser of two orders of human beings who did not have either the credentials or the capacity to be full adults.

## A SCHOLARLY AND INDEPENDENT INTELLECTUAL LIFE

The very scope and volume of her work was overwhelming. She was an intellectual, a composer, an encyclopedist who wrote the only two medical texts produced in twelfth-century Germany. She was a scientist who understood ecology and sustainability and the "web of creation" and the life of the universe before ecology was a word and despite the theology of domination that had become the clarion cry of a patriarchal worldview. She was the dissenting feminine voice of God in a world that defined men, the males of the species, as agents of God free to control, horde, consume, and destroy the natural resources of the human race. Hildegard's theology of *viriditas*—of the greening power and purpose of all life—redefined what it means to be "reasonable" in the face of a rationality now defined as dominion without limits and control without benefit of compassion.

Greater intellectual dissent than hers at that time is difficult to imagine.

She was a visionary, a mystic, a justice seeker, a Benedictine woman steeped in the psalms and the scriptures who saw life through the eye of God and named injustice, indifference, and corruption wherever she found it. She chastised popes and kings, priests and emperors to right a world rife with Crusades, ecclesiastical corruption, and civil carnage.

At the age of sixty she began four speaking tours of the Rhine, speaking from castles and cathedrals about the sins and errors of the time, regardless whose. She was a prolific writer who not only called sin wherever she saw it but raised the best of Christian ideals in everything she did, for everyone to see. A "prophet" they called her as she called for the reform of the Church and honesty in high places.

She wrote about the priests of the time:

*But because they have the power of preaching, imposing penance, and granting absolution, for that reason, they hold us in their grasp like ferocious beasts. Their crimes fall upon us and through them the whole church withers, because they do not proclaim what is just; and they destroy the law in their drunkenness and they commit copious adulteries, and because of such sins, they judge us without mercy. For they are also plunderers of their congregations, through their avarice, devouring whatever they can; and with their offices they reduce us to poverty and indigence, contaminating both themselves and us. For this reason, let us judge and single them out in a fair trial for they lead us astray. . . .*

She wrote to Pope Anastasius IV:

*So it is, O man, that you who sit in the chief seat of the Lord, hold him in contempt when you embrace evil, since you do not reject it but kiss it, by silently tolerating it in depraved men.*

And though she revered Bernard of Clairvaux, whose words inspirited the misbegotten Crusades, she spoke out against the participation of the clergy in the militarism of knighthood:

*How can it be right that the shaven-headed with their robes and chasubles should have more soldiers and more weapons than we do? Surely, too, it is inappropriate for a cleric to be a soldier and a soldier a cleric?*

The system simply could not break her. Justice was her passion, her impulse. Her writings reek with it and her life was exhausted in its service.

Right to the end, she strove against the clergy of the area because of what she saw as an unjust demand. Ordered to remove from the community cemetery the body of a man whom the local bishop had excommunicated, she refused. In fact, in order to protect the corpse from abuse, Hildegard herself at the age of eighty walked among the headstones using her cane to destroy all sign of the man's fresh grave and marking so it could not possibly be moved.

She wrote of that situation:

*I saw in my soul that if we followed their command and exposed the corpse, such an expulsion would threaten our home with great danger, like a vast blackness—It would envelop us like a dark cloud that looms before tempests and thunderstorms. . . . So we did not dare expose him lest we seem to injure Christ's sacraments.*

They punished her for that by putting the entire community under interdict that denied this community the right to have Mass, receive communion, or sing the Divine Office, a deprivation that would wound the soul of any Benedictine community of women to this day. They tried to starve her spiritually, to reject her totally. And still Hildegard and her community would not relent in their commitment to the Law above the law.

## THE SANCTITY OF STRUGGLE AND SIGN OF THE TIMES

Within months of this last great struggle for justice and compassion, Hildegard died, unbeaten and unbroken. Why? Because as a Benedictine woman, steeped in the scriptures every day of her life, she could not, with integrity, do less.

Surely this great Benedictine woman is a woman for our own times, one who knows sexism and decries it, knows militarism and deplores it, knows clericalism and rejects it, knows corruption and unmasks it, knows faith and puts the gospel above the institution.

Hildegard, a dissenter of the first class, is, the Vatican itself assures us, a blazing sign of spiritual brilliance for us all. Even here. Even now.

In her own time, Bernard of Clairvaux himself begged Pope Eugenius "not to allow such a brilliant light to be covered by silence. . . ." Now, in this century, in our time, this silence is finally officially broken.

The only question now is whether or not we will do the same.

# STIRRED INTO FLAME

## MONSIGNOR JOHN V. SHERIDAN

*Paul J. Contino*

> The fruit of the Spirit is love, joy, peace, patience, kindness,
> generosity, faithfulness, gentleness, and self-control.
> There is no law against such things.
>
> —*Galatians 5:22–23*

ONE MORNING, just after 8:00 A.M. Mass at Our Lady of Malibu Church, I was thinking about Monsignor John Virgilius Sheridan, now deceased for two years. I stopped at a nearby coffee shop for rumination and sustenance. The young man at the cash register took my order and asked, "Do you still give those talks at the church?" He was recalling mornings seven years past. Then in elementary school, the young man had attended Mass with his grade-school classmates, and Monsignor Sheridan, then in his late eighties, would look up from his reading of the Gospel, catch my eye, and say in his distinctive Irish brogue, "Ahh, Professor Paul, would you come up and say a few words to these good people." I never refused. Having reflected on the readings beforehand, I would improvise a brief homily that—I hoped—would resonate with the schoolchildren and the more seasoned congregants.

I told the young man that I hadn't given such a talk in a while. I didn't explain why, but as I recall it, a friend had e-mailed a citation of canon law forbidding homiletic incursions by a layperson, and another parishioner had protested more vociferously, so I asked Monsignor to no longer extend his spontaneous invitations. As always, John—as I will call him for the remainder of this essay (although I always called him Monsignor while he was alive)—understood.

Why recount this memory? To highlight a quality of Monsignor John Sheridan and, I venture to say, any saint: He was a personalist, never a legalist. If the Holy Spirit moved him to call a parishioner to the pulpit—and he called others, too—he listened to the Spirit. The Spirit guided him in decades of pastoral counsel and in his voluminous writings, which, at least on one occasion, pressed against the limits of law. Above all, John strove to be kind. He wore his kindness lightly, claiming that it "came not from the struggle great Christians make with themselves to be Christlike, but from temperament and heredity, from a deep almost reckless confidence in God's unlimited kindness, and from an indigenous indisposition to be legalistic or even logical in my own life and counseling."

John exaggerates his aversion to logic. In the heady years

before and after Vatican II, he served as answer-man for
the U.S. Catholic Church, responding to hundreds of questions about the faith—be they on scripture, liturgy, or moral
theology—in the Los Angeles diocesan paper, *The Tidings,*
in the nationally syndicated *Our Sunday Visitor,* and in the
two substantial volumes that collected his columns. John's
writing was always lucid and direct. But his keen sense of
paradox could frustrate adamant adherents of the principle of
noncontradiction. He understood the perennial pull between
law and spirit, institution and *charism,* the gracious limits of
form and the divine call to freedom. He loved the Church
for its sacramental life, but also for its culture and teaching.
Rooted in the reality of the incarnation, John trusted that the
finite things of this earth—including law—can mediate the
infinite and serve as a means of grace. But an incarnational
faith is always receptively aware of life's comic surprises and
ironies. From his youth, John remained open to the way
God's plans might unexpectedly usurp his own. Consider the
irony of the incarnation: who expected the Messiah to come
as He did, "infinity dwindled to infancy" (Gerard Manley
Hopkins), a poor carpenter from Nazareth, crucified like a
criminal? John lightened life's gravity by his attunement to
grace, and his own graceful good humor.

When he spoke, one could hear John's incarnational embrace of paradox, his Trinitarian sense of unity in particularity. Whether from the pulpit or during a brisk walk across
the Malibu bluffs, one might lose the thread and suppose
a non sequitur had slunk into the dialogue. One would be
wrong. John's utterances freely linked the homely-wondrous
events and entities of creation. To revise Dr. Johnson, John

yoked by gentleness the most heterogeneous ideas. Such connections might be made elliptically; you had to pay attention. Father Farrell Sheridan, his ever-practical beloved brother and fellow priest, once observed that John was "always interrupting himself," that his discourse could take the form of "an endless complex of plots, sub-plots, parentheses and adjectival clauses." But consider this analogy: if God is the Word, the Logos, might Farrell's description of John suggest the way God speaks and sustains the blooming buzz of creation?

So, allow me to interrupt myself and present a sketch of John's life. He was born to a loving family in Carrickmaquirk, County Longford, the rural midlands of Ireland where the Sheridans had deep roots. His father, a devout, melancholy farmer, was married to a younger, ever-hospitable wife, for whom he was ever grateful. Of seven children, three became priests and one a nun; his ancestors included persecuted clergy forced to celebrate Mass hidden in the Irish woods. John entered a seminary college, but, after his first year, became gravely ill with then-incurable *tubercular peritonitis.* He prepared himself for imminent death. But God surprised him. After three years of hospital and home care, addicted to prescription morphine, John knelt and prayed that God would send a sign that he was indeed called to be a priest. Within a week, the wounds in his viscera completely healed. His doctor had no medical explanation and wrote him a personal note: "John, I am convinced it was someone greater than all of us who brought you this far. You really should not be here. Your intestines were literally jelly. If this is not an answer to prayer, then prayer is meaningless. Be grateful, do God's work, man, and pray for us."

John obeyed each of the good doctor's prescriptions, including his insistence that he move somewhere warmer. So John came to Los Angeles. He attended St. John's Seminary and, in 1943, was ordained and assigned to Holy Cross parish. In his hale heyday—indeed, throughout his life—he was a good-looking man. Old photos seem issued by central casting. In fact, handsome Father Sheridan, going his way, soon met Bing Crosby and introduced him to his parish youth group. His first of many honors came from the L.A. Police Department, which acknowledged his work in steering kids away from gangs. After he had served other parishes—St. Elizabeth's, St. Basil's—Cardinal James Francis McIntyre appointed him director of downtown L.A.'s new Catholic Information Center. Father Sheridan soon became known for his radio and TV programs, pamphlets, books, and, of course, his nationally syndicated question-and-answer column. Each thoughtful response was marked by careful reading and research; John always sought to think and feel with the Church.

But in August 1969, the Church, in its hierarchical form, pushed back. A year after *Humanae Vitae* was issued, Monsignor Sheridan published a response that acknowledged the inevitable "tension between authority and conscience, between superior and subordinate," observed that human persons are not angels, and lauded a form of authority "exercised concentrically rather than pyramidally." The archbishop was not amused. Four decades later, John recalled the episode to his friend, Doug Kmiec (who had supported presidential candidate Barack Obama and been chastised by some Church authorities):

*Throughout our lives in our Faith, our beliefs and morals are often tested, sometimes to the crisis point. It's then, [Saint] Paul tells us, to stir up into flame this priceless gift, our Faith. . . . An article of mine in* Our Sunday Visitor *circulated nationally, and . . . was sensationalized. . . . It so upset the late Cardinal McIntyre that I was notified under threat of suspension from my priestly ministry to retract immediately and publicly what I had written. The Cardinal, my superior, was a holy and highly respected, very conservative man with whom I continued to enjoy a warm relationship. Now by his orders I [had to] retract something which the vast majority of theologians and I believed, and believed sincerely, to be eminently correct and within the authentic teaching of the Church. . . . It was a period of great depression for me, but I obeyed, and wrote my final article in* The Tidings *quoting from Saint Paul and his admonition that we "stir into flame this gift of God," our Faith. (2 Tim. 1:6)*

John was hurt by Cardinal McIntyre's response, but, as always, sustained by the Spirit. In his memoir, *From Malibu with Love* (1993), he remembers his friend, the cardinal:

*Not a professional theologian, exegete or historian, McIntyre was however gifted with an intuitiveness for which he was never given credit. . . . Dorothy Day . . . was a lady whose opinions the Cardinal's worst critics would never dare to question. On one of her last visits to Los Angeles, while McIntyre was being harassed by the media, she had dinner with us. Coming from an afternoon spent with the Cardinal, she showed us a personal check for $15,000 which he had given her. I remember distinctly how concerned she* *was about him. A prophet herself, she saw with insight and sadness what was happening. "Some of us," she said, "may disagree with Cardinal McIntyre on how we see or promote the Kingdom. I personally will always be in his debt for his understanding, his wisdom, his compassion and his honesty." My heart went out to, and I always defended, the great creative community of the Immaculate Heart Sisters, and indeed, many others with whom the Cardinal was in conflict, but I resonated with Dorothy Day's appraisal.*

John always exercised such generosity of spirit. I remember driving him somewhere, and suggesting that *Humanae Vitae* was prophetic in its rejection of a contraceptive culture that divorces sexual relations from the gift of children, but that it articulated an ideal, perhaps even a counsel of perfection. As pilgrims we limp toward the ideal—"Be ye perfect, even as your heavenly Father is perfect"—and are called to employ *phronesis,* practical wisdom, when we hit the muddy interstices of life. By grace, we achieve the good by degrees. John sat in the passenger seat and hummed in affirmation. I remember another time, sitting at the little kitchen table in his "chambers" and declaring, "The Church needs to recover and articulate its rich tradition of culture and teaching!" John paused, put his tea cup down, straightened, looked me in the eyes, and with his faux barrister's baritone replied, "You speak to me as one who needs to be convinced!" He embodied the very thing I was smugly contending, and here I was preaching to him! I laughed hard, and so did he. With John, laughter was always a fruit of the Spirit.

John was well known in Los Angeles. Once named the city's "Man of the Year," he was honored by presidents, popes, and Pepperdine University, where I teach. The latter award points up his profound gift for ecumenism, for reaching out to people of different religious traditions, or none at all. At the second of his two funerals, I met a rabbi who spoke of his deep gratitude for John's friendship. Above all, John was a parish priest. In 1965, he was named pastor of Our Lady of Malibu. He'd go on to write many books—on saints, psalms, his pilgrimage to the Holy Land, and a nourishing book on accepting death, *And When It Is Dawn* (1980), that was recommended by hospice centers around the country. But in his face-to-face pastoral role, he "stirred into flame" the faith and love of countless people to whom he made himself available.

Availability is integral to the work of the parish priest. In her essay on "School Studies," Simone Weil extols the attention of Saint John Vianney, the "Cure d'Ars," patron of parish priests, and suggests that his capacity to attend to others was sharpened by his struggles to learn Latin. (I suspect that John's attentiveness to others was, in part, honed by his years at the Moyne Latin School. Surely his studies enabled him to coach his friend Martin Sheen through the Latin soliloquy he delivered in the "Two Cathedrals" episode of *The West Wing.*) As a priest, John modeled *availability,* in the sense that one of his favorite thinkers, Gabriel Marcel, emphasized that word. John always reached out in relation to and often friendship with others. Any person with him participated in John's deep sense that life was a mystery to be lived, not a problem to be solved.

John deeply valued the availability priests offered in the confessional. As he wrote in his memoir, "I can attest with the utmost conviction, as a sinner approaching the Sacrament of Reconciliation, and as a confessor who spent countless hours in those downtown confessionals, that there is no comfort, no consolation, no experience in human life, to equal the graced penitent walking out of the confessional, with a radically renewed awareness of being forgiven, of being loved unconditionally." People have told me that talking with John literally saved their lives. His graced presence gave them the hope to begin again. The abuse scandal made him very angry, but he worked through his rage with the help of his own Italian confessor.

And John was available in his celebration of the Eucharist. Before daily Mass, he'd arrive early to recite the Morning Prayer, using a simpler form of the Liturgy of the Hours. After the psalms, he'd turn slowly and greet whomever was in the pews beside and behind him. One morning, I remember the sun's slanting rays beaming through the church windows, and a beautiful woman walking gracefully up the nave of the church to greet him with a kiss. He accepted that kiss, as he always accepted the love of others, with calm, grateful eyes. Children loved the way he'd begin the liturgy by wishing everyone "a blessed, blessed day." His homilies, crafted yet improvisational, were always inspired by his love for God's word and for God's people. At the Offertory, he'd summon any sleepy-heads with gusto: "Lift up your hearts!" Later, he'd place the host in the communicant's hands, give them a little tap, and say his or her name. My father-in-law, an old Marine with three tours of duty behind him, said he'd never felt so moved as when he received communion from Monsignor and heard him say, "Peter."

After Sunday Mass, Monsignor would stand at the back of the church and greet each person: "Ahh, but do you know this fine creature," he'd say, introducing strangers (and sometimes married couples) to each other. I've never known anyone who forged so many friendships with such a wide array of people—from children to the elderly. After daily Mass, I'd often meet Monsignor back in the sacristy, where Bill, our steadfast server, would read a post-communion prayer that hung on the wall, translated by Hopkins: "Lend this life to me then: feed and feast my mind, / There be thou the sweetness man was meant to find." Monsignor would gaze intently out the window, deep in prayer. Sometimes I'd wait for him outside in the parish garden. He'd emerge—one hand on his cane, the other on the arm of a friend—and exclaim with dramatic flourish, "Ahh, Mister Paul, I desire to greet you!" Then he'd pause to greet the flowers. "Just look at that fine person!" he might say, addressing a lily or a rose. And he'd greet the weeds, "And how are you, you villains?" John wasn't a pantheist, but he discerned God's presence everywhere. He lived the deep insight of Saint Thérèse of Lisieux, the Little Flower, who, near the end of her short life, observed, "All is grace."

On Holy Thursday 2010, John was unsteady on his feet and he asked me to stand by his side during the liturgy, in case he needed to be caught. As during those impromptu homilies, I felt a bit awkward, standing behind the altar at the celebration of the Lord's Supper, as if encroaching upon the priestly role. But John made tangible the Church's teaching that all believers share in Christ's priesthood, just as we share in His Body. In his final year, I'd often be last in line to receive communion so I could take his arm and help him back up the stairs to the altar. I'm thankful to have done so on the morning of August 25, 2010, as that would be the last Mass Monsignor celebrated. That afternoon, he and two beloved friends were in a terrible automobile accident. Sister Mary Campbell, his close friend and graceful helper for many years, died immediately. Ambassador Doug Kmiec suffered serious physical injuries, and great spiritual pain, as he relates in his memoir, *Lift Up Your Hearts* (2012). John lingered in UCLA hospital for three weeks.

In those final weeks, John taught his many friends about suffering. When one saw his broken, bloodied body a few days before he died, it was, at first, hard to say, "All is grace." And yet it was so. When John heard the familiar voice of a visitor to his hospital room, his eyes opened wide—pained yet alert, receptive, always loving. To the end, John Sheridan saw grace in every person, and thus he helped us to see it in each other—whether we were running or limping, laughing or weeping, whole or broken, or—to use two of his favorite adjectives—"saintly" or "wretched," often both on the same day. That's what saints do: by the beauty of their holiness, they draw us in, and inspire us to be better. Our pastor, Father Bill Kerze, put it well: All who knew John "encounter[ed] a person of compassion, a fellow sinner who is really a saint, an *Alter Christus,* a living bridge to a God of goodness and life." John saw the mystery of God's love at work in "the wondrous universe," and in ready response, he prayed, "*Quid retribuam? What can I give?*" Anyone who knew him continues to feel

John's presence and, thus, to have been granted a task: to give as he gave, to be kind as he was kind.

Immanuel Kant claimed, "From the crooked timber of humanity nothing straight can ever be made." Paul Claudel popularized the proverb, "God writes straight with crooked lines." Allow me to amalgamate: Through John Sheridan, God built straight with crooked timber. No matter how broken or bent, after being in his presence, people felt edified—built up, more whole, more holy. The saints are the Church's greatest apologetic. Like so many, I'm grateful to have known the saintly Monsignor John Sheridan.

# PHILOSOPHER OF
# THE HEART

---

## MAX SCHELER

---

*John Cornwell*

THE PHILOSOPHER MAX SCHELER (1874–1928) was a combative, constructively critical temporary Catholic convert who eventually apostatised, yet he exerted a seminal influence over the delayed Catholic renewal of the 1960s. He helped shape the thought of many leading Catholic figures, including Romano Guardini, one of the century's great philosophers of religion, and Edith Stein, the Jewish convert, Carmelite theologian, and death camp martyr.

Scheler's vision for Catholicism in Germany during the second and third decades of the twentieth century anticipated the spirit of the Second Vatican Council. He advocated a united Europe imbued with the Judaic Christian spirit, free of British utilitarianism and the excesses of American materialism. He critiqued both capitalism and communism and promoted an expression of Catholicism that was pluralist and inclusive, antipathetic to clericalism, dogma, false Catholic victimhood, and the siege mentality.

Born in Munich in 1874 of a Lutheran father and an Orthodox Jewish mother, Scheler was an enthusiastic Marxist as an adolescent. This background enabled him to appreciate the scope within Catholicism for engagement with society and politics. He was the son of a land agent for the grand Duke of Saxe-Coburg and a socially aspiring mother, who persuaded her husband to move from the duke's rural estates to Munich to enjoy a more cosmopolitan lifestyle. Fiercely independent, he was raised an Orthodox Jew but rejected the faith of his birth to embrace Catholicism in his early teens, drawn by the Church's liturgy, the cycle of the worshiping year, and the Bavarian expressions of Church ceremonial. Physically impressive, with a massive head, immortalized by the painter Otto Dix, Scheler was charismatic. An ebullient and brilliant teacher, a courageous and original intellect, he went against the tide during the turbulent epoch that spanned the Great War and the Weimar period in Germany as Nazism began its inexorable rise. The philosopher Martin Heidigger said on Scheler's death in 1928 that he was "the strongest philosophical force in modern Germany, even in contemporary Europe and in contemporary philosophy." Scheler spoke out boldly and prophetically against the Nazis in the late 1920s. Eventually he would abandon his formal membership of the Church, but his vision of a socially and politically engaged Catholicism of the people would persist.

Scheler was no plaster saint. His early days as a student were fragmented and wayward. As an adolescent he read and was influenced by Friedrich Nietzsche; he believed that philosophers need to purge their minds of early influences to be open to original thinking. Where Nietzsche argued for the will to power, Scheler argued for the power of love. He was baptized a Catholic at age fourteen.

He studied philosophy at Munich University, then moved after a year to Berlin, where he began to pursue medicine, then switched to sociology. After two years he enrolled at the University of Jena to complete his doctorate in philosophy before returning to the University of Munich, where he eventually acquired a teaching post and married. He had a weakness for women and was a heavy drinker. He was married at thirty, but the relationship did not prosper; the couple separated in 1910 and eventually divorced. He was accused perhaps unjustly of impropriety with students—"moral turpitude." He sued a Munich newspaper for libel but lost. The university, which had a strong formal Catholic ethos, sacked him. Marital troubles would dog his life: he was married three times, a circumstance that led, inevitably for those days, to exclusion from the Church. And yet, Scheler had strong moral principles within sexual ethics and would develop a much cited distinction between "sexual shame" and "moral shame." Sexual shame for Scheler is not an admission of moral wrongdoing, of being judged as a moral subject; it is a consciousness of revulsion against the human body being used as an object. Scheler describes sexual shame as a *Schutzgefühl*—a shield emotion. Loss of a sense of sexual shame means vulnerability to being preyed upon sexually, or preying on another.

He moved to Göttingen and lectured in cafés. The students flocked to his unscheduled seminars. When the Great War broke out he was rejected for military service because of eye problems. At first he defended Germany's role in the war; later he became a leading figure in bids for peace, traveling in Holland, Austria, and Switzerland to encourage negotiations between Germany and the Allies. He campaigned relentlessly for the development of democracy after the Versailles treaty and argued for a United States of Europe to prevent further war.

Scheler's academic preoccupation was the development of the philosophy of phenomenology associated with Edmund Husserl (1859–1938). Phenomenologists were intent on studying the nature of knowledge and personhood through ruminative subjective experience. This involved a rejection of the dry, impersonal, unemotional, logical, linear, abstract, and objective approach of scholasticism—the philosophy that dominated Catholic seminaries and Catholic dogma. Scheler saw values as socially embodied and emotional. Values are not unchanging abstract entities; a person is not a substance but a conscious "doer," both an individual and a member of a community. He emphasized process over immutable universal concepts. His thinking and influence are best appreciated in contrast to those who opposed him.

No one stood in greater opposition to Scheler at the end of the First World War than Eugenio Pacelli, the future Pius XII, who had arrived in Germany as papal nuncio in 1917. He was to represent a Vatican version of Catholic identity in Germany through the Weimar period. Having lost the war, Germany in 1918 found itself close to social, political, and economic collapse. Revolution loomed; cynicism clashed with fanaticism; the rival claims of the extreme right and the extreme left to resolve Germany's problems soon brought the country to the brink of civil war and economic ruin. Yet, by the mid–1920s, Germany, and Berlin especially, was becoming a hub of modernist artistic expression, experiment in film, art, literature, drama, and risqué night-clubbing. Pacelli condemned what he saw as the degenerate climate of the Weimar Republic, blaming it on the freedoms of democracy. Scheler saw in the Weimar a potential for the drama of ideas.

As papal nuncio, Pacelli (who had been an architect of the 1917 Code of Canon Law, an instrument of hierarchical centralization), was tasked with renegotiating many ancient treaties between the German provincial states and the Holy See. This involved the elimination of many jealously held local ecclesiastical privileges. For example, the new code insisted, unprecedentedly, that only the pope now had the right to nominate new bishops, whereas bishops in German states had formerly been nominated by the canons of the cathedral and lay entities. At the same time, he was keen to curb the power and influence of the Catholic Center Party. Following the lead of Pius XI (1922–39), Pacelli was uncomfortable with an alliance between the Church and democratic Catholic political parties that could not be controlled from the Roman center.

While committed to Catholic spirituality, liturgy, and ethos, Scheler stood at the opposite extreme to Pacelli's vision of what it means to be a Catholic. He had a powerful influence over the leading Center Party representatives, who numbered no less than five chancellors during the Weimar period, all of them antagonistic to Pacelli's aims. Scheler believed that Catholics should offer Germany and Europe neither Roman Catholic apologetics nor papal power from the Vatican, but a beneficent, self-determining influence rising from the smallest groups and communities. The influence of Catholicism, he believed, could be "generous and gentle rather than harsh," "concrete rather than abstract," "rooted in people and lived tradition rather than ahistorical principles," "more attached to the organic than artificial elites." The litany of contrasts revealed the gulf that had opened up between social Catholicism and the pyramidal ideology of papal supremacy that saw the pope as an initiating ecclesiastical autocrat ruling from the apex. Scheler saw the future of the Catholic Center Party in Germany and Catholic workers' unions, moreover, as rallying points for Christian democrats of every stripe; nor were Jews to be excluded. Catholicism could offer a focus for pluralism in the social and political sphere. Catholic influence, he insisted, must not stand merely alongside something called nationhood: "rather it must be woven into it and be evident in international relationships." With the end of the war and the exile of the Kaiser and his family, Scheler saw the prospect of a Catholic "moment" in Germany, combining reconciliation and international outreach.

Yet even as a new engagement seemed possible between Catholics and the rest of German society, a historic Vatican initiative was subverting the process. Pacelli's mission as papal nuncio eventually matured into a bid for an overarching church–state treaty, a *Reichskonkordat,* that would recall the four hundredth anniversary of Luther's Reformation by reversing its symbolism and significance. It was on December 10, 1520, at the Lestertor in Wittenberg that Martin Luther and his students had burned the corpus of Catholic canon law in token of their rejection of papal autocracy over the German Church. The act symbolized not only Luther's defiance of papal authority but his conviction that Rome "exalts its own ordinances above the commands of God." The volumes of canon law, Luther had complained, "say nothing about Christ." That historic act of apostasy, sacred to German Protestantism, lent immense import to Pacelli's scheme: the bid, after four centuries, to achieve official government recognition of, and indeed acquiescence in, the imposition upon German Catholics of the 1917 Code of Canon Law with its concentration of legalism, summitry, and Vatican hegemony. His hope was for a Vatican-controlled German Church that would dissociate itself from the nation's political life. In 1933 Pacelli would negotiate a deal with Adolf Hitler granting imposition of canon law over Catholics in exchange for their withdrawal from social and political action. Encouraged by Pacelli, the Center Party would vote for the bill that gave Hitler dictatorial powers, then dissolve itself.

Scheler's vision for a Catholic renaissance in Germany and Europe was inclusive, pragmatic, pluralist, communitarian, politically involved. He summed up his vision in a single, breathless description of Catholicism's true potential distinctiveness. Catholicism, he wrote, was

> *not the content of our faith . . . but the Catholic style of life and culture, the special form of Catholic humanity, its greater generosity, gentleness, softness, peacefulness, let us say quietly also its gentler tempo in response to work and ambition, so often criticized even within our own ranks as "inferiority"; its more devoted joy in the world and its serene harmony; its more concrete realism over against the abstract notions of order and unity; its innocence more rooted in the*

*people, and its more trustful and less complicated way of*
*living resolutely by living traditions; always to love what has*
*grown up more than what has been made, however cleverly.*

Among Scheler's many books, his lasting masterwork, first
published in 1913 and still in print in English, is *The Nature
of Sympathy,* an exploration of empathy—an appreciation
of the feelings and viewpoints of others. He offers a powerful critique of thinkers such as the British utilitarians, and
of Sigmund Freud, who argued against altruism, claiming
that fellow feeling is driven by self-interest. The book surveys
notions of love throughout the history of religion, concluding
that empathy is the basis of our knowledge of persons. Scheler
offered in *The Nature of Sympathy* a powerful antidote to the
later domination of logical positivism and behaviorism, as expounded by figures like A. J. Ayer and Gilbert Ryle.

In speeches he gave in 1927 Scheler argued that capitalism was a disposition of "mind" rather than an economic system. While granting with Max Weber that capitalism owed
much to Calvin's notion of prudence, he insisted that the true
origins of twentieth-century capitalism are to be found in
modern *angst,* a subconscious insecurity leading to a mania
for self-protection against all eventualities. In the same year
he warned against the impending dangers of Nazism.

If Eugenio Pacelli defined Scheler in terms of his opposite,
John Paul II would define him in terms of an unfortunate
amalgamation of Schelerian philosophy with ideas antitheti-
cal to the spirit of his thinking. While it is clear that John
Paul's principle of solidarity expounded as a bishop in Poland
owed much to Scheler, his attempts in his academic writings

to combine Scheler with the philosophy of Thomas Aquinas proved an unfortunate travesty. Admirers of John Paul's philosophical meditations down the years have claimed that he redressed and enlivened the inflexibility and austerity of scholasticism. Yet, to others, he had adopted the worst of both worlds. As one Jesuit scholar commented, "I often have the impression of banging into scholastic steel as I wander through the phenomenological fog."

Dogged by ill health, no doubt unhelped by his eighty-a-day cigarette habit, Scheler died at age fifty-four in 1928. Five years later the Nazis would ban and burn his books.

———————

My admiration for Max Scheler stems from personal experience of living through periods of disillusionment with the dry abstractions of scholastic thought. He made available to me a refreshing philosophical perspective with an emphasis on process rather than unchanging substance that enabled me to find my way back to the Church after an absence of twenty years. He also saw individual conscience as, in the final analysis, more crucial than blind obedience to authority. In this he was reminiscent of John Henry Newman. Following his conscience he left the Church eventually, unable to accept its more authoritarian strictures. I suspect that had he lived longer he would have been reconciled once again. Some of his statements toward the end of his life showed that he was moving in that direction. What is certain is that his disillusionment with Catholicism arose from a courageous determination to follow wherever his intellectual and spiritual integrity led him.

# SPEAKING THE
# TRUTH IN LOVE

## BERNARD HÄRING

〜〜〜

*Charles E. Curran*

I N 1993 POPE JOHN PAUL II issued his encyclical *Verita-tis Splendor* (The Splendor of Truth) on moral theology, which strongly condemned many developments in Catholic moral theology and the crisis that had been brought about by the fact that many Catholic moral theologians disagreed with and dissented from some moral teachings of the hierarchical Church *magisterium* (teaching office).

Bernard Häring, the foremost Catholic moral theologian in the second half of the twentieth century, reacted to the encyclical with an anguished *cri de coeur:* "Let us ask our Pope: are you sure your confidence in your supreme human, professional and religious competence in matters of moral theology and particularly sexual ethics is truly justified? . . . We should let the Pope know that we are wounded by the many signs of his rooted distrust and discouraged by the manifest structures of distrust which he has allowed to be established." Häring ended this article by insisting on the need to honor God's gracious forgiveness by forgiving each other for the harm we have inflicted on one another and the anger we may have harbored in our hearts.

This stinging criticism reflects Häring's insistence on the need for the virtue of loving criticism within the Church. Such an attitude does not entail a loveless or consistently negative criticism. Only those who appreciate and praise what is good in the Church can offer a healthy criticism of what is not in keeping with the gospel and the signs of the times. Blind conformity is not a virtue. Without absolute honesty and sincerity Catholic theology will never be credible. Häring has insisted that creative freedom and creative fidelity should characterize both the Christian life and the role of theology reflecting on that life.

Who was Bernard Häring, and how did he himself strive to live out creative freedom and creative fidelity as a Catholic Christian? The biographical facts of his life furnish the setting within which he made his significant contributions to the Church. Häring was born in Böttingen, Germany, the eleventh of twelve children, to devout Catholic parents in 1912. He entered the Redemptorist order and was ordained a priest in May 1939. He was drafted into the German army as a medic and served in France, Russia, and Poland. After the war he received his Ph.D. in theology at Tübingen University and taught moral theology at the Redemptorist Theologate in Gars-am-Inn in Upper Bavaria. His most important teaching role was at the Alphonsian Academy in Rome for more than thirty years before retiring to Gars in 1986. He was a *peritus* (expert) and active participant in the work of the Second Vatican Council (1962–65). He died in Gars on July 3, 1998.

## HÄRING'S CONTRIBUTIONS TO
## THE CATHOLIC CHURCH

Häring's major gift to the Church was his work as a moral theologian reflecting on the Christian life, but he also was a most significant voice for Church reform and the development of the spiritual life of Christian people. As a moral theologian Häring wrote the most significant book in Catholic moral theology in the second part of the twentieth century: *The Law of Christ,* originally published in German in 1954 and translated into fifteen languages. *The Law of Christ* proposed a biblical, liturgical, christological, and life-centered moral theology. He pioneered a new approach to moral theology that opposed the method of the manuals of moral theology with their concern only for training confessors for the sacrament of penance by learning how to distinguish what is sinful and the degrees of sinfulness.

Häring's moral theology was based on the good news of God's loving gift for us and our grateful response. We are called to be perfect as the gracious God is perfect. Christians have to experience growth and continual conversion in their moral life and in their multiple relationships with God, neighbor, world, and self. Häring staunchly opposed any legalism that made God into a controller rather than a gracious savior.

Nearly twenty-five years after having published *The Law of Christ*, Häring published first in English his completely new three-volume synthesis of moral theology: *Free and Faithful in Christ*. He continued to publish many other volumes and articles in the area of moral theology. His 1972 book on medical ethics appeared in six languages and was the occasion of a very painful investigation of Häring by the Congregation for the Doctrine of the Faith. This investigation was going on at the same time that Häring was suffering from throat cancer and at times very close to death.

The fact that Häring taught at the Alphonsian Academy in Rome from 1954 to 1986 gave him both prominence in Rome and the opportunity to teach many students (nearly all of whom were clerics) from all parts of the world. A significant development over the years in his moral theology was his emphasis on the healing power of nonviolence.

There is some truth in the criticism that Häring's moral theology at times lacked academic rigor and was too homiletical in style. Häring was not an academic writing primarily for fellow academicians but was a Church person writing for the Church. His moral theology came from a deep and creative intelligence and included significant dialogue with philosophy, sociology, psychology, and medicine.

A second contribution of Häring's, in addition to his moral theology, was his work for Church reform. He was a most active participant in Vatican II. Pope John XXIII read his 1963 book on what the council should do and sent him a message expressing his joy in reading the book and his complete agreement with it. Häring worked on the documents on the Church in the Modern World and the Decree on Priestly

Formation. Cardinal Fernando Cento, the co-president of the mixed commission working on the document on the Church in the Modern World, publicly called Häring the "quasi-father of *Gaudium et spes.*"

In addition to his work inside the council, Häring carried on an indefatigable mission outside the council. He frequently addressed various groups of bishops from all over the world. The fact that Häring was fluent in eight languages made him a much-sought-after speaker to explain the implications of reform in the Church for the bishops at the council. He also frequently commented to press panels in all these different languages and was recognized by all as a very competent and forthright proponent of reform in the Church. In many publications and lectures, Häring ceaselessly pointed out the dangers of legalism and pharisaism in the Church. He frequently differed, even at times publicly, with some leading figures in the Church but always made an effort to avoid making enemies of anyone.

Häring was an early advocate for change in the papal teaching condemning artificial contraception for spouses and had a great influence as a member of the commission that was established by the popes to study this issue. When Pope Paul VI issued *Humanae Vitae* (On Human Life) in 1968 reaffirming the teaching, Häring forthrightly and publicly disagreed. His differing positions on contraception, sterilization, the pastoral care of divorced people, and some aspects of medical ethics made it inevitable that he would ultimately come under investigation by the Congregation for the Doctrine of the Faith. Until his death, Häring remained an important voice throughout the world for reform in the Church.

His intense love for the Church at times compelled him to be a loving critic.

Third, Bernard Häring was an intrepid proponent of a renewed spirituality in the Church. Anyone who ever met him realized he was a person of prayer. His own spirituality permeated all that he did. His theoretical understanding of moral theology insisted on the intimate connection between the moral life and the spiritual life of the Christian. In 1963, in Paul VI's first year as pope, he asked Häring to give the annual Lenten retreat to the pope and the Roman curia.

In his summer vacations and at other times, Häring traveled the world, not only giving lectures in moral theology but also giving retreats to all the people of God as well as clergy and religious. Even in his retreat work, Häring carried out an ecumenical ministry. For example, at the invitation of Dr. Douglas Steere, the Quaker observer at Vatican II, he gave spiritual exercises at the Dayspring Retreat Center outside Washington, D.C., every year until his larynx was removed. Häring also encouraged religious orders of women throughout the world to establish houses of prayer.

## HÄRING'S INFLUENCE ON ME

This sketch of Häring's life and work has given a basic understanding of his contributions, but Häring has played a very significant role in my personal life and work. My appreciation for Häring was summed up in the dedication of my 1972 book, *Catholic Moral Theology in Dialogue*—"To Bernard Häring CSsR—teacher, theologian, friend, and priestly minister of the Gospel in theory and practice on the occasion of his sixtieth

birthday." As a very young priest of the diocese of Rochester, New York, I was doing doctoral work at the Alphonsian
Academy in Rome from 1959 to 1961. I was scheduled to teach
moral theology at the diocesan seminary in Rochester. After
four years of theology at the Gregorian University, I was opening up somewhat from my conservative theological orientation
and my commitment to the moral theology of the manuals.
I did not write my dissertation with Häring, but I was truly
thrilled and nourished by his classes (in Latin) in which he developed his approach to moral theology. At my invitation many
fellow priests living with me at the American college in Rome
came to hear him and were greatly impressed.

In 1961 I started teaching in the seminary in Rochester,
trying to emulate the approach of Häring. One year early in
my teaching the two-semester course I did not open the required manual until March 1. I first wanted to show the full
depth and breadth of the Christian moral life before getting
into the manual. I later read in Häring's autobiography that
he had done the same thing when he began teaching moral
theology. I was the primary mover in bringing Häring to the
United States in 1963 to give lectures and workshops during
the summer. In subsequent years Häring came back many
times to the United States during the summer, and he also
traveled through many parts of Africa, Latin America, and
Asia giving lectures and retreats.

On July 29, 1968, Pope Paul VI's encyclical *Humanae Vitae*
reiterating the condemnation of artificial contraception for
spouses was publicly released. I was the leader and later the
spokesperson of what started as a group of ten of us, mostly
from Catholic University, who read the encyclical that night

and drafted a response to it. Our ten-paragraph statement concluded that Catholics could responsibly decide to use birth control if it were for the good of their marriage. After finishing the statement we called a number of other theologians in the country looking for more signatures. I reached Häring in California, read him the statement, and was ecstatic when he agreed to sign. On the morning of July 30 I acted as the spokesperson for the then-eighty-six Catholic scholars, including Bernard Häring, who had signed the statement. Ultimately more than six hundred signed. This forthright and early response to the encyclical gained worldwide attention. Häring himself then and later without doubt became the most prominent and public proponent in the Catholic world for disagreeing with the conclusion of the encyclical.

In the summer of 1979, I was informed that I was under investigation from the Vatican Congregation for the Doctrine of the Faith for my dissent on a number of moral issues. That fall I went to Rome to consult with Häring and others. Throughout the process I stayed in close touch with Bernard. After much correspondence back and forth it became clear in late 1985 that the Congregation for the Doctrine of the Faith was going to take action against me, which they ultimately did in declaring that I was neither suitable nor eligible to be a Catholic theologian. However, they did agree to have an informal meeting of myself with Cardinal Joseph Ratzinger and some officials of the Congregation in March 1986. I was able to bring one advisor. All along Häring had agreed that if there were such a meeting he would accompany me.

Häring's presence was a source of great strength and consolation to me. He began the session by reading a two-page paper entitled "The Frequent and Long-Lasting Dissent of the Inquisition/Holy Office/CDF." It was Häring at his forthright best at speaking to power. In the end he strongly urged Cardinal Ratzinger to accept a compromise that I would not teach sexual ethics at Catholic University and there would be no condemnation. The meeting ended without any solution or action.

The next day, the fourth Sunday of Lent, six of us went to Häring's religious house to celebrate a liturgy at which he presided. The Gospel was the parable of the prodigal son. Häring in the homily looked at me and said that the Church was the prodigal son who had taken all my treasure and my work for moral theology and fed it to the pigs. But the Holy Spirit was calling on me and the others present to take the role of the Father and forgive the Church. Only with a spirit of forgiveness and hope can we continue to celebrate the Eucharist. He ended the homily by repeating twice that Christians are people who have hope.

In the past few years I have often been encouraged by the witness of Bernard Häring. These are not good times for us progressive Catholics who are working for Church reform. The Vatican resolutely opposes any attempts to bring about progressive change in the Church. A defensive centralization continues to mark the attitude of the Vatican to any attempts to bring about change. John Paul II recognized there was a crisis in moral theology because many moral theologians today dissent from papal teaching. But the popes have adamantly fought such change and even taken punitive action against those who have dissented on matters that are not essential to the Catholic faith. Meanwhile all of us have seen family and friends leave the Catholic Church because of its intransigence. Many people have asked me if I see any signs of hope in the Church today. I remind them and myself that hope is not hope if you see it in front of you. Saint Paul tells us that hope is hoping against hope. Hope is believing in light in the midst of darkness and life in the midst of death.

Bernard Häring was truly a person of hope. He faced death many times during World War II. He almost died during the operations trying to cure his cancer of the throat. The person who spoke in more languages to more people in all parts of the world than any other theologian, preacher, or missionary later had his vocal cords removed and had to learn to speak from the esophagus, which was not easy either for him or for his listeners. In the last years of his life he experienced the return of a centralization and authoritarianism he thought had been vanquished by Vatican II.

Häring's witness of critical love for the Church, his forthrightness, and his hope even in the midst of darkness enabled him to continue the struggle for Church reform. His witness gives hope and strength to all who work for reform in the Church.

# LOVE AND VIOLENCE

## MICHELANGELO MERISI DI CARAVAGGIO

*Paul Elie*

G OD DOESN'T RAPE; GOD WOOS, Augustine of Hippo says somewhere. But Michelangelo Merisi di Caravaggio says otherwise—says that God has it both ways.

In Rome you can see it one way and then the other in the space of an hour.

First to San Luigi dei Francesi near Piazza Navona: grey stone, short porch, curt signage, beat-up green doors. This church is open for just a few hours in the morning and a few in the afternoon. The doors are locked as often as not, but as you pass, going to lunch in full sunlight across cobblestones baking in the heat, you can feel the radiation coming from Caravaggio's *Calling of St. Matthew* inside—can feel a life changing at the tip of the extended finger behind which Jesus, with a look not a word, says "Come away with me."

Then to Piazza dei Popolo on the rim of the historic center. This piazza is as endowed with art as any in Rome: twin baroque churches, an obelisk, the imperial arch that for 750 years has served as a portal for pilgrims arriving from the north. But the holy of holies is inside the church on the far corner: Caravaggio's *Conversion of St. Paul*. The painting pulls you like an electromagnet across the piazza—pulls you as the force of grace, so called, pulled Saul of Tarsus off his horse and left him flattened and immobile, legs and arms spread skyward.

The God of love, and the God of violence: this is the primordial pairing at the heart of Caravaggio's work.

What is it (the art historian asks) that makes Caravaggio's work so convincing, and so recognizable that he seems to belong to us and our times as much as to Counter-Reformation Rome? Is it the pinpoint lighting of the paintings, together with the surrounding darkness, like black box theater? Is it the tight focus, the caught-by-surprise quality of the action, akin to the "decisive moment" that Henri Cartier-Bresson sought with his photographs? Is it the stress on the poor and ordinary rather than the grand and iconic? The attention to the pale, ribbed, hirsute human body? The doleful candor of the embedded self-portraits?

It is all those things. And all through them, it is Caravaggio's pairing of love and violence that joins his world to ours. For Caravaggio love and violence—not faith and doubt, not salvation and damnation, not orthodoxy and heterodoxy—are the extremes of religious encounter. They are opposed so relentlessly in his work as to make those other dichotomies seem small and dry. The emphasis Caravaggio gives them is an act of fidelity and a mark of personal style.

Flannery O'Connor remarked that reading Kafka "makes

you a little bolder as a writer." She read Kafka at the Iowa
Writers' Workshop, and there she began to go boldly into the
territory of violence, a place where "the kingdom of heaven
suffereth violence, and the violent bear it away." More than
most writers of her time and place, certainly more than any
other American Catholic writer, she recognized the violence
of contemporary life; and she made the struggle between love
and violence akin to the struggle in the individual soul between belief and unbelief, piety and blasphemy. A moment
of graced insight in a flurry of gunfire, a son's tenderness
called forth at last during a mother's heart attack: O'Connor
grasped that only in moments like these would her people—
her characters, and her readers—"feel, in [their] bones if nowhere else, that something is going on here that counts."

That is how it is with Caravaggio. When you stand in
front of his painting of a dead man being raised, a holy
woman being buried, a bearded elder straining against the
cross to which he has matter-of-factly been nailed, you know
that something is going on here that counts. You can see the
violation of the laws of nature that a full-body resurrection
would require. You can see, in the holy woman's sickened
complexion, the awful death that preceded this grim act of
burial. You can see in that elder's rippled midsection, straining upward against the force of gravity and the agony of crucifixion, a man who is every believer's bearded uncle, at once
less than and more than an apostle.

The maxim *amor vincit omnes* was etched into a wall
of one of the palaces in Rome where Caravaggio lived as a
cardinal's kept artist. It would take this artist—a religious
artist—to plumb the depths of the classical maxim. Love

conquers all—but by conquering, not by proposing or persuading. Love works in the way of violence. It acts in opposition to violence. It is like violence in its abruptness and lack of proportion.

God writes straight with crooked lines, as the poet Paul Claudel had it (and the remark itself runs in a crooked line back as far as Augustine). Caravaggio paints love with violence. His brush is reed and sword alike. With it he welcomes Christ into Jerusalem and challenges the faint of heart.

---

His life was closer to *Pirates of the Caribbean* than *Diary of a Country Priest*. He was born in Milan in 1571 and grew up there and in the village of Caravaggio in Lombardy. He lost family in the plague of 1576–77: his father, a grandfather and grandmother, an uncle. He arrived in Rome, gifted and lightly tutored, in 1592, as the city prepared for the holy year of 1600, which would be marked with pilgrimages and public executions. He wore a thick dark beard beneath his sad, all-seeing eyes. He liked weapons, and he was arrested for carrying sword in the streets without a permit. He kept company with prostitutes, male and female, and made a female consort the model for the Virgin Mary. He went about with a teenage boy and painted him nude—painted him head-on and with relish. He once struck a waiter who suggested that he couldn't tell one kind of artichoke from another. He killed a man, probably in a duel; convicted and sentenced to death, he fled Rome for Malta, the island fortress in the south, and sought to become a knight there. After a fight he was jailed. One night he bribed or overpowered a guard, slipped out, descended a high wall to a boat offshore, and escaped to Sicily. From there he persuaded his cardinal friend to get his sentence lifted and to arrange his return to Rome in exchange for new paintings.

It is a life as full of incident as any artist's. And yet even in the best biographies (by Helen Langdon, by Andrew Graham-Dixon), Caravaggio the person is notably less vivid than the people in his paintings. As with Johann Sebastian Bach—another religious artist who at once defines and transcends the term—the particulars of the life seem wan and fragmentary in comparison with the work: its originality, its intensity, its controlled excess, captured in the theological term *supererogatory,* or "more than is necessary for salvation."

As with Bach, too, the particulars of the life do not begin to account for the work's intensely religious character. Never was an artist so wholly resident in a Catholic society as Caravaggio was in Catholic Italy circa 1600. (Michelangelo and Raphael, pre-Reformation, were dual citizens of Catholic Italy and classical antiquity.) But no amount of information about the era—the Counter-Reformation, the Inquisition, the severe piety Cardinal Carlo Borromeo enjoined on the region's Catholics—can account for the high wattage of Caravaggio's religious insight.

A man who wanted to marry a woman who preferred to sleep with Caravaggio called him "an excommunicant and cursed man." In his way of life, the painter was something other than orthodox. And yet his paintings are among the few from the Catholic tradition that people of all shades of belief recognize right away as definitive. Religious art is not conclusive evidence of religious belief, but the paintings suggest that

Caravaggio, no matter how he lived, saw life from the point of view of Christian belief as clearly as anyone ever has.

For his use of living models, his attention to light and its effects, his scrutiny of the body, he is called a naturalist. For his attention to ordinary people—poor, humble, everyday people—he is called a *pauveriste,* an artist working in a tradition that developed in the spirit of Saint Philip Neri and his community's embrace of the poor who came on pilgrimage to Rome. But Caravaggio's approach is more complicated than those terms suggest. I would suggest that it is best understood in terms of fidelity. He paints crucial episodes in the Christian adventure. He paints them in a way faithful to scripture, to human action, to the claims and burdens of the flesh. He paints in fidelity to his gifts for precise rendering, portraiture, and dramaturgy. He paints in fidelity to the body of belief that he carries with him, which at once sustains him and maintains him through employment and patronage. And he paints in fidelity to his experience of love and violence; without making his experience the measure of belief, he makes it belief's probe and guarantor.

The paintings are beginnings and endings at once. His attention to biblical scenes and episodes from the early history of the Church makes them feel early, as if they precede the tradition of Christian iconography that developed in the Middle Ages. Somehow he got back behind the long, grand tradition of Christian art and made it new. That is what you feel when you look at the paintings, at any rate. Never before have you seen a biblical scene shown this way. No one before Caravaggio saw it this way. The paintings, breakthroughs four hundred years ago, look like breakthroughs today. The ancient faith is made new and arresting again; the whole epistemologically strained religion is grasped as if for the first time.

At the same time, the paintings exhaust the incidents they depict. A writing teacher once said that most writers begin their stories too early and that Ernest Hemingway, for example, knew to begin a story near the end. Well, so did Caravaggio. His biblical scenes are all but over as he paints them. Lazarus is being raised. Christ is being taken. Catherine sits calm and sexy before the wheel of her impaling. Matthew, Peter, and Paul are being killed in action. Lucy, dead already, is being laid in earth. An epochal action is ending. The hour is getting late.

The paintings, a religious artist's acts of fidelity, at once depart from artistic convention and defy the conventional presentation of Christianity. With them Caravaggio rejects the identification of Christian belief with good taste and good behavior, with the forces of order and propriety and appropriateness. And he stands aside from the identification of Christianity with history—from the sense of the Church as a superintending agency executing a mission that extends from the time of Christ up to the present.

To say this is not to scant the role of the Church in Caravaggio's work. The Church was his sponsor and protector. The episodes he painted as crucial are identified as such through doctrine and tradition and were cherished by the churchmen who commissioned him to paint them. The power of the paintings derives in large part from their objectivity: you feel, looking at them, that something is happening there that counts because of the Church's teaching, maintained against forceful opposition, that the something happening there really happened—that sacred history is history, not metaphor or myth.

Fidelity, for Caravaggio, involves putting some things in and leaving others out. He rejects what is false and trivial in Christianity by dramatizing the Christian adventure at its most intense. For the most part the body is brought in and the appurtenances of the Church are left out. In a Caravaggio Christianity exists here and now, once and for all. There is no horizon of history or society. There are no patrons crowding the outskirts. A sacred action is taking place in a dark rectangle of space. It has not happened before. It will not happen again.

Such fidelity brings about a change of emphasis both for the painter and for the person who sees the paintings. That is a pattern that runs right through the history of Christian belief. Prophets and saints shift the emphasis. So do doctors of the church. So do religious artists. All these in their different ways see unseen aspects or dimensions, fresh conflicts or sites of drama, in the body of belief. Thomas Aquinas, turning through Averroës to Aristotle, emphasized the natural order as the substrate of the supernatural. Hildegard of Bingen perceived a mystical order in sacred music. Peter Maurin and Dorothy Day saw in poverty an opportunity for communal self-sufficiency and so conjoined slum and farm. Angelo Roncalli looked past the theology of fixity and recognized the Church as a congregation of people on the move, an insight made dramatic in Karol Wojtyla's journeys.

So it is with Caravaggio. He shifts the emphasis in Christian art from piety to fidelity. He turns our attention from good and evil to love and violence. His fidelity to these aspects of the encounter—found in scripture, known from experience—is the religious artist's act of conscience.

---

You can see this in those two Caravaggios in the center of Rome.

In Rome no one church or bridge or palazzo stands out in independent glory. The effect is of all of them put together, of the city as an all-encompassing work of art with a life of its own. This effect reduces most paintings in Rome to secondary works: accessories in churches, treasures on palace walls, frescoes incorporated into the city body and soul. It is as if the painters knew the futility of artistic independence and opted ruefully to subsume their talents to the civic good. Paintings in Rome illustrate episodes in the story the holy city embodies. They accessorize and adorn.

Except for the Caravaggios. The Caravaggios dominate their churches and haunt the streets surrounding them. They are as dark and hidden as the catacombs; they are black holes, packed with significance until their gravitational force is strong enough to withstand the gravity of Rome as a whole.

In one of his memos for the next millennium Italo Calvino characterized Saint Ignatius Loyola as the first modern person. He meant that Ignatius was the first to grasp the power of the individual imagination as an aspect of our everyday mental life. In the Middle Ages the crucial episodes of the Christian adventure were represented for the believer in painting and sculpture and decorative arts. With Martin Luther they were recounted verbally in the German vernacular. With the

*Spiritual Exercises* Ignatius invited the believer to devise his own images for those crucial episodes and screen them on the insides of his head.

If Ignatius was the first modern, Caravaggio was right behind him. He figured out how to be bold in Rome, where religious art was everywhere. In the city of public art, his paintings are interiors; in the eternal city, a site transcending time, his paintings take place in the middle of the night. For all their action, they are images of the interior life. The believer is knocked off his horse, or is beckoned to come closer—is converted through love or through violence.

The *Calling of St. Matthew* at San Luigi dei Francesi is a work of love. Strictly speaking, it is about obedience. The teacher points a finger in the darkness, and we are to understand that the tax collector will obey. But what passes between Jesus and Matthew is love. Jesus makes his appeal from the shadows—the margins—rather than from the center of the painting. His hand is extended but relaxed, not in anger or accusation. The clear-eyed regard shown to Jesus by the boy to Matthew's left—who is so handsome, so stylishly dressed and plumed, and so brilliantly lit as to be the center of the painting—shows that there is nothing to fear here. The light of the whole, the diagonal sweep from the right-hand corner across the window in the center, suggests the steadiness of the love in Jesus's request and command. The accepting gaze of the eventual evangelist, the eternal "Who, me?"—eyebrows raised, eyes soft and wet as if tears are forming—makes clear that he knows his life is changing. So do we: but we feel his old life ending more than his new life beginning.

The *Conversion of St. Paul* is a work of violence. Literally, it is the scene of an accident. A rider has been thrown off his horse. A bald and bearded old minder is settling the horse down. But the rider is in agony. He is flat on his back on the ground. His helmet is thrown off, his sword unsheathed, the saddle blanket scattered underneath him. His skin is pallid; his arms and hands are veined with tension. His face is flushed red; his eyes are lidded shut. Only his arms and legs, spread toward the blackness at the top edge of the painting— spread sexually, or crucifically, scholars suggest—indicate that he is alive. Only the presence of that old minder suggests that the horse, whose right foreleg stirs just above the fallen rider, will not stomp the rider to death.

Here is the other form love takes. This rider's journey is finished. Wherever he was headed, he is not going to make it there. He has survived an act of violence, but he will have to start over again. He is a body of broken bones. He will heal along the way.

---

Caravaggio never made it back to Rome. In July 1610 he went ashore south of Rome with the boat bearing new paintings for his cardinal friend, the price of his return to the city. Onshore, he got in a quarrel and was thrown in jail. The boatman sailed for Rome without him. Sickened by this separation from his work—to him, it was an act of theft and left him without a ticket back into Rome—he bribed his way out of jail and set off for Rome on foot. He never got there. He died of a heart attack or exhaustion. He was thirty-eight.

His paintings were scattered. Many are in the churches and galleries of Rome. Others are in Sicily. But there is a Caravaggio in Fort Worth, one in Kansas City, one in Detroit. Caravaggio's *Taking of Christ* hung for two hundred years in a monastery refectory in Dublin before it was identified as a Caravaggio.

It is evidence of the paintings' self-sufficiency that they travel well, and the loss of several Caravaggios is further evidence. Caravaggio's painting of *Christ at the Mount of Olives,* long in Berlin, was destroyed in an Allied bombing. So was a painting of *St. Matthew and the Angel.* A *Resurrection,* with saints, was destroyed in an earthquake in Messina. An *Adoration of the Shepherds* that hung in a Franciscan oratory in Palermo was stolen and has never been recovered. We can imagine it hanging on the wall of a Mafia redoubt, akin to the severed head of John the Baptist in Caravaggio's two paintings of *Herod and Salome*—a figure of extraordinary beauty taken and displayed as a prize.

The losses are terrible but apt. Caravaggio's paintings are works from the struggle between love and violence, not paintings of the struggle rendered from the outside. Works of love, those lost Caravaggios were reclaimed by violence. Love conquers all, but violence will have plenty of victories along the way.

---

How can Caravaggio's fidelity serve as a model for ours? How can his anguished life edify and inspire? What does his work, violent and ardent, tell us about our own generally less convulsive religious lives?

The question of why the Church in age after age tends to become a school for obedience, a facility for the maintenance and transmission of values (that term of barter and exchange) rather than a point of entry for the Christian adventure—that is a question for a different piece of writing. Here the question is narrower, a question for the religious artist.

How to be a little bolder after seeing Caravaggio? How to learn from his tableaux of love and violence?

The place to begin, I think, is with the recognition that for the religious artist fidelity is a calling unto itself. To stand in Rome before the Caravaggios there is to understand that the crucial episodes of the Christian adventure happen once and for all in every age. Seeing them, the religious artist understands that the maintenance and preservation of Christianity must be left to others. That those episodes still matter to us is owing to the Church, no question, but also to the religious artist. The artist must see and show those episodes in the present age—must find them, in many instances, where others are not looking. This artist must work by reorienting our attention. So it may be that in our time this artist will recognize love in gym or rave or nightclub, will recognize violence in the walk-in clinic or the humanitarian's laboratory. When first confronted, this artist's work will look irreverent to those called to maintenance and preservation. But the artist, eyes open, hand extended, knee bent, is striving for perfect fidelity.

# GOD OR GOLD

## BARTOLOMÉ DE LAS CASAS

### Robert Ellsberg

Christ did not come into the world to die for gold.

—*Bartolomé de Las Casas*

THE ARRIVAL OF THREE small Spanish ships on the blue
shores of the Bahamas in 1492 marked the beginning
of an unprecedented collision of cultures. For the Spanish
explorers and their royal patrons, the "discovery" of "the
new world" was like the opening of a treasure chest. But for
the indigenous peoples, whom Columbus called "Indians," it
marked the onset of oblivion. For most of the invaders, this
was not a serious consideration. In their view, the Indians
were a primitive, lesser breed; as Aristotle taught, some
were born to be slaves and others to be masters. While the
Church endorsed the Conquest as an opportunity to extend

the gospel, there were few theologians of the time prepared to see the Indians as fully human and equal in the eyes of God. One who did was the Dominican friar Bartolomé de Las Casas, who was so affected by what he had seen during the early decades of the Conquest that he devoted his long life to raising an outcry and bearing witness before an indifferent world.

To an extraordinary degree the life of Las Casas was bound to the fate of the Indians. As a boy of eight, he witnessed the return of Columbus to Seville after his first voyage to the New World. With fascination the young boy watched as the "Admiral of the Ocean" paraded through the streets, accompanied by seven Taino Indians (the surviving remnant of a larger number who began the voyage). As he recalled, they carried "very beautiful, red-tinged green parrots," as well as jewels and gold "and many other things never before seen or heard of in Spain."

Bartolomé's father quickly signed up for Columbus's second voyage, and in 1502 Bartolomé made his own first trip to Hispaniola (present-day Haiti and the Dominican Republic). After later studies in Rome for the priesthood he returned to the New World, where he served as chaplain in the Spanish conquest of Cuba. Though a priest, he also benefited from the Conquest as the owner of an *encomienda,* a plantation with Indian indentured laborers.

In these years, he witnessed scenes of diabolical cruelty, later chronicled with exacting detail. He described how the armored Spaniards would pacify a village by initiating massacres; how they would enslave their captives and punish any who rebelled by cutting off their hands; how they would consign them to die before their time through overwork in the mines and plantations. His account, based, as he frequently noted, on "what I have seen," included accounts of soldiers suddenly drawing their swords "to rip open the bellies" of men, women, children, and old folk, "all of whom were seated, off guard and frightened," so that "within two credos, not a man of all of them there remained alive."

Such scenes, replayed constantly in his memory, haunted Las Casas for the rest of his life. They also began a process of conversion, as the Spanish priest gradually defected from the cause of his own countrymen and identified with those who were treated as nonpersons, of no account, of "less worth than the dung in the street."

In 1514, at the age of thirty, Las Casas gave up his lands and the Indians he possessed and pronounced that he would refuse absolution to any Christian who would not do the same. Eventually, he joined the Dominican order and went on to become a passionate and prophetic defender of the indigenous peoples. For more than fifty years he traveled back and forth between the New World and the court of Spain, attempting through his books, letters, and preaching to expose the cruelties of the Conquest, whose very legitimacy, and not merely excesses, he disavowed.

On one occasion, a bishop became bored with his account of the death of seven thousand children, and interrupted him to ask, "What is that to me and to the king?" With fierce indignation, Las Casas replied, "What is it to your lordship and to the king that those souls die? Oh, great and eternal God! Who is there to whom that *is* something?" To Las Casas the Indians were fellow human beings, subject to the same sadness, entitled to the same respect. With this insight it followed that every ounce of gold extracted by their labor was theft; every indignity imposed on them was a crime; every death—whatever the circumstances—was an act of murder.

Although the main attraction for the Spanish in the New World was gold, the Conquest was ostensibly justified by evangelical motivations. The pope had authorized the subjugation of the Indian populations for the purpose of implanting the gospel and securing their salvation. Las Casas claimed that the deeds of the conquistadors revealed their true religion: "In order to gild a very cruel and harsh tyranny that destroys so many villages and people, solely for the sake of satisfying the greed of men and giving them gold, the latter, who themselves do not know the faith, use the pretext of teaching it to others and thereby deliver up the innocent in order to extract from their blood *the wealth which these men regard as their god.*"

With shame, he recounted the story of an Indian prince in Cuba who was burned alive. As he was tied to a stake a Franciscan friar spoke to him of God and asked him whether he would like to go to heaven and there enjoy glory and eternal rest. When the prince asked whether Christians also went to heaven and was assured that this was so, he replied without further thought that he did not wish to go there, "but rather to hell so as not to be where Spaniards were." Las Casas notes, with bitter irony, "This is the renown and honor that God and our faith have acquired by means of the Christians who have gone to the Indies."

But Las Casas's theological insights went far beyond a simple affirmation of the Indians' human dignity. In their

sufferings, he argued, the Indians truly represented the crucified Christ. So he wrote, "I leave in the Indies Jesus Christ,
our God, scourged and afflicted and beaten and crucified not
once, but thousands of times."

For Las Casas there could be no salvation in Jesus Christ
apart from social justice. Thus, the question was not whether
the Indians were to be "saved"; the more serious question
was the salvation of the Spanish who were persecuting Christ
in his poor. Jesus had said that our eternal fate rests on our
treatment of those in need: "I was hungry and you gave me
food . . . naked and you gave me clothing. . . . Truly I tell you,
just as you did it to one of the least of these who are members
of my family, you did it to me" (Matt. 25:31–40). If the failure
to do these things was enough to consign one to hell, what
about the situation of the New World, where Christ, in the
guise of the Indians, could justly say, "I was clothed, and you
stripped me naked, I was well fed, and you starved me . . ."?

Las Casas did not oppose the goal of evangelization. But
this could never be achieved by force. "The one and only
method of teaching men the true religion was established
by Divine Providence for the whole world and for all times,
that is, by persuading the understanding through reason and
by gently attracting or exhorting the will." Needless to say,
such views on religious freedom, the rights of conscience, and
the relation between salvation and social justice were far advanced for his time; indeed, they were scarcely matched in
the Catholic Church until the Second Vatican Council. Even
then, they were bitterly debated.

Nevertheless, Las Casas did win a hearing in Spain and he
was named "Protector of the Indians." With the passion of

an Old Testament prophet, he proclaimed, "The screams of so much spilled human blood have now reached heaven. The earth can no longer bear such steeping in human blood. The angels of peace and even God, I think, must be weeping. Hell alone rejoices." But his efforts made little difference.

In 1543, with court officials in Spain eager to be rid of him, Las Casas was named a bishop. He spurned the offer of the rich See of Cuzco in Peru and accepted instead the impoverished region of Chiapas in southern Mexico. There he immediately alienated his flock by once again refusing absolution to any Spaniard who would not free his Indian slaves. He was denounced to the Spanish court as a "lunatic" and received numerous death threats. Eventually he resigned his bishopric and returned to Spain, where he felt he could more effectively prosecute his cause. He took part in an epic debate with one of the leading theologians of the day, defending the humanity of the Indians, their right to religious liberty, and challenging the legality of the Conquest. He also fought to abolish the *encomienda* system, and wrote voluminous histories of the Conquest and "the Destruction of the Indies." By this time, he charged, the once-vast indigenous population of Hispaniola had been reduced to two hundred. Las Casas died in his monastic cell on July 18, 1566, at the age of eighty-two, confessing to his brethren his sorrow and shame that he could not have done more.

---

Five hundred years after the "discovery" of America, what are we to make of this life, this witness? Clearly for his writings on human equality and his defense of religious freedom,

Las Casas deserves to be remembered as a political philosopher of extreme significance in the history of ideas. But in decisively challenging the identification of Christ with the cause of Christendom, he proposed a recalibration of the gospel that continues to provoke a response. In 1968 the bishops of Latin America, meeting in Medellín, Colombia, examined the social structures of their continent—in many ways, the ongoing legacy of the early Conquest—and named this reality as a situation of sin and institutionalized violence. To preach the gospel in this context necessarily involved entering the world of the poor and engaging in the struggle for justice.

In undertaking such a shift in perspective and allegiance, the bishops were renouncing their age-old identification with the rich and powerful, and their new stance provoked a furious reaction. As Dom Helder Camara, a courageous Brazilian bishop cut from similar cloth as Las Casas, observed, "When I feed the poor they call me a saint. When I ask why there are so many poor and hungry they call me a Communist." In subsequent years many priests, sisters, and lay Catholics raised this same question, and with fateful consequences. In the words of Oscar Romero, the prophetic archbishop of San Salvador, "One who is committed to the poor must risk the same fate as the poor. And in El Salvador we know what the fate of the poor signifies: to disappear, to be tortured, to be captive, and to be found dead."

In the decades of the 1970s and '80s the truth of those words would be played out in the lives of tens of thousands of Christian martyrs in Latin America. They included Archbishop Romero himself, a bishop, like Las Casas, whose conversion had been prompted by his encounter with the "scourged Christ" of the poor. He was assassinated in 1980 while saying Mass in El Salvador, and he became a symbol of a new Church born of the faith and struggle of the poor. His death was a potent sign of the lingering contradictions implied in the original "evangelization" of the Americas— that five hundred years after the arrival of Columbus, in a land named for the Savior, a bishop could be assassinated by murderers who called themselves Christians, indeed faithful defenders of Christian values.

The story of such witnesses of our time later inspired me to travel to Latin America in the 1980s to experience first-hand the face of this changing Church. And that experience later led me to work at Orbis Books, publishing arm of the Maryknoll Fathers and Brothers, the publisher of Romero and a whole library of books on liberation theology. One of Orbis's authors, the Peruvian theologian Gustavo Gutiérrez, traced his own work to the prophetic witness of the sixteenth-century friar. Through his book, *Las Casas: In Search of the Poor of Jesus Christ,* I encountered the story of this great and prophetic soul.

Las Casas lived in a time of epochal change, in which new, unprecedented realities posed new questions. Were the Indians truly human? Over time, that question has been definitively answered—at least in theory. But in practice? Slavery in the United States was abolished only 150 years ago; legalized segregation in our own lifetime. But to what extent do we truly consider the lives of those designated the "other" as equal to our own? In a global economy that largely functions to siphon wealth and resources from the world's poorest to its wealthiest inhabitants, who can say whether it is God or gold that we truly worship? As we steadily ravage the irreplaceable natural resources of the planet and recklessly undermine the fabric of sustainable life on Earth—all for the sake of short-term profit—who can say that we have advanced beyond the rapacious conquistadors, whom Las Casas depicted as "wolves, tigers, and hungry lions" feasting on the blood of their victims?

Long after Las Casas's death, his writings became the basis of the "Black Legend," a potent weapon in the service of Protestant anti-Catholicism and anti-Spanish propaganda. In light of the bloodstained history of the past century, it is harder to ascribe his testimony to some peculiar Iberian aberration from the land of the Inquisition. In fact, his writings pose the deepest challenge to the role of the Church in our time. In the face of today's injustice and violence, in the face of all the threats to human survival, do Christians stand on the side of the victims or with those who profit from their suffering? The Jesuit theologian Ignacio Ellacuría of El Salvador, another author who would join the company of martyrs, spoke of the "crucified peoples of history." Like Las Casas, with his talk of the "scourged Christ of the Indies," Ellacuría compared the poor with Yahweh's Suffering Servant. In their disfigured features he discovered the ongoing presence and passion of Christ—suffering because of the sins of the world. In this light, he said, the task of the Christian was not simply to worship the cross or to contemplate the mystery of suffering, but "to take the crucified down from the cross"—to join them in compassion and effective solidarity.

Five centuries before the phrase was coined, Las Casas's "preferential option for the poor" continues to trouble the conscience of all who turn their gaze from the sufferings of the "other," whether in our midst or across the sea, while daring to ask, "What is that to me?"

# THE SAINT OF
# THE IMPOSSIBLE

SIMONE WEIL

*Mary Gordon*

W HO WAS SIMONE WEIL? To what category should
we link her name? Philosopher? Political activist
and theoretician? Factory worker? Farmworker? Christian
mystic? Self-hating neurotic? Self-hating Jew?

The thinkers and writers who have given serious attention
to Simone Weil give some indication of her complexity. They
range from T. S. Eliot and Malcolm Muggeridge (who tried
to ignore her left-wing politics) to Mary McCarthy, Susan
Sontag, Alfred Kazin, Leslie Fiedler, and Adrienne Rich
(who didn't want to dwell on her religious vision). It would
be difficult to imagine another figure uniting these radically
divergent sensibilities.

She was born in Paris on February 3, 1909, the daughter of
a doctor and a devoted full-time mother. Her older brother,

André, would grow up to become a world-famous mathematician. Simone Weil always considered herself intellectually inferior to her brilliant brother; this was a cause of great shame and feelings of unworthiness. By all accounts, the Weil family was warm, loving; the parents were greatly encouraging of their extraordinary children's intellectual lives. The sources for Simone Weil's later sorrows cannot, it would seem, be traced to an unhappy family life. As an adolescent, she developed severe headaches that would plague her for the rest of her life. Her parents unceasingly sought treatment for her, but nothing was successful.

At the prestigious École Normale Supérieure, she studied with the renowned philosopher Émile Chartier, who was known as Alain. Her dissertation subject was René Descartes. She set herself the task of mastering all the great thinkers of the European tradition, reading and writing on an astonishing variety of topics, from ethics to aesthetics, to sociology and political theory.

But from an early age, her astonishing intellectual commitment (she became fluent in ancient Greek by the age of ten) was joined with a heartfelt identification with the poor and suffering. Always, her imagination was seized by the situations of what she would later call "affliction." At the age of six, she gave up sugar in solidarity with soldiers fighting in World War I. Simone de Beauvoir, a fellow student at the École Normale, encountered Simone Weil weeping after learning of the deaths of victims of Chinese famine. Simone Weil told Simone de Beauvoir that the most important thing in the world was the coming revolution that would feed all the starving people of the Earth. De Beauvoir responded that the most important thing was to help people find a reason for their existence. Simone Weil snapped back: "It's easy to see that you've never gone hungry."

She saw herself allied with the politics of the left, but always on her own terms. At the age of ten she declared herself a Bolshevik, but she earned the enmity of committed communists when she repudiated Stalin in the early 1930s, among the first to see in him the same tyranny of force that marked Hitler. She talked her parents into letting Trotsky stay in an empty apartment that they owned, but she argued even with him, finding in any form of Marxism a love of force that she could not tolerate. As early as the 1930s, she was writing against the evils of French colonialism, meeting with Vietnamese and Algerians working in Paris for the liberation of their homelands.

In 1931, she got her first job as a teacher in the lycée of Le Puy, a small city in the Haute Loire region in the south of France. By all accounts, Simone Weil was a greatly beloved teacher: utterly devoted to her students, demanding but kindly, careful, encouraging, exact. At the same time, she was intensely involved both in the complicated politics of the French labor movement and in the movement for workers' education. She would travel long distances, carrying fifty-pound sacks of books, to teach economics and philosophy to workers, who returned her devotion with a thorough-going loyalty and admiration. This political activity did not, however, please the authorities in the French educational bureaucracy; she was often in danger of losing her job, and she moved among several different lycées in the course of her career.

In 1933, convinced that she had no right to speak about the lives and conditions of workers unless she had shared their lot, she worked for a year at a series of factories owned by the Renault company. Physically clumsy, with unusually small hands, she suffered greatly from the physical demands of factory work, which dreadfully exacerbated her headaches. She was changed irrevocably by this experience, the experience of being turned, in her words, into "a thing, a slave." From then on, the vitality and indomitability upon which everyone who knew her has remarked seemed diminished. She was perceived to have visibly aged and weakened.

In 1936, she joined the forces of the anarchists in fighting on the Republican side in the Spanish Civil War. Once again, her clumsiness was a problem. She stepped into a vat of hot cooking oil, badly burning her leg. Her parents had to come to her rescue, traveling into war-torn Spain to bring her home. Unlike most of the participants on both sides of the Spanish Civil War, she was able to see the horrors inflicted not only upon but by her comrades, whose casual brutality shocked her. She felt compelled to bear witness to the lust for violence that appalled her on both sides but was particularly painful to her when she observed it among the anarchists whom she had idealized. She wrote a letter to novelist Georges Bernanos, who had been a supporter of Franco and then became shocked by the brutality of the right. She tells him that she had thought that his political positions as a right-wing monarchist would necessarily make him her enemy. But now, she says, she thinks of him as her brother.

In 1937 she had experiences of a mystical and visionary nature, in which she felt herself penetrated by the presence of

Jesus Christ. The first was in Assisi, the second in the Abbey of Solemes, inspired by Gregorian chant and the introduction by an Englishman of the poem "Love" by George Herbert. From then on, her life changed radically. Not abandoning her commitment to the poor and suffering, she increasingly turned her attention to spiritual matters, immersing herself in Christian tradition, but also exploring other religious traditions, particularly Hinduism. In order to read the Bhagavad Gita in the original, she studied Sanskrit.

Deeply drawn to Catholicism, she met with priests and spiritual advisors, particularly a Father Perrin to whom she opened her mind and her heart. During this period, she also worked as an agricultural laborer, developing an intense friendship with a religious Catholic, Gustave Thibon, with whom she explored the question of conversion. But she would not submit to baptism in the Catholic Church because, she said, of its history of *anathema sit,* of excommunication on intellectual grounds, the Church's insistence that Catholicism had a monopoly on truth. She said she could not be part of an institution that deprived anyone of intellectual liberty.

Devoted to solidarity among the oppressed and suffering of the world, she nevertheless failed to identify with the plight of Jews under Nazi persecution. She would not wear a yellow star; threatened with the loss of her job, she wrote to the Ministry of Education explaining why she did not define herself as a Jew, since she had had no contact with the Jewish religion and considered her intellectual formation Christian and French. But her alienation from Judaism was more thoroughgoing. She was deeply critical of Jewish tradition, referring to Yahweh as a God of force and punishment and the Jewish people as devoted to exclusion and persecution of the other. She traced all the evils in Western thought back to the Jews and the Romans, the following of whom, she believed, led to the rejection of the tradition of the Greeks, which stood, in her mind, for purity and freedom.

In 1942, her parents had the opportunity to flee occupied France for America where André Weil had a position at Haverford College in Pennsylvania. Simone was unwilling to leave France, wanting to put herself in the position of greatest danger to cast her lot with her beloved France in its hour of trial by the Nazis. But she knew her parents wouldn't leave without her, so she sailed for New York, where she lived for three months, all the time working tirelessly to get back to Europe, particularly England, where she hoped to work with Charles De Gaulle and the Free French.

At that time, she was obsessed with a plan to parachute nurses into dangerous battle situations; she insisted that she be among those parachuted in. It was an impractical plan, and De Gaulle referred to her as "absolutely crazy." Nevertheless, after three months, she sailed to England, where she worked in the Propaganda Department of the Free French. There, she was diagnosed with tuberculosis and hospitalized. Always uncomfortable with many kinds of food, with everything having to do with eating, she worsened her condition by refusing to eat what the doctors recommended, insisting that she eat only what she imagined was the ration of those suffering in occupied France—an amount that she had arbitrarily decided upon. She died in Ashford, Kent, in August 1943, at the age of thirty-four. The circumstances of her death were as controversial as the rest of her life: some, particularly her doctor, believing she starved herself, others insisting that there was nothing that could have prevented her death by tuberculosis.

The work on which her reputation is based was published posthumously. Among the strongest supporters of the publication of her work was Albert Camus. Camus paid a visit to the Weil apartment on his way to receive the Nobel Prize in Stockholm, asking Simone's mother if he could have some time alone in Simone's writing room. Camus referred to Simone Weil as "the only great spirit of our age."

To all the descriptions that have been applied to Simone Weil, is it proper to add "heretic"? Probably, she would have applied it to herself and taken pride in the applications. Among the Christians she most admired were the heretical Albigensians and Cathars. She even had a soft spot for the Manicheans.

But before we consider whether or not to apply the term *heretic,* we should examine what we mean by it. The category of heretic can only exist in relationship to an opposite category: orthodoxy. There is no noun that can be formed for the word *orthodox* and applied to a person. One can be a heretic; no one can be an orthodox. The noun, *orthodoxy,* attaches not to a person but to a system of thought.

Orthodoxy insists that there is one right system of thought, one right way of thinking, one single truth, *The* truth, with a capital *The,* definite article required. And this insistence is precisely why Simone Weil refused to be baptized in the Catholic Church. In her *Spiritual Autobiography,* addressed to Father Perrin, she wrote:

*I should like to draw your attention to one point. It is
that there is an absolutely insurmountable obstacle to the
Incarnation of Christianity. It is the use of the two little
words* anathema sit. *It is not their existence but the way
they have been employed up till now. It is that also which
prevents me from crossing the threshold of the church.
I remain beside all these things that cannot enter the
Church, the universal repository, on account of those two
little words. I remain beside them all the more because my
own intelligence is numbered among them. Christianity
should contain all vocations without exception since it is
Catholic. In consequence the Church should also. But in
my eyes Christianity is catholic by right but not in fact.
So many things are outside it, so many things that I love
and do not want to give up, so many things that God
loves, otherwise they would not be in existence. All the
immense stretches of past centuries, except the last twenty
are among them, all the countries inhabited by the colored
races, all secular life in the white peoples' countries, in the
history of these countries, all these traditions banned as
heretical, those of the Manicheans and the Albigensians
for instance.*

As is so often the case with Simone Weil, she was ahead of
her time in her insistence on the importance of non-Western
religious traditions and the aggressive implications inherent
in a sense of Western superiority. And she not only challenges
the notion of heresy, she reinvents it, insisting that it is only
in heresy, or an acceptance of it, that genuine truth may be
found.

# SACRED SLOTH

## MICHEL MONTAIGNE

*Patricia Hampl*

> If my mind could gain a firm footing, I would not
> make essays. I would make decisions. . . .
>
> —*"Of Repentance"*

FOR MONTAIGNE, it starts with death. But maybe the act of writing is always a hedge against oblivion.

He suffered many deaths before he embarked on his career of daydream. For daydream—not philosophy, where his work was catalogued before literature claimed it (and certainly not theology)—was his métier. *This daydream of meddling with writing,* he said.

Jottings, tries (*essais*), he calls his writing. The very word he employs, *essai,* is not to be confused with our idea of a freshman theme. His word is purposely unliterary, almost a refusal to *be* literary. To essay is, for him, just to give something a whirl. Only later usage turned his casual term into a genre—and into our own French-borrowing English term: the essay. This offhandedness accounts for his uncanny premodern postmodernism, allowing us to imagine he's one of us. He anticipates Forster's instruction to *only connect*. But as the twentieth century showed, only connecting usually means, paradoxically, deconstructing—trusting association, refusing linear order. Montaigne's jumps and starts, his digressions, his very contradictions earn him his union card into the ranks of the future.

But first, death. In swift remove, he lost his adored father Pierre, five infant daughters, a brother, absurdly, from a tennis ball to the head (sixteenth-century tennis balls were made of wood). Most harrowing of all, his beloved friend Etienne de La Boétie, whose intimacy the *Essais,* in a sense, attempt to replace or replicate. All these gone before or soon after he retired to his Périgord chateau. He was thirty-eight.

France was enduring its own mortality, beset by pestilence and, worse, by the wars of religion. A healthy man of thirty-eight could think, without melodrama, that he was teetering near the grave. Death, perhaps, launches him into his curious vocation.

*Perhaps*—one of his favorite words, pivot of possibility, the ignition revving the engine of thought. Most agnostic of words. Modest, throat-clearing, almost unnoticeable as it tips the sentence off the high dive of articulation, plunging into possibility, rippling with arrays of notions, observations, contradictions. *Perhaps. Or—perhaps not.*

His project—not to write his life, but his mind. *Je ne peints pas l'estre. Je peints le passage.* I don't portray being. I portray passing. (The lovely immediacy of his verb—he doesn't say he writes, but *paints* passing, the faint echo in the French suggesting, as the English *portray* does, a sketch).

*I portray passing.* To snag perception as it flares across the horizon of observation, rainbowing into thought. He was attempting (that word! attempt, try, *essai*) to describe "man" not in the great abstract project of philosophy but in his own eccentric particularity. He was, therefore, inevitably, an apostate. Never mind that all his life he remained a professing Catholic (while three of his siblings became Protestants) at a time when the choice of religion could be a mortal one.

Having chosen the first-person voice and stipulating himself as the only human specimen he could fairly report on, he was a man of moderation in an age of deathly polarization. Death again: the dueling certainties of orthodoxy and reformation (a.k.a. heresy) raised against each other, weapons separated by mere paces on the French landscape.

Montaigne's first work was not written on the page. It was installation art, painted on his library wall in the tower of the ancestral chateau where he had retreated to daydream:

*An. Christi 1571 aet. 38, pridie cal. mart., die suo natali, Mich. Montanus, servitii aulici et munerum publicorum jamdudum pertaesus, dum se integer in doctarum virginum recessit sinus, ubi quietus et omnium securus (quan)tillum in tandem superabit decursi multa jam plus parte spatii: si modo fata sinunt exigat istas sedes et dulces latebras, avitasque, libertati suae, tranquillitatique, et otio consecravit.*

*In the year of Christ 1571, at the age of thirty-eight, on the last day of February, his birthday, Michel de Montaigne, long weary of the servitude of the court and of public employments, while still entire, retired to the bosom of the learned virgins, where in calm and freedom from all cares he will spend what little remains of his life, now more than half run out. If the fates permit, he will complete this abode, this sweet ancestral retreat; and he has consecrated it to his freedom, tranquility, and leisure.*

Strange that he announces his plan in the third person. That seigniorial authority is just what his *essais* will dismantle. In place of the magisterial third person, "omniscient" as they used to say in English departments, he descends to the limitations of the first. This is the compositional compass whose poles he will magnetize.

Stranger still: in 1571 to write of living in *tranquility and leisure*. Just a year later the fragile détente between Catholics and Protestants is shattered by the St. Bartholomew's Day Massacre, causing ravage and rampage in Paris and then throughout the heretic-hunting countryside. His wall art, announcing his tranquility and leisure plan, is a very pre–9/11 manifesto. But the curious thing—Montaigne went ahead and lived and wrote from this insouciant intention into a rapacious post–9/11 world anyway.

He chooses to write his *essais* in—better to say *from*—the first person, apparently for the freedom of it. *Freedom,* a word he tattoos twice on the wall in that inaugural text. A heretic's word. Every day he faced this paragraph—more private contract than public manifesto—as he sat at his desk in the tower. It is a covert farewell to omniscience, an abdication from the aloof declarations of philosophical inquiry and theological certainty.

Another farewell hides in clear view: the words on the wall are Latin, but the *essais* will be written in French. Here too he descends to the common ground. For Montaigne this descent to the demotic is not heretical as it was for some earlier reformers, but still, it made an unsponsored claim for the individual voice. People had died for this: in 1415 Jan Hus was burned at the stake in Constance, in part for translating scriptural texts and preaching in Czech, an act that gave faith to the folk, undermining priestly hegemony.

The testament on Montaigne's wall announces his project not as a search for truth as philosophers pursue it, not as theological apologia. He is recording the soul's chaotic apprehension of reality. His is the dream of the golden age—to live at one's ease, free.

It is one of the curiosities of Catholic ferocity against heretical texts that reference the classics—pagans, after all—elicits no wrath. Montaigne could quote away from the Stoics, whole swathes of text and stanzas of poetry he had by heart, gods and goddesses winding around his own words, Jesus nowhere to be found, the prophets of the Old Testament absent too. Fight as they might over heaven and hell, the learned orthodox and their reforming adversaries apparently reached détente about limbo. The pagan divinities and their poets could abide unharrassed.

Montaigne's tranquility was edgy. A man careful of the margins. He was trusted by all sides, by the Catholic King Henri III and his scheming mother, Catherine de Medici, but also by Henri Navarre, the Protestant heir. Montaigne's chateau was a neutral safe house, never torched when others around him were burnt and pillaged.

The bliss of his freedom was leisure, not action. Flight of the mind—the paradox of traveling by sitting still. But how do you attain this freedom from certainty, from "making decisions," and still *matter,* avoid triviality? What he seeks—and comes to embody—is freedom from the blinders of orthodoxy while sustaining fealty to the tender beauty of a home tradition. Not revolution, but evolution—his position, an ever-changing one. He was, after all, portraying passing.

Montaigne is often called a skeptic—a patronizing modern compliment—as if this were his great prophetic achievement (making him look like us). But he was far too subtle—and ardent—to settle for that chilly selfhood. His greatest heresy, if it can be called that, was to write in the first person, to observe the self as it passed along. His project was so anomalous it took the Vatican almost two centuries to put the *Essais* on the Index of Forbidden (and therefore tantalizing) Books. It was there from 1767 to 1854.

There is only one way to achieve the freedom he posted on his tower wall: by claiming time. In the end, time is all we have. In the end and at the beginning, time's meter is ticking down. While the Catholic League (the rigid Church party) claimed the voice of orthodoxy, determined to influence forever not only religion but the future, Montaigne demurs at the beginning of his book that he has *no goal but a domestic and private one.* He just wanted his time.

Free time, we call the best kind. *What do you do with your free time?* As if time were a possession, which it is. Meaning how do you spend the sliver of autonomy you have cadged for yourself (*spend* being the operative word—time is money, as everyone knows). Montaigne jingled the silver in his pocket while there was some left (*in calm and freedom from all cares he will spend what little remains of his life*). He decided to spend it all before it was taken from him.

He made an exotic escape, even as he retired to his birthplace. The Muses' bosom is not the girl next door. His "retirement" was mind travel, stalking the beast of private thought, which is to say candor, as it awaits levitation into language. Famously, *I am myself the matter of my book.*

To daydream is to lift off, not to stay but to embark.

He wanted, no doubt, to achieve the blank regions, the margins of Renaissance maps, province of monsters and improbable sea creatures, the uncharted territory where imagination engulfs experience. The unknown. Orthodoxy has trouble with the unknown, especially an orthodox religion that asserts not only infallibility, but immutability. Orthodoxy doesn't portray passing; it enshrines a tableau, beautiful but brittle.

Divested of "servitude," and "public employment," sitting solo in a room lined by bookshelves packed with the wisdom of the past, the walls ringed with Latin and Greek quotations from the sages he'd read since childhood, frescoes of rosy-fleshed gods and nymphs painted on the walls—languorous nudes mostly—he settled in. But in spite of all this company, alone.

He was placing "a consciousness astonished at itself at the core of human existence," the philosopher Maurice Merleau-Ponty writes of him, reminding us that "to be conscious is, among other things, to be somewhere else."

Montaigne's vocation is astonishment. To go where none has gone before. And where is that?

Within.

To daydream, to meddle with writing. To try, to test, to essay. The sensation is not psychological, not private. It is out *there*. The *there* of observation. Yet also within. You watch yourself. No, not quite—you watch yourself watching the world. You report back from that distant realm, so little traveled.

———

When you visit the statue of Montaigne in Paris, you find him amidst greenery, sequestered in the bushes across from the Sorbonne, as if preferring, in bronze, the margin he chose in life. The first thing you notice is his shoe. Even at night, when I come upon him, the shoe emerges first, golden against the dusky bronze of his casually seated self, cross-legged, bending forward as if to catch what you might be saying there on the sidewalk.

People rub the shoe for luck. A shoe-rub is said to assure a good exam result. It glows from all this human touch, an elegant sixteenth-century Mary Jane dancing slipper, blushing from generations of twentieth-century fondling. The sculptor, Paul Landowski, is better known for his gigantic 1931 Flash Gordon statue of Christ the Redeemer overlooking Rio de Janiero. Montaigne's statue was done two years later, in 1933, perhaps to commemorate the four hundredth anniversary of his birth.

Something of the dandy about that shoe. Then you notice the face, surprisingly intent, looking back at you. The face of a man who appreciates the finer things, but wryly amused by this weakness for pleasure, not haunted by his appetites. Landowski has given Montaigne a twentieth-century face, nonchalant, worldly, warm—almost an American face. A humanist face. This Montaigne, like the one I've been reading in recent years, sees it all and accepts it all in advance— the "all" of human perversity and contradiction played out on the field of avidity and longing.

It was raining that night, and though I'm urging a visit to the statue as if to a shrine, I didn't *visit* it. I just happened upon it, running late, trying to locate a fish restaurant recommended by a friend. Dripping in his leafy bower by the university, gleaming with rain—or maybe because I'd been living with his sinuous sentences in my head and had no idea the statue existed—this bronze Montaigne had something of the apparition about him. Like Walt Whitman, another eccentric of the first-person voice, he was loafing by the side of the road.

Out with the iPhone. Snap snap. Got the shoe. Didn't, couldn't quite, get the face. I had made an earlier pilgrimage to the tower near Bordeaux, had stood alone in the rounded room, the stony enclosure where he devised his pieces, some shorter than a page, others long enough to make a chapbook. He had refused to outfit this study with a fireplace (imagine the cold in winter) in order to safeguard his precious library.

I also entered the adjacent cramped alcove where he had allowed a fireplace. On the walls I made out what was left of painted frescoes (naked nymphs and godlets, bundles of chipped floral décor) and graffiti of earlier visitors—boldly scrawled *Emma 1882,* faint *Pierre 1920,* and someone whose message I couldn't decipher, the date *1989,* the most recent I found.

I looked out the window of the alcove to experience (or think I was experiencing) his view. May, a great blossoming *marronnier,* part of an allée of chestnuts marshaled along a gravel roadway leading to the tower. Nearer by, just below, an untended trapezoidal parterre garden where I imagined herbs (surely he ate well—he tells us he loved rich sauces). I turned back toward his writing room to take some notes, hoping for an insight (an earnest essayist acting the part). Turning quickly, gaze angled down to my notebook, I misjudged the space (an earlier century, a smaller scale) and smacked my head into the stone wall.

You do see stars. Or bits of white, spinning, that you could take for stars.

Then, in my bell-ringing, star-shooting brain, I remembered Montaigne had whacked his head too, colliding with another rider, knocked semiconscious from his horse as he rode his wooded property. He was taken for dead as his men carried him, insensible, back to the chateau. It is one of the few recognizably "memoiristic" vignettes in the *Essais,* a scrupulous reconstruction of this pivotal episode, a bit of *story* in the midst of all his musing, pondering, wondering—what used to be called philosophizing.

Why did he honor this moment, so uncharacteristically, with narrative? Because, no doubt, it was a near-death experience. But even more, it was unbiddable, decisive, causing him to pierce to the core of the creative imagination, perhaps for the first time. In being knocked off his horse, Montaigne experienced the doubleness that empowers personally voiced writing, maybe any writing. This apparently modest voice assured his honor—and his safety—on the margins, friend to the orthodox and to the heretical, as he wrote of his "domestic" business.

He experienced the fall—but he also *observed* the experience. The shock of double register galvanized him to apprehend the parallels of experience and observation. It was a conversion moment. (No wonder that most notorious conversion—Saint Paul's—is represented as a fall from his horse. Neither the fall nor the horse is mentioned in the Bible, but this is the standard image of his change of heart, as if the violence of being knocked from a height were the only way to express it adequately. Paul's fall is the spark moment of Christianity, a drop from the power ride of orthodoxy, a thump out of self into a vision of a new world order.)

You get knocked off balance, off your assumptions. You see stars. Or what you take for stars. Your perception changes, is changed. Even in our homely cliché we routinely speak of being *struck* by this or that. The point is you *see*—a fresh, startled seeing that feels accurate. The self is not, for once, a burden you lug around, slave to dogma (in Montaigne's time) or to experience (in our super-psychologized age), the dog's body of a life it must either endure or enjoy. The self in the *Essais* is revealed, instead, as an instrument for rendering—if not "reality," then the experience of reality. The poetry of experience fastens to the reportage of the world.

To perceive accurately you must, paradoxically, be knocked out of yourself—knocked out of the inevitable narcissism and egotism that is our narrative lot. This quicksilver experience has been given, by literature and psychology, the lackluster label *detachment*. John Keats called it "Negative Capability," another awkward term. Because it is essentially spiritual, the experience is impossible to corral in language. But once felt, there is nothing—not even love—to compare.

Americans revere the first-person voice. It unites high culture and pop culture—"Call me Ishmael," the great novel begins, and on Dr. Phil people yap with abandon about themselves. Maybe we don't love the personal voice—we just trust it. It feels authentic to us, a people given the charge in our founding document to pursue happiness, always an individual (another age would say an heretical) enterprise. It may be our greatest fiction—to believe the personal voice is more "authentic" than other narrative modes. We'll take it, most of the time, over "omniscience." Not only because we are a notoriously self-regarding people, but because the first-person voice opens the narrative door to speculation. Not to declaring, but to wondering. Perhaps we don't just want a story. We want how it feels, how it seems. We want the story of thinking.

*This is my letter to the world that never wrote to me*—another American parent of the personal voice, speaking in her sidelong, lyrical, heretical way *(Tell the truth, but tell it slant)*.

Rather coquettishly, Emily Dickinson also said, *I'm nobody—who are you?* That apparent self-revelation (really a self-screening) and its waggish question display the economy shared by the personal voice in lyric poetry and the personal essay (two forms up to the same business). Of course you're nobody (so am I). But that fragile voice reveals more than a self. It holds the mirror up—not to itself but to the world.

Montaigne made the first modern move in this direction, in the midst of the bloodiest wars of religion till the ones of our own age. His dancing slipper makes what he claimed was a "private" pirouette, but the glowing footstep emerges onto the public street, still golden in the dark.

# A COLLISION OF SYSTEMS AND TENDENCIES

## GEORGE TYRRELL

*Ron Hansen*

H E WAS BORN IN DUBLIN in 1861, the fourth child of English parents Mary Chamney and William Henry Tyrrell, a journalist with the *Evening Mail,* the foremost Protestant-Tory newspaper in Ireland. William was talented but ill-tempered and domineering, and he left his family penniless when he died two months before George's birth. Thence forward Mary and the four children were vagabonds, shifting homes and schools sometimes two or three times in a single year. Witty, friendly, if often aloof, George found friends at school but thought their games, so governed by rules, a form of humbuggery and sought instead the wilder excitements of, as he put it, "gymnastics and fighting and tearing about, and climbing and courting danger."

At the age of eight, he enrolled in Rathmines School and found such ease and success in his classes that he succumbed to what he later recognized as flaws of character: "first, a confirmed habit of idleness; secondly, an overweening conceit of my own powers." But it was there that his headmaster acquainted him with an evangelical, High Church Anglicanism that fascinated him but left him skeptical and basically godless until he met Anne Kelly, a Roman Catholic and the Tyrrell's maid-of-all-work whose kitchen became his afterschool haunt. Lovesickness caused him to defend her against the fervent Protestant accusations of his mother, and he felt an "anxiety to say something in favour of so preposterous a religion as Popery; while my secret unbelief made me find little objection to the gnats of Romanism after the camels of Christianity."

Ever more entranced by a Catholicism that he found "dangerous, wicked and forbidden," George first tried a religious half-measure of secretly attending a Church of Ireland where the ministers wore birettas and cassocks and instead of a communion table there was an altar of sacrifice. With feelings of sinful mischief, George hid crucifixes and images of saints in his room, slept on a board, and flagellated himself with a handmade discipline in a fantastic impersonation of faith that fixed on extremes of piety but had nothing to do with the spirit.

Uprooted again, the family rented a furnished apartment from a Miss Lynch, a Roman Catholic landlady whom George adored, and, as he confessed in his autobiography,

"This quiet, holy, unselfish little woman had more to do with my destiny than any other" force.

Within a half-year, George's agnostic brother Willie, who was not yet twenty-five, died following a sudden, desperate illness. Rocked by the tragedy, his fifteen-year-old brother flung himself into hagiographies and histories, including Charles Montalembert's six-volume *Monks of the West*. Reading Compline in Latin one night, he found himself praying to Saint Benedict "straight in the teeth of my Protestant conscience," and when his eyes fell back on the page of his Latin breviary, he read the concluding verses of Psalm 91: "Because he hoped in me, I will deliver him; I will protect him, because he hath known my name; he shall cry out to me, and I will hear him; I am with him in tribulation, I will deliver him, and I will glorify him."

Having failed a sizarship examination that would have granted him free tuition to Trinity College in Dublin, George felt excused to sail to England to help the poor of the city slums, but with an ulterior notion of religious conversion and even, perhaps, ordination to the priesthood. And fortuitously, in a London bookshop, he happened upon Paul Feval's *Jesuits* and recalled how Miss Lynch once counseled him to join the Society of Jesus, for "they are very learned and very holy men." With that in mind, he took catechetical instruction from a Jesuit in the Farm Street residence in Mayfair, and on Sunday, May 18, 1879, George Tyrrell was received into the Roman Catholic Church.

He was eighteen then, blond, frail, and homely, with a face like a caricature, but with a winsome goodness, intellect, and sincerity that earned him the sympathy and affection of others. Jesuits at Farm Street urged him at once to join their order, but canon law forbad a convert from entering religious life for at least a year. The English province superior therefore sent Tyrrell to work on a Jesuit mission in Cyprus as a lay volunteer, and then to the English College in Malta, where some Jesuits treated the convert "not as one who had courageously embraced a more difficult and somewhat paradoxical position, in lieu of an easier and more obvious one; but rather as a drunkard who had come to his senses—a repentant fool, if not a repentant rake."

Yet, with some misgivings, in September 1880 Tyrrell entered the Jesuit novitiate in the pastoral southwest London suburb of Roehampton, and there he was forever changed by the *Spiritual Exercises* of Saint Ignatius Loyola, the founder of the Society of Jesus. The purpose of those four weeks of silence and contemplation on the mysteries of the Trinity, humanity's sin, and the life, death, and resurrection of Christ was to free the new Jesuit from addictions and worldly attachments, to help him develop an intimate friendship with Jesus, to avail himself of deeply personal mystical graces, and to choose rightly, based on Ignatius's rules for discernment of the spirits of good and evil. Those and other retreat experiences would be found imprinted on each page of Tyrrell's future writing. But also incipient then were his dissatisfaction with a hollow, mechanistic asceticism and an inflexible, irrational orthodoxy. Each would prove to be his undoing some years hence.

Still, in 1882 he professed his first vows of poverty, chastity, and obedience as a Jesuit, and he was sent up to Stonyhurst College in Lancashire ahead of his class for philosophical studies that his superiors hoped would focus his restless mind. But instead of the favored neoscholastic *interpretation* of Thomas Aquinas by the sixteenth-century Spanish Jesuit Francisco Suárez, happenstance permitted Tyrrell to concentrate enthusiastically on the Thomistic sources themselves. And the lazy, often indifferent scholar fell in love with learning while earning the confidence and praise of Jesuit professors who hailed him as the finest mind in his class.

His philosophate was completed in 1885, and for his regency he requested a return to the English College in Malta, where he taught elementary schoolboys for a fulfilling three years. His final education as a seminarian was at the Jesuit theologate of St. Beuno's in North Wales—where Gerard Manley Hopkins had matriculated fourteen years earlier—and at last, at age thirty, George Tyrrell, S.J., was ordained a priest of Christ by the bishop of Shrewsbury.

His first apostolate was at Saint Aloysius parish in Oxford, followed by a quick reassignment to an intellectually backward and financially strapped congregation in Lancashire's coal country that would surprisingly offer him the happiest year of his life. In those hectic days of the ever-growing English province, few Jesuits stayed on a job long—Hopkins shifted houses so frequently that he called himself "fortune's football"—so, too soon and against his wishes, Tyrrell was given a chair in philosophy at Stonyhurst College, where he'd been judged a rising star nine years earlier. He was thirty-three.

Eloquent, incisive, challenging, and clever, he was a natural as a teacher, exciting in his thought, accessible and pastoral with his students, ever self-effacing, but also humorously sardonic about his far less popular fellow professors and their stiff fidelity to Suárez rather than the originator of his teaching, Thomas Aquinas. Within just two years Tyrrell had won the love and loyalty of the seminarians but the envy and enmity of faculty, who feared, he told a relative, that "I was turning the young men into Dominicans."

It was determined he could not stay.

Looking for a happier spot for him, his Jesuit superiors decided to fit him into the staff of editors on the Jesuit journal *The Month,* headquartered at Farm Street, so he could occupy himself full-time with writing. Even in the theologate of St. Beuno's he'd been fluent and tireless with his pen, often filling whole holidays with trenchant papers—three articles ran in *The Month* but some others were jests and opinions meant only for his classmates—on a stunningly wide array of topics, from biblical criticism to socialism to the harm in cramming for exams. And now he was given free license to publish and a friendly, if vigilant, journal for his many lucubrations.

At first there were cogent, often generous, but increasingly acidic reviews of theological and philosophical texts, then a series of rather quarrelsome articles on Anglicanism that some Roman ecclesiastics possibly smiled on, and he even shuffled up two collections of intellectual catechesis and piety—*Nova et Vera* and *Hard Sayings: A Selection of Meditations and Studies*—intended for the enrichment of highly educated Catholics. Still smarting over his ejection from Stonyhurst, he was cautious about rousting his censors.

Then in 1899 he delivered a series of eight Lenten lectures to the Roman Catholic undergraduates at Oxford University, which he published in book form as *External*

*Religion: Its Use and Abuse.* His Jesuit superiors found no reason to censure the book, but it would arouse the vigilance of the Holy See because he spoke of the Church not as a fine philosophical construct nor a majestic political force, but as a *sacrament* intended by Christ to help and grace human beings. Maude Petre, Tyrrell's good friend and first biographer, wrote, "The Church for him was a lowlier, and yet, in the best sense, holier creation, standing on the ground, at the level of the weakest, its doors wide open, its pavement soiled by the feet of the poor and miserable; ready to learn, even while she taught, to serve while she commanded." She had long been an *Ecclesia docens,* a Church teaching, but she needed also to be an *Ecclesia discens,* a Church learning.

Tyrrell continued to publish widely, often at the rate of two books per year. *The Faith of Millions* was a collection of meditations inspired by his prayer with the *Spiritual Exercises* and the book called for, in part, a greater appreciation of the vital and telling religious experiences of ordinary Christians.

Writing to a friend about his work on *The Church of the Future,* Tyrrell noted that "I make the saints and not the theologians the teachers of Christianity. The Spirit of Christ rather than Christ Himself is the creator of the Church."

Tyrrell considered *Lex Orandi, or Prayer and Creed,* a book of pastoral theology on our human longing for a transcendent God. Tyrrell noted in his preface, "That we are dissatisfied, not only with what the ideal gives us, but, by anticipation, with all it could ever possibly give us, is proof that there is a higher love-power within us which must seek its object elsewhere."

The title came from the Latin saying, *Lex orandi, lex credendi,* which can be translated "As the Church prays, so she believes."

And he next wrote the sequel, *Lex Credendi,* in which he argued that the Spirit of Christ depicted in the Gospels was also revealed in the lives of the saints, each adapting the Spirit to their own time and place and providing a guide for the Church's "really fruitful and lasting decisions. . . . The Pope is in theory no irresponsible absolutist who can define what he likes, who can make truth and unmake it. He is but the interpreter of a law written by the Holy Ghost in the hearts of the saints. He is bound by this living book."

Even the section titles of Tyrrell's *The Church of the Future* hint at disputations that the Holy See could not overlook: "Catholicism as Officially Stated; or, the Theory of Ecclesiastical Inerrancy"; "A Liberal Restatement of Catholicism"; and "The Ethics of Conformity." What Tyrrell was arguing throughout was that the deposit of faith was a Spirit, an idea, that grew organically and changed over time, and only holiness was proof for deciding whether conscience and religious experience truly conformed to the Spirit of Christ.

All his ideas were incendiary to ecclesiastics only a century removed from the slaughter of clergy and religious during the French Revolution. They saw Marxism on the rise across the continent; priests and seminarians executed or expelled from Spain during the *gloriosa revolución* of 1868; anticlericalism becoming public policy in Otto von Bismarck's Reich; there was, as the Holy See called it, "a ferocious war against the Church" in South America; and enflaming the memories of those in the Roman hierarchy was the recent seizure of the wealthy papal states by the Italian army, with the result that the only sovereign entity of the papacy was the Apostolic Palace and the loop of fortifications on Vatican Hill.

The *Ecclesia docens* felt under siege.

An initial response was the Syllabus of Errors issued by Pope Pius IX. ("The ninth" in Italian is *nono,* so wags were soon calling him "Papa No-no.") The syllabus was sub-divided into ten sections in which a host of false statements were made and then condemned by citing earlier papal documents that had considered the error. So, for example, "All truths of religion proceed from the innate strength of human reason," or "Protestantism is nothing more than another form of the same true Christian religion," or "The Roman Pontiff can, and ought to, reconcile himself, and come to terms with, progress, liberalism, and modern civilization."

In the squint of ecclesiastical prejudice and suspicion, Tyrrell's intricate philosophy of religion would be corrupted and misconstrued until it seemed in itself a syllabus of such errors. But accusations became more telling with Pius X's 1907 decree *Lamentabili Sane Exitu* (With Truly Deplorable Results) by which the Holy Office condemned and proscribed sixty-five errors of modernists in biblical exegesis and the interpretation of the mysteries of the faith.

Without naming the offenders, the Holy Office left little doubt that it was condemning and consigning to the Index of Forbidden Books the biblical criticism of Alfred Loisy, a French Catholic priest and professor of Hebrew who maintained, for instance, that the first five chapters of Genesis are only figurative history, that Moses was not the author of the Pentateuch, that scripture shares the problems and limitations of all other ancient texts, and that Jesus did not intend an organized Church.

And of course *Lamentabili* was also meant to anathematize the writing of George Tyrrell. Soon after reading it, Tyrrell sent a confidential letter to his superior general in Rome, the Spanish Jesuit Luis Martín, offering to formally request release from the Society of Jesus, which he felt was "leagued with those who are doing everything to make faith impossible."

Already he'd left Farm Street and his work on *The Month* for the rustic tranquility of a small Jesuit parish in Yorkshire's Richmond-in-Swaledale where his job was to simply be a good priest, and it would consume a full two years of worrying over his Jesuit status before he finally received his dismissal from the order, with the conditions that he could receive communion but not celebrate Mass, and that he could be reinstated to the ministry and the Society of Jesus only through formal applications.

Tyrrell wrote Luis Martín that

> *I shd. like to assure you, now that I stand outside the Society, how completely I realize that we have both of us been driven to this unpleasant issue by the necessities of our several minds & consciences; & Y[our] P[aternity] still more by the exigencies of a most difficult position. . . . Nothing cd. be further from my sentiments than any sort of personal rancour or resentment. I feel that it is a collision of systems & tendencies rather than of persons; & that many such collisions must occur before the truth of both sides meets some higher truth.*

Even as Tyrrell was seeking a way to reestablish himself as a priest by consenting to censorship of his writing, Pope

Pius X issued his September 1907 encyclical *Pascendi Dominici Gregis* (Feeding the Lord's Flock), which focused even more militantly on those deemed modernists, condemning their teaching as the "compendium of all heresies," calling them "enemies of the Church," and viciously describing these still-unnamed theologians in terms generally applied to Satan.

Tyrrell felt the need to comment and did so in an extensive letter to the London *Times* that was printed in two installments. Writing of the encyclical, he said, "As an argument it falls dead for every one who regards its science theory as obsolete; for all who believe that truth has not been stagnating for centuries in theological seminaries, but has been steadily streaming on, with ever increasing force and volume, in the channels which liberty has opened to its progress." Noting that it was not a statement *ex cathedra,* that is, infallible, he called it "a disciplinary measure preceded by a catena of the personal opinions of Pius X and his immediate *entourage*." Any "modernist," he wrote, could now expect censure, suspension, and excommunication. "They were the portion of his spiritual ancestors, who in past ages so often saved the Church, sick unto death with the pedantries of scholastic rationalism and the *rabies theologorum*" [madness of theologians]. And just when the people were hoping that the Church "might have bread for the starving millions, for those who are troubled by that vague hunger for God on which the Encyclical pours such scorn . . . Pius X comes forth with a stone in one hand and a scorpion in the other."

Recognizing that there would be dire consequences for an ordained priest who publicly rebuked the Holy Father,

Tyrrell was not surprised to hear in October 1907 that he'd been given a "minor" excommunication. Afterward he was frequently urged to rejoin the Anglicans, but Tyrrell would not, for "I feel my work is to hammer away at the great unwieldy carcass of the Roman Communion and wake it up from its medieval dreams."

He was a houseguest of friends in Clapham when, in 1909, he fell seriously ill with a kidney malady that was later correctly diagnosed as the final stages of Bright's disease. Even from his sickbed he produced *Christianity at the Cross-Roads,* a book that avoided criticism of Roman Catholicism to instead examine its riches and use it as a comparative measure of other religious expressions. In it he wrote, "It is impossible to deny that the revelation of the Catholic religion and that of Jesus are the same. . . . It was in the form of such a tradition that He necessarily embodied His Gospel, and the Catholic Church has preserved the earthen vessel with its heavenly treasure."

After signing the preface to the book in June, he went to Maude Petre's home in Storrington and fell critically ill with a stroke that paralyzed his left side and garbled his speech. A friendly priest was called in and heard Tyrrell's confession, and just before headaches, nausea, and internal bleeding finally rendered Tyrrell comatose, another priest, who'd been hostile toward him from the pulpit, found the pastoral grace to administer the sacrament of extreme unction.

On July 15, 1909, George Tyrrell died at age forty-eight.

Rome issued instructions that he should be denied the Catholic funeral rites, so after fruitless appeals to the bishops of Southwark and Westminster, his friends Maude Petre and Baron Friedrich von Hügel arranged for a burial in Storrington in the Anglican churchyard. Henri Bremond, a French former Jesuit and modernist, but still a priest with full faculties, recited the familiar prayers over Tyrrell's coffin and gave a eulogy that ended, "To realise that we shall never hear him again on earth would entirely darken our lives, if he had not taught us his own bitter, but triumphant, optimism and the present duty of hoping against hope. Hope! This must be our parting word and feelings."

In 1910, Pius X signed a *motu proprio* insisting that all clerics in major orders and professors on Catholic faculties of philosophy and theology swear an oath against modernism. In 1912 Maude Petre published *The Autobiography and Life of George Tyrrell* and soon saw the two volumes placed on the Index of Forbidden Books.

High ecclesiastical authorities may have gloated that they'd annihilated the life and writings of George Tyrrell, but as David G. Schultenover, S.J., points out in *George Tyrrell: In Search of Catholicism,* "Anyone who has studied both him and the documents of Vatican II will recognize his principles reborn on nearly every page. Thus was fulfilled the prophecy that Tyrrell applied to himself and inscribed in his breviary" when he left the philosophate at Stonyhurst. It was a lesson first given to Moses: "Thou shalt see from afar the land which the Lord God will give to the children of Israel, but thou shalt not enter therein."

as dark and expressionless as a silhouette, taunting me with her opacity. How foolish to have imagined her death might release me, or that I might enter a church without her at my side. Within me is the other kind of labyrinth, like the trap Daedalus designed to stymie the Minotaur and contain his rage. I haven't yet learned that I, not the one who has injured me, am the person who suffers my withholding forgiveness.

My mother was seventeen when she discovered she was pregnant. Her parents, who argued against an abortion, raised me in her stead, and she lived with us until I was five. After that, Sunday was the only day of the week I could expect to see her, the hour of Mass the single one I dependably shared with my mother. I never paid attention to the liturgy, my attention fixed on the remote young woman at my side.

---

By the time Joan of Arc was seventeen and had proclaimed herself the virgin warrior sent by God to deliver France from her enemies, the English, she had been obeying the counsel of angels for five years. Until then, the voices she heard, speaking from over her right shoulder and accompanied by a great light, had been hers alone, a rapturous secret. But in 1428, when they pressed her to undertake the quest for which they had been preparing her, they transformed a seemingly undistinguished peasant into a visionary heroine who defied every limitation placed on a woman of the late Middle Ages.

At God's behest, Joan ran away from home. She nagged at her uncle, who lived in Burey, a village near her hometown of Domremy, until he agreed to take her to Vaucouleurs. She had been visited by angels, she told him, and they had directed her to speak with Robert Baudricourt, the captain stationed there. Baudricourt, the angels said, would provide her the means of getting to Chinon, where the French dauphin had taken refuge upon the English occupation of Paris. But once he learned what the peculiar girl in the red homespun dress wanted of him, and what authority she claimed, Baudricourt told Joan's uncle to give her a sound thrashing and take her back to her parents.

Joan would not be dissuaded; she returned twice more to Vaucouleurs, causing enough gossip and curiosity that Baudricourt asked a local priest to perform an exorcism to be sure Joan wasn't keeping company with demons rather than angels. The priest's judgment that there was no evil in the girl, her claim that she and no other could save France, and the captain's desire to end her months' long campaign for his support convinced Baudricourt to provide Joan an escort to Chinon. The journey through enemy territory took eleven days on horseback, and concluded without so much as a skirmish. Once Joan had at last penetrated the French court, she presented Charles, the fainthearted dauphin, with a private miracle, one that neither ever revealed. Whatever it was, it convinced the dauphin that Joan was in truth heaven-sent, it was God's will that he wear France's crown, and it was she who must lead what was left of his army to recapture all the territory the English had annexed.

Given a warhorse, armor, and some ten thousand soldiers, Joan took up the sword her angels provided. She was frightened of the enormity of what God asked of her, and she was feverish in her determination to succeed at what was by anyone's measure a preposterous mission. As Joan herself protested to her voices, she "knew not how to ride or lead in war," and yet she roused an exhausted, underequipped, and impotent army into a fervor that carried it from one unlikely victory to the next. Most famously, she turned the tide of the Hundred Years War when she raised the siege of Orléans by defying the cautious strategies of seasoned generals to follow inaudible directions from invisible beings.

By their "angels' speech and tongue," she told the inquisitors who sent her to the stake. That's how she knew the voices were heaven-sent.

---

Perhaps it's a small thing I don't want to lose, or maybe I think of it as currency. In either case, I keep it in my wallet's zippered pocket. There was no occasion warranting a gift, and I remember she said I was too old to beg and wheedle and make a scene. A woman made of painted wood with hair as dark as hers, smiling and round under her red dress and apron: a mother, clearly. The wood squeaked when I twisted the halves apart. Seven of her, one inside another, ever smaller and rendered with less detail until the smallest's face had room for only dot eyes and a mouth like an eyelash. That was the only one I'd wanted, really, the seamless kernel that didn't come apart in my hands.

I wonder now if my attachment to that most rudimentary incarnation, fetal in its lack of distinguishing features, was a way of wishing myself back inside her, the larger dolls a series of wombs, one giving birth to another.

Imagine the safety of a child so protected.

What did it feel like to be my mother? The question dogs

my heels, turns each corner with me as I slowly approach the labyrinth's center. I'm convinced that if I knew what she hid from me—if I knew her—I'd have what I needed to banish her.

---

By angels' speech and tongue. Joan of Arc testified under oath that it was during her thirteenth year that she first received what she described as "a voice from God to help her and guide her." The voice came toward noon on a summer's day, when she was in her father's garden. As it was noon, church bells began to ring, but Joan hadn't even the chance to cross herself before the garden vanished, and the sky and the earth as well. No river, no houses, no green pastures with their white spatter of sheep. There was nothing but light, "a great deal of light on all sides, as was most fitting," she told her examiner, reminding him tartly that "not all the light came to him alone!"

The voice's arrival was of consuming interest to Joan's inquisitors. How could it not have been? Over and over they questioned her in the attempt to access, or construct, evidence that might be used to prove its source demonic. But all it had given Joan on that first afternoon was the kind of mild direction a clergyman might extend to any child. "Be good," it had said, and "go to church often."

After it had fallen silent and the garden emerged from the flood of light, Joan found herself "much afraid." The visitation preoccupied her, as would anything so unexpected and overwhelming. Already what happened had slipped between her and the life she used to have. For the remaining seven of her nineteen years, Joan's daily companions, whose company she chose before that of mortals, and whom she obeyed as she did not any mortal, were angels. Asked if she believed she had sinned in leaving home secretly against her mother's and father's wishes, Joan answered that had she a hundred parents or been the daughter of a king she would have left nonetheless. Whatever she did, she insisted, was at the command of God.

The clergy couldn't tolerate Joan's belief that she had access to God outside the authority of the Church—outside their control.

Still, it wasn't Joan's inquisitors who led her to the pyre. It was her angels.

---

I'm irritated by other people on the path, whispering together or wandering off before reaching the labyrinth's center. Even more I'm irritated with myself, always chasing—like my mother—after whatever ineffable something might reveal life's purpose. My mother was born a Jew, indoctrinated as a Christian Scientist, converted to Catholicism, orbited through Transcendental Meditation and into the gardens of Los Angeles's Self-Realization Fellowship only to, in the end, drift out a Catholic who watched TV evangelists on her death bed, a scrap of paper bearing a Buddhist chant—*nam renge myoho kyo*—hidden under her pillow. When will I stop following in her wake, sifting compulsively through life's details to find the one where God is hiding? I should be outside, taking pleasure in this foggy city's rare sunny afternoon instead of advancing a few steps only to turn back on myself in a twisted circle.

It's not hard to dismiss Joan's voices, to reduce them to a symptom and her life to a case study. The judges to whom we commend Joan are doctors of medicine rather than the church. She's been handed retroactive diagnoses of hysteria, schizophrenia, epilepsy, even tuberculosis.

Academics don't judge; they interpret. Feminist scholars posit a Joan calculating enough to costume herself as a visionary, like Saint Catherine of Siena or Saint Bridget of Norway, during an era when mystical revelation was one of the few routes a woman might take to political power. Cultural anthropology reminds us that it is at times of overwhelming social crises—like that of fifteenth-century France, staggering in the wake of war and plague and famine—that visionaries arise. Ethnographers identify shamanic figures as a feature of successful societies; granted passage to states of consciousness that elude the vast majority of us, they are the repository of our fears and hopes as well as our means of petitioning the divine. Neurotheology has discovered a "God spot" in the human brain. Four out of five people experience feelings they identify as rapture when specific areas of their temporal lobes are stimulated by a magnetic field. If the brain is wired for faith in a higher being, it must be that faith conveys an evolutionary advantage.

"The first maker of the gods," William James wrote, "was fear."*

---

*William James, *The Varieties of Religious Experience* (New York: Library of America Paperback Classics, 2009), 74.

---

One foot in front of the other. The path is too narrow to accommodate more than one person at a time, and so we wind on, single file, a sparse and straggling queue of supplicants. Halfway through the maze, I've yet to free my thoughts from workaday cares and reproach myself for failing to arrive at anything resembling a meditative state. What is this emptying one's mind business? I can't even slow my thoughts down, let alone exile them.

Abruptly, a voice comes not from above but from all around me, its volume one of magnitude more than sound. Later, when I try to remember the voice, I'll think of dancing in front of the speakers at a rock concert and feeling sound too loud to hear, feeling how my bones vibrated within their envelope of flesh. It's a terrible analogy, and I can't do better. The few people walking the labyrinth, the nun sitting in the pew by the exit, the sacristan replacing candle stubs with fresh tapers: not one of them looks up. They haven't heard a thing other than the careful, nearly silent tread of feet or the clicking of rosary beads in the hand of whoever walks behind me.

*You want to know?,* the voice demands, and its tone chastises. It tells me I've asked and asked and asked again, like a whining child, for something from which I have been protected, for knowledge withheld to spare me pain. *I'll give you what you think you want.*

Even as the voice falls silent I'm filled—stricken—with a fear worse than any I have ever known or imagined. Depthless, black, and cold, it crowds my chest, pushing everything aside. Fear makes me nothing but chest. No brain with which to reason, no legs to carry me away, no hands to shove it away. Only a pair of lungs that have forgotten how to inhale. I stop moving long enough that the clicking rosary, having grown weary of waiting behind me, steps off the path, and reenters a few paces further ahead.

---

The primary aspect of a mystical state is ineffability. "It defies expression," James tells us, "no adequate report of its content can be given in words."*

As Joan's trial for heresy progressed, so did her descriptions of the voice or voices that guided her evolve. The longer and harder she was pressed to describe what couldn't be described, the more fully she characterized what she called angelic, in that it conveyed messages from God. A single voice accompanied by a great light evolved into a trio of voices that could be distinguished from one another, those of the archangel Michael and the virgin martyrs Saint Catherine and Saint Margaret, all widely venerated in Joan's place and time. The voices conjured beings with lips to speak, bodies she could see and touch and even smell, creatures with wings and crowns.

A few of Joan's biographers attribute her summoning more and more details to desperation. The weeks of the trial's public sessions were followed by more weeks of private interrogation in the dank cell where Joan spent the better part of a

---

*William James, *The Varieties of Religious Experience* (New York: Library of America Paperback Classics, 2009), 343.

year, shackled to her bed, threatened officially with torture, unofficially with rape. As it was believed that the devil could have no commerce with a virgin, her persecutors had motive enough to establish that Joan was not, as she claimed, inviolate, penetrated only by female hands searching to ascertain the truth. Against protocol, she was guarded not by women but by men who had opportunities to rape her. When she asked for a confessor, she was given a false one whose directions were to extract information for the eavesdropping inquisitors spying through a chink in the wall.

Who was it that persuaded her to have angels with their arms, feet, legs, and robes painted on the standard Joan carried into battle, her judges wanted to know? She "had them painted in the fashion in which they were painted in churches," she said.

It's typical for visitations such as those Joan experienced to accrue definition and detail. She'd had an experience, hundreds of them, in fact, that required explanation. What if her sojourn among French royalty, passing through castles and cathedrals filled with paintings and tapestries accomplished under the court's patronage, gave her an idiom with which to explain her voices? Familiar figures, holy and God sent, they provided the vessels in which she could safeguard what she didn't want to forget or deny, rapture so overwhelming and potentially disorienting that it required containment.

Did she herself ever see them in the manner in which she had them painted? This is among the questions Joan refused to answer. Under no circumstances would she disclose her visions and revelations. "Truly," she said to the judges when they showed her the rack that waited for her, "if you were to tear me limb from limb and separate my soul from my body, I would not tell you anything more: and if I did say anything, I should afterwards declare that you had compelled me to say it by force."

---

So this is what she hid from me, the monumental goddess of my youth, at whose feet I fell. How is it possible to live with fear like this? How did my mother carry it, putting one foot in front of the other? It's primal, almost animal—the inarticulate fear of a child lost in a crowd, blind with panic, groping for a familiar hand. The fear of annihilation.

I've wondered at the cost to a child of losing—at two, at seven, and at twelve—three beloved governesses, with whom she shared an intimacy she didn't have with her mother. By the time my grandmother held me on her lap, there wasn't any money for a governess. I claimed more of her attention than my mother ever had.

Epiphany. A manifestation of the divine. Is this what I've been given, reluctant, naysaying Catholic that I am? That my child mother—and how much younger she grows as I age— was afraid, not fearful but broken by fear, doesn't answer to every hurt, but it explains enough. I don't need to twist her apart anymore so I might look inside.

Stopped in my tracks, I keep my head bent, my eyes no longer cast down to guide my feet but to hide the tears that drip from my nose and make dark circles on the stone underfoot. My prayers are not sophisticated; reduced by panic to begging, they're barely coherent. All I can muster is some version of *Take it away, take it away, please please take it away. I under-stand now, take it away.*

As it is: the fear lifts. But not before it has settled into me, teaching me, in as much as I can be taught, what it felt like to be my mother.

Later, I won't be able to remember what happened during the remainder of the afternoon. I'll be able to picture the too-deep stairs on Taylor Street and revisit my irritation with how awkward they made the climb, but I won't remember walking back down. I won't know if I completed the labyrinth, or if I, too, wandered away, annoying those who remained on its path. I suppose I sat in a pew to gather my wits before going to whatever appointment waited. Or maybe I canceled it. Maybe I just went back to my hotel.

———

Asked how she was sure from the beginning that the source of her voices was divine, Joan said she "had the will to believe it."

Child that I am of an age when plagues are caused by germs and not God's wrath, and the divine right of kings has yielded to the election of presidents, I want not to believe. As soon as I characterize what I heard as having issued from beyond my own consciousness, I begin arguing against the possibility of its being so. My objections are, of course, entirely reasonable. That's just what's wrong with them.

———

It's courage that Joan is remembered for, her selfless physical courage in battle and, even more, the courage of her convictions. She had the audacity—some would say the insanity—

to face down and defy dozens of Sorbonne-trained judges who intended to put her to death. As for Joan, she preferred death to a life in which she betrayed all she loved most. That she was sure she was bound for paradise was considered a heretical presumption.

On May 30, 1431, Joan of Arc, nineteen years old, was led to a pyre built upon a high platform so the jeering crowd could watch her burn. But among even the English, who sent her to her death, there were many who succumbed to "great weeping and tears" and "made professions of faith" before the spectacle was concluded. After it was, the executioner went to the Dominican convent. "He greatly feared he was damned," he told his confessor, and he told him he knew "he had burned a saint."* Joan died nobly, her dignity unassailable, praying and calling on Christ before she finally expired. Like Christ, she asked for God's mercy on those who had persecuted her.

Although aspects of Joan's life will always be beyond our power to understand, her courage is not among them. Its magnitude reflects that of her faith.

———

Another gift from my mother, a necklace, lost for so long now I'm surprised I can picture it at clearly as I do. A fine gold chain bearing a glass orb the size of a cherry stone. Within it was a single yellow mustard seed suspended in a drop of glycerin.

So I had it once, and could carry it with me: the measure of faith enough to move a mountain.

---

*Regine Pernoud, *The Retrial of Joan of Arc* (San Francisco, CA: Ignatius Press, 2007), 254, 247, 253.

# DO I STAY OR
# DO I GO?

## SISTER CORITA KENT

*Melinda Henneberger*

Do I STAY OR DO I GO? In a sense, Corita Kent did both.

Neither the Church nor the art world knew quite what to make of Sister Mary Corita Kent or her playful, devotional, political 1960s pop art. Her eye-popping serigraphs of repurposed ad slogans and scribbled Bible verses borrowed from pitchmen and then were infused with, as one of her prints says, "the big G stands for goodness." God.

Because there was nothing else quite like her work, it was hard to categorize, and that always makes the critics nervous. Her focus on Christ, in efforts like *Jesus never fails,* and *that man loves,* must have come off as uncomfortably reverent to some in the secular world, where she nonetheless caused a sensation. Yet she was much too irreverent to suit her bishop and others in the Church, where she was rightly seen as a threat to order. At the chancery, her wimple fooled no one.

What most speaks to me about Corita Kent—very much a forerunner of today's American women religious, who are living the Sermon on the Mount but stand accused of heresy by the Vatican—is her emotional shrug of a reaction to the situation, both at the time and later in her life. Though she eventually left the convent, she wasn't broken or run off by anybody, and she never lost either her faith or her joy.

Born Frances Elizabeth Kent in Fort Dodge, Iowa, in 1918, Corita grew up in the heart of Hollywood and followed her older sister Ruth into the convent straight out of high school, apparently without too much agonizing. "My very closest friend was just utterly shocked when I told her, during the summer after we graduated, that I was going to enter this community," Corita told an interviewer for the UCLA Oral History Project in 1976, a decade before she died of cancer. "I don't remember keeping it a secret, but I guess I just didn't talk about it. And she said, 'When did you make up your mind?' And I said, 'I don't know. I think I just always have wanted to be.'"

If she never questioned her calling, though, she routinely questioned her assumptions, in a way that made others want to follow suit. The truly radical thing Corita taught her students at Immaculate Heart College in Los Angeles, where she headed the art department, was to see with new eyes, through exercises like peering through a tiny square cut in a piece of paper so as to take in just a sliver of the world at a time.

People of all ages and backgrounds made unlikely changes

in their lives after meeting or even corresponding with Corita, and this, too, vexed the higher-ups. "I never would have become an artist if she hadn't taught me how to see," says my friend Dale Loy. In the early '60s, Dale interviewed Corita for a profile in *Sunset* magazine and ended up becoming her student, her friend—and before long, an ex-journalist. "She taught me how to see the wholeness of life—to draw upside down or see fifty things in your room you've never really looked at before—an incredible way to jostle our closed circuit of doing things the way we've always done them."

Really, you couldn't even give Corita a simple assignment like planning the school's traditional "Mary's Day" celebration without her turning what had always been just a march and a mumbling of the rosary into such an all-in celebration, riotous in the best way, that 1960s activists modeled their "happenings" on it.

The writer Samuel Eisenstein was so moved by a "Mary's Day" à la Corita that he went home and wrote her a letter proclaiming the mother of Jesus "the juiciest tomato of all"— a phrase she then made the theme of one of her best-known, and most provocative, serigraphs.

Even the suggestion that the Virgin Mary might be seen as sexual or "juicy" infuriated the bishop of Los Angeles at the time, Cardinal James Francis McIntyre, an ultra-traditionalist who opposed Vatican II reforms and tried to bar her from displaying the work.

On one of the UCLA Oral History Project tapes, she talks at some length, and without rancor, about the controversy and McIntyre's multiple attempts to throttle her.

In Eisenstein's letter after Mary's Day, she says, he

*included this marvelous thing which he had written on
Mary; and one of the phrases that really made it memorable
was "Mary was the juiciest tomato of all." And in the context, it was really beautiful. The whole thing was gracefully
done. So I made a print from it, using those words. Well,
I was aware of how "tomato" was used colloquially, but I
felt—you know, at that time, language was taking a turn
you could hardly use a word without it having some other
meaning. And I figured that wasn't fair for people to destroy
words that—and at that time, I did a lot of research into
tomato, and Sam did some for me, too, and found out that
it really had a marvelous history and was connected in fact,
at one point, I'm quite sure, with the mystical rose. But that
caused just more trouble than could be imagined over such a
simple thing, because people said, you know, "That's a dirty
word. How can you use that in connection with the Blessed
Mother?"*

Tomatoes, roses, humanity, and all of creation were connected for Corita. The trouble that came to her because she
was so open to all of it never knocked on her door directly,
she said, but was communicated through the chain of command: "Well, they had a funny way of acting," she says of
Church officials. "I suppose it was very normal, because it
was a very hierarchical way. *I* never got into trouble: the
head of the community and the head of the college got into
trouble. . . . They wouldn't bother dealing with me."

It wasn't only her art that caused the bishop such *agita*.
After Vatican II invited religious women to step into the modern world, Corita was among the Sisters of the Immaculate

Heart of Mary who began thinking seriously about adopting modern dress and adapting to modern life.

In response, McIntyre fired those sisters who worked in local Catholic schools in 1967. Though the women appealed their case to the Vatican, they lost there, too, and were ordered to either abide by the bishop's rules or seek dispensation from their vows.

The remove with which she talked about the ultimatum later was not much different from her feeling at the time, her friends say, and though she was so exhausted that many were worried about her, that was not a function of worry, she says, but of many years of overwork and lifelong insomnia. So many people wrote to her that even keeping up with her correspondence could have occupied her around the clock, and her fame was perhaps more of a burden than the bishop's various edicts.

Again in the UCLA interviews, she uses the word *funny* to describe the spot she was in with the hierarchy.

*Well, I think that it was a funny situation, a rather unique situation, because I think we were used to being in trouble. . . . If the top man is a progressive person, then the changes come much more gradually and gently. But in the Los Angeles situation, there was an extreme rigidity on the part of the hierarchy. So that what should have been very normal growing—organic changes were not allowed to be organic because everything that changed created such a big sensation that it blew it out of proportion. . . . We thought it was normal to change. But the people who were more conservative—I think they often feel that one little change is going to lead to many others, and they're certainly right. I think that's why they're so frightened by little changes.*

Corita left the order in 1968, two years before it split apart entirely, with 90 percent of its members leaving to create a new independent group. Her older sister, Ruth, stayed on in the original order, and Corita moved to Boston, where she continued to work but made a far quieter life for herself, and found this more contemplative and private time a great relief.

After I first wrote about Corita, in *The Washington Post,* following a local exhibition of her work, the question everyone seemed to want answered was whether she'd lost her faith in God, either before or after walking away.

But her friends say just the opposite happened. And in fact, her decision to leave the convent doesn't seem to have been much more fraught than the decision to enter had been when she was only seventeen.

"She continued to be a woman of deep faith," says one of her closest friends and fellow sisters, Lenore Dowling, "but she wasn't a 'catechism Catholic,' and therefore wasn't rebelling. When one's belief in God and humanity have such deep roots, conflicts and turbulence remain on the surface." Dowling sees today's conflicts between American religious sisters and Church officials playing out that way, too, with the women more peaceful and less reactive than those who've charged them with "radical feminism" might imagine: they continue to do what Christ asked of all of us, in hospitals and soup kitchens and shelters and "in the streets," Dowling said, "and the bishops are in the cathedrals. Even though externally, you'd think they'd be angry, they too are on a steady keel. There's not a compliance, but there is a consistency."

When Corita left Los Angeles for Boston, she thought she was only taking a rest and leaving for a sabbatical: "Well, in a way I supposed when I left that summer, it was only for the summer," she said in the UCLA interviews.

*And then when I got back East and was all quiet and peaceful, it just seemed that it wasn't possible to go back. So in a sense, I made the decision after I had gotten out, or after I had gone away. And I think the decision was then made in the years that followed, rather than the years that preceded, with a lot of the thinking. Because I had never thought of leaving up 'til that point, so I wasn't having any difficulty with the thought. But after I left, I looked back. And I've never had any regrets about leaving, even though there have been difficulties.*

She was someone who naturally "did enliven people, and put them in touch with their deepest selves," Dowling says. "I don't think anybody ever had a class with her who doesn't still feel her presence." Yet as an introvert, she'd paid a price for that, and was happier out of the public eye. Her later work changed in a way that reflected that, and she moved from brighter colors to pastels in keeping with the softer tone her life took on.

"I'm learning to sleep now," she said in the UCLA tapes.

*I just sleep at different times—whenever I feel like it. I think I have a calmer life, and a chance for more inner development, which I think is not only different but also normal for a person. As you know, you finish the extreme active part of your life, the part that is outward, you then want to develop more inwardly than I had before.*

Nor does Corita seem to have been anguished by the prospect of death, and before she died, she wrote this extraordinary letter:

*I wish to thank my family and friends, known and unknown, who have had a part in forming my life up to this point, and to ask that by your prayers and thoughts, you continue to help me in the new life I begin now. I feel this new life is just a next step and that I will still be knowing and caring for all of you forever. With love and hopes for your futures, Corita.*

So many of us in the Catholic Church are preoccupied with natural, perfectly valid questions about staying or going, fighting or steering clear. But what Corita reminds me is that the answer may only become obvious later. Of the ten rules posted on the wall of her classroom, number five was "To be disciplined is to follow in a good way. To be self-disciplined is to follow in a better way." And ninth was "Be happy whenever you can manage it. Enjoy yourself. It's lighter than you think."

# THE BURIED LIFE

## BEDE GRIFFITHS

~~~~~

*Paula Huston*

I'D ONLY JUST TURNED TWENTY but thought of myself as much older than my peers, who, unlike me, had actually listened to the advice of their elders. This meant that while I'd been working full-time to get my husband through college, they'd been happily matriculating at prestigious campuses around the country. I consoled myself with the notion that, unlike them, I was an adult. And also that my time would come, which finally it did.

I enrolled myself at the local city college and on day one of the new semester arrived on campus as thrilled as a freshly scrubbed first grader, energized by the semi-guilty thought that my *real* life, or rather that cluster of potentialities that lay like a vein of unmined ore somewhere deep inside me, was finally about to reveal itself. Who would I turn out to be? Though I had assumed I would discover this when I became a grown-up (one of the reasons I'd found the supposed emancipation of teenage marriage so compelling), so far I didn't have a clue.

My first class was biology. The professor, reedy and earnest and not much older than the rest of us, announced that we would not, as I had expected, be studying mitosis, but rather something he called "environmentalism." For it was 1972, and Planet Earth was in peril; if our habits did not change dramatically, within thirty-five years we'd be coping with the harbingers of an environmental apocalypse.

Shocked and upset—my most profound religious experiences had come during childhood as I communed with nature, and even though I could no longer believe in the Christian God, the only place I felt close to being whole and good was in the natural world—I went home that night, sewed myself a crude backpack of sailcloth, and unearthed my ancient bike lock. And for the next two semesters, I peddled to school along boulevards jammed with carbon monoxide–spewing traffic, eleven miles each way, because knowing what I now knew, there was no other choice.

————

Forty-two years before my own great awakening, a young Englishman named Alan Griffiths, along with two friends from Oxford, embarked on what he called an "experiment in common life." The three were appalled at the environmental degradation caused by the Industrial Revolution, but even more so by the resulting damage to the culture. They set out to recapture some of what had been lost by adopting a premodern way of life "primeval in its simplicity," as Griffiths puts it in his autobiography, *The Golden String*.

After some months of searching, they bought a small Cotswold cottage without electricity or running water near a village called Eastington. Griffiths, committed to walking rather than driving or taking trains, made the daily trek each day to fill their clay pitchers at the village pump. The three of them cooked their basic meals on the fireplace: porridge in the morning, vegetable stew and cheese cut from a great round of Double Gloucester at midday, and four eggs, laid by their foraging ducks, in the evening.

Griffith's visionary enthusiasm occasionally proved too much for his companions, who found themselves struggling with the extreme austerity of their adopted lifestyle. However, he loved the sense of being at one with nature, which at seventeen had given him his first genuine religious experience, an event so overwhelming that the post-Victorian Christianity in which he'd been raised paled in comparison. His new spiritual guides had become the great Romantics: Samuel Coleridge, John Keats, Percy Shelley, William Wordsworth.

Yet at Eastington, even these nineteenth-century poets were too recent. Wanting as authentic an experience of premodern life as they could get, the three limited themselves to books from the 1600s or earlier, often reading these in their original languages. This misty, bygone world still shimmered in the great medieval churches that loomed like God over nearby Cotswold towns and villages. Soon, as though it were a natural next step, they were spending part of each morning, "while the porridge was cooking on the fire and the candles in winter shed their mellow light on the crockery," immersed in their Bibles.

By the time the grand experiment ended less than a year

later, they were praying on their knees and fasting, and Griffiths had begun worshiping at the village church. That he'd not only undergone a shift in worldview but made a connection with what Matthew Arnold calls the "buried life" was clear; where this would lead, he could not yet discern.

---

Not long after that biology class, I found my own late-twentieth-century version of Eastington: an acre and a half on the central coast of California, hours north of the industrialized harbor city of my youth. We were starting to think about kids. And if we were going to have them, they were going to grow up where you could breathe the air. School, I told myself firmly, could once again wait.

We both worked full-time to make our new mortgage payments and spent the weekends rototilling, planting, and weeding a sprawling organic garden; we raised chickens, composted our kitchen scraps in a worm box, and assiduously recycled. I learned to bake bread, served our homegrown produce for dinner, and canned and preserved what we couldn't eat fresh. When I got pregnant, I dragged my reluctant husband to natural childbirth classes, and after our baby was born, nurtured her on breast milk and pureed apricots from our trees.

Though it would be easy to blame the zeitgeist—it was the height of the '70s, after all—there was more than hippiness afoot.

---

Griffiths, forty years before me, was in the midst of a frightening free fall. Not long after the Eastington experiment ended, he'd returned to the Cotswolds on his own, adopting the severely ascetical life of a hermit and devoting most of his time to prayer. Yet something was clearly wrong; the more he fasted, the more he hungered for fasting. The more he prayed, the more he longed for prayer. He began to fear that in his zeal his mind was becoming unhinged.

In desperation, he decided he must not rise from his knees until God gave him clear direction. Almost immediately, he was "carried away by a great wave of prayer," and when he finally returned to consciousness eight hours later, he had a new understanding of the spiritual life: "There is an inner sanctuary into which we scarcely ever enter. It is the ground or substance of the soul, where all the faculties have their roots, and which is the very centre of our being. It is here that the soul is at all times in direct contact with God."

He consulted with a sympathetic priest—it took some doing to find a Catholic priest nearby—who took him to a Benedictine monastery. The countryside around Prinknash Priory was still unspoiled, the white habits of the monks were simple and clean, the daily schedule of chanting and sacred reading soothed his ravaged psyche, but most important, the fifteen-hundred-year-old monastic lifestyle helped him understand why he had for so long been anguished and confused: "It was the absence of prayer as a permanent background to life which made modern life so empty and meaningless."

He was first baptized into the Catholic Church, then became a monk—Brother Bede—and after that took holy orders, steadied by the knowledge that here among those who practiced the Benedictine way of *ora et labora,* prayer and work, he would remain until he died.

My own free fall, when it finally came, took the form of a love affair and guilt-shot divorce, followed by a stint as a single mother of two, a second marriage that included stepchildren, and finally a return to academia to finish my degree. Ten years of turmoil had taken their toll, but though I no longer fantasized that college would show me who I was, though I could feel, right through my clothing, the brittle fragility of my once-hopeful heart, I could still find some peace in the miracle of sunlight and seeds.

Then, at nearly forty, I underwent another classroom awakening, this time in an ethics course taught by a Christian who recognized the sad hungers that burned within me. He introduced me to his Catholic wife, who drove me to a Camaldolese Benedictine monastery on the Big Sur coast, 860 acres of redwoods and blue flowering ceanothus beside the shining sea. After years of self-imposed exile from God, I was finally home.

Though I'd never be a nun—How could a married divorcée with four kids be a nun?—during these few hours in a wilderness hermitage, the seeking eye within, so clouded by disillusionment and regret, began, on its own, to drink in the light.

In 1993, nearly sixty years after he made his permanent vows at Prinknash Priory in England, Bede Griffiths died in a Christian ashram at Shantivanam in South India. Here, after a rocky start, he had been the monastic superior and a widely respected swami for the previous two and a half decades. The young idealist from Oxford who had once walked the seventy miles from Eastington to London in order to avoid riding the train had become a prolific writer, a friend to the Dalai Lama, and, in his role as an international guru to thousands of young seekers, a frequent flyer. It had been years since he'd worn the white Benedictine cowl; instead, he lived in the *dhoti,* or Hindu loincloth, and the *kavi,* or saffron robes of a Hindu *sannyasi* ("renouncer"). He went barefoot. He sat on the floor. He ate with his hands.

He was not a Christian missionary—he had not come to India for that—but despite his incorporation of ancient Sanskrit traditions into the daily Eucharist, not to mention his vocal criticisms of what he saw as an increasingly moribund Church, he was still very much a Catholic. He spent two hours a day in the lotus position, silently repeating the Eastern Orthodox Jesus prayer ("Lord Jesus Christ, son of the living God, have mercy on me, a sinner"). People said that simply being in his presence could open you to an experience of *darshan,* or spiritual "seeing." Shortly before he died, a fellow Benedictine, Laurence Freeman, sat beside his hospital bed with the Gospel of John: "When I read the words, 'This is my commandment that you love one another', [Bede] caught his breath and lifted a finger with emphasis and said 'That is the whole gospel.'"

At his funeral, throngs of grief-stricken Christians, Hindus, and Muslims from the surrounding villages laid flowers at his feet, washed them with milk, and marked his forehead with sandal paste and red *kumkum* powder. Then, one by one, they kissed him farewell and carried him to his grave.

Not long after Bede's passing, I went on a solo pilgrimage around the world, spending a week in India in hope I might make it down to see his by-now famous ashram at Shantivanam, the "Forest of Peace." This was not to be. However, the soul-sucking heat, the camel carts, the women stacking water buffalo patties for winter fuel, the roadside idols wearing *tika* powder and *malas* of flowers helped me see why Bede considered India such fertile spiritual soil. Despite the inroads of high technology, vast portions of India remain completely intertwined, in the most elemental of ways, with nature.

I was forty-six when I hit the pilgrim trail; Bede was forty-nine when he left England to take up life in an alternative universe; both of us, in our own ways, were seeking answers to the same questions, the questions we had not been able to put into words when, in our twenties, forty years apart, he moved to a Cotswold cottage without running water or electricity and I so fiercely embraced a modern version of my pioneer ancestors' life.

What is it about Western culture that makes it so difficult to "taste" God? Why would we in the West rather prove theological propositions than experience the holy? Certainly, the irreversible developments in philosophy, science, psychology, and politics that culminated in the worldview we call modernism have contributed to our dilemma. But at the heart of the issue, I have come to believe, lies the unmooring of creation from its origin in God. When we began looking at nature with a calculating rather than a contemplative eye, we were, without knowing it, abandoning a sacramental view of reality. When we began to see ourselves as monads, autonomous and self-contained, we were, without knowing it, relinquishing the vision of heavenly participation that nourished and sustained Christianity for nearly fifteen hundred years.

God looks upon the earth and it trembles. He touches the mountains and they smoke. He makes springs to gush forth in the valleys and causes the grass to grow. He sets the boundaries for the seas and sends the rain to fall upon the good and the evil alike. He forms our inward parts and knits us together in our mother's womb. If we are fearfully and wonderfully made—just ask any neuroscientist or orthopedic surgeon—it is because the creator of the universe has taken a personal interest in our flourishing. No wonder that in him we live and move and have our being. We are temples of the Holy Spirit, no longer imprisoned by the boundaries of chronological time; we are members of the Eucharistic Body of Christ, intimates in a vast *koinonia*.

What modernity and its corresponding disenchantment of the universe has cost us is nothing less than this.

---

Somewhat amazingly, Bede Griffiths never did run afoul of Rome ("We are too far away," he once quipped rather smugly). Though he certainly precipitated considerable controversy in both the Catholic and Hindu worlds—his wearing of the saffron robe and use of Sanskrit scripture deeply offended some swamis, and his incorporation of Hindu practices such as the *arati,* or the waving of the flame, during Mass horrified certain Catholics—his writing was never censored, even that which posited a universal religion and a Cosmic Lord.

He is considered by many to be an important pre–Vatican II pioneer of ecumenism, and thousands of people around the world still employ the meditation techniques he taught at Shantivanam.

For me, however, his significance lies in a different direction. I honor him as one of the few modern Christians who recognized that the loss of a sacramental worldview has seriously diminished our capacity for faith. Yet for some people, people like Bede and me, nature still triggers the primary religious experience. Bede had his at seventeen; I had mine, when, as a child of ten, I lay on my back beneath the giant sequoias. When nature lights you up that way—when you feel as though you've seen, however briefly, into the Wordsworthian "life of things"—your spiritual path is pretty well laid out for you. When you finally meet God, it will almost surely be as a contemplative. One who flourishes in the wilderness. One who craves, like some half-mad hermit, significant amounts of a solitude and silence nearly impossible to find in our frenetic, urban society. A person whose primary mode of prayer is meditation.

————

Not long after the pilgrimage, I became an oblate of the Camaldolese community and thus a member of Bede's monastic family, vowing before my brother monks to live, as well as a busy mother, wife, and grandmother can live, by the Rule of Saint Benedict and the Brief Rule of Saint Romuald of Ravenna, tenth-century founder of the order. The Benedictine way of manual work and prayer in a rural setting has come fairly naturally: for the past twenty-seven years, my family has lived on four acres in the country where we grow fruits and vegetables, press the olives from our trees, make wine, keep chickens, and harvest honey from our hives. Not as Luddites (the challenge these days is how to keep the dirt out of the iPhones) but instead as pilgrims on the way.

Romuald's contemplative rule is a little more difficult to follow, given the busyness of our lives, but as the years have passed—and I am sixty now—it has become the bedrock of my existence, that which unites my beloved natural world, the roving eye within, and the God who gives everything life. Not surprisingly, what I am most drawn to in the Rule are its references to nature as sacrament:

> Sit in your cell as in a paradise. Put the whole world behind you and forget it. Watch your thoughts like a good fisherman watching for fish. . . . Empty yourself completely and sit waiting, content with the grace of God, like the chick who tastes nothing and eats nothing but what his mother gives him.

I believe that this ancient Christian way of prayer, developed by the fourth-century desert fathers and rediscovered seven hundred years later by an Italian monk who could not imagine the extent of the assault creation would someday undergo, encapsulates one of Bede's most important spiritual insights:

> Nature comes into being in the Word and expresses the mind of God to us, and nature is moved by the Spirit, which brings all things to maturity in Christ. This creation is in evolution towards the new creation, and man is [meant to be] the mediator, the high-priest, who unites [it] with God.

# EVERY DAY,
# YES OR NO?

## DOROTHY DAY

*Patrick Jordan*

ONE OF THE MOST STRIKING things about Jesus as recorded in the Gospels—at least to me—is how directly he speaks to people. Yes, he often taught through parables—paradoxical, sometimes funny stories that continue to generate endless interpretations. He was canny, particularly so when dealing with the authorities, religious and secular. When they tried to trip him up, his rhetorical response could put them to scorn. Still, in most of his recorded sayings, Jesus's yes is *yes* and his no is *no:* "No one can serve two masters" (Matt. 6:24). Yes or no? We're still dancing around that one. Perhaps the most direct, haunting question he asked, toward the end of his life, remains "When the Son of Man comes, will he find faith on earth?" (Luke 18:8).

In his *Tales of the Hasidim,* Martin Buber tells the story of a young man who left home and journeyed far to meet the famed preacher of Mezritch, Rabbi Dov Baer (d. 1772). He did so, the tale recounts, not to "learn Torah" (the study and interpretation of the Sacred Law) from the great seer, but to see how he "unlaced his felt shoes and laced them up again." When I first arrived at the Catholic Worker house in New York as a volunteer in 1968, I could never have imagined it would be to learn how Dorothy Day (1897–1980) tied her shoes.

Seventy at the time, taller than I had expected, Dorothy had pale blue eyes masked somewhat by her heavy-rimmed editor's glasses. She wore a bandana that only partially concealed a magnificent crown of braided white hair. The new First Street house (St. Joseph House), just off Second Avenue a block from the Bowery, was in a teeming ghetto of older Italians (too weary to escape with their children to the suburbs), newly arriving Puerto Rican and Dominican families, and the off-scouring of the city—the unemployed and the alcoholics and drug addicts who lived in the alleys and flophouses nearby. They would panhandle and war against one another 24/7, but each day they would drag themselves over to the Catholic Worker for bread and a sobering bowl of soup.

When I arrived at the new St. Joseph House, it was still empty, awaiting an occupancy permit from the city. Dorothy was sitting at a spare desk on the ground floor of the five-story walkup, waiting for a delivery for the contractor. She was talking with two young draft resisters. It was during the Vietnam War and she had publicly encouraged young men to burn their draft cards. (In 1941, the very day after Pearl Harbor, she had told a New York audience,

"You young men refuse to take up arms. Young women, tear down the patriotic posters. And all of you, young and old, put away your flags!") With the seasoned ease of someone who had been welcoming strangers for generations, she quickly welcomed me and included me in the conversation, inquiring about mutual friends on the West Coast. A lifelong reporter and editor, she could unobtrusively find out more about a person in fifteen minutes than I would in a month. Rather quickly, she then shifted the discussion and told me where I could locate a bed on the floor of a Catholic Worker apartment six blocks away (in a building where she was also living at the time). After leaving my bag there, I could retrace my steps a few blocks to the existing Worker house on Christie Street and pitch in serving the evening meal. It was the shortest interview/job orientation of my life, and the most significant. As one of Dorothy's granddaughters wrote later, but I was yet to learn, "To have known Dorothy means spending the rest of your life wondering what hit you." (Dorothy herself once cautioned the young son of a coworker as they were crossing a busy Manhattan avenue: "If I'm going to get run down, I want it to be by a Mack truck.")

The basic outlines of Dorothy Day's life are well known. A radical and a journalist who converted to Catholicism in 1927 (following the birth of her daughter a year earlier), she co-founded the Catholic Worker movement in 1933 with an itinerant French Catholic social thinker, Peter Maurin, twenty years her senior. Together they started a newspaper, opened houses of hospitality to respond to the immediate needs of the urban poor, and established farming communes to house and give work to the unemployed. The aim was and continues to be to foster an understanding of Catholic social teaching, to promote personal responsibility for the common good rather than relying on the state, and to exemplify in one's daily life the voluntary poverty and pacifism of the earliest Christian communities. In short: "to create a new society within the shell of the old." Day has been called the "most significant, interesting, and influential person in the history of American Catholicism," and the Catholic Worker has been described as "the most important radical Catholic movement in American history."

But you might never know that from meeting Dorothy herself, although I did experience occasions when an entire roomful of people would fall silent even though she had entered unobtrusively. While not generally one to put herself forward, when praying and fasting in Rome for ten days in 1965, she wrote the bishops at the Second Vatican Council she would be praying that the Holy Spirit might "enlighten your minds and inflame your hearts with the courage to proclaim peace and love to the world. Hear the voice of suffering people, starving while billions are being spent for armaments."

What Dorothy did convey unabashedly in person was an uncommon intelligence and complete attention to whatever was at hand. Her look could be so focused that many thought her severe or unsmiling, but that was not the case. She had a youthful voice, a lilting, if reticent, laugh, and her blue eyes could sparkle. There was in her a modesty that was nearly elemental. I think it had to do with an always near-to-hand self-awareness about past failures—personal, moral, and spiritual—and about the daily, ongoing failures of the Catholic Worker movement as well. (She liked to quote G. K. Chesterton to the effect that if something was worth doing, it was worth doing badly.) Once, after a particularly horrendous week at the new First Street house (bedlam, drunkenness, and a full moon), she told me pointedly, "The Catholic Worker is madness," but then added immediately, "There is so much suffering in this place I cannot help but think it is redemptive."

"Where there are slums," she had written, "we must live in them and share the conditions of the poor." Why? Because Christ chose to be poor—or, as she put it, because "poverty is so esteemed by God." It is something to be sought after, worked for, the pearl of great price. In fact, she noted, "It is our greatest message: to be poor with the poor." But for all that, as her granddaughter Kate observed years later, Dorothy "turned the life of poverty into something dynamic, full of richly simple moments for those who have nothing."

Most of the clothes Dorothy wore were hand-me-downs from the Catholic Worker clothing room, but she also had some lovely outfits, gifts from her sister Della, and a set of everyday dresses made by a Catholic Worker friend. The fact was Dorothy looked great in just about anything. One summer, it was in 1972, another friend had sent her a check for "wine and roses," which meant Dorothy could use it for herself. So she invited Kathleen and me (we would be married later that fall) to see *Fiddler on the Roof* with her and to have a cream cheese sandwich at Chock full o'Nuts beforehand. Who could refuse?

*Fiddler* is a rousing musical comedy, based on Sholem

Aleichem's Tevye stories, which Dorothy loved. The play concerns nineteenth-century shtetl life, and how the Hasidic families of the period were attempting to cope with the growing encroachments of modernity and a czarist state. The curtain goes up with a rousing anthem and circle dance, "Tradition!"—a notion dear to Dorothy ever since she had first lived among poor Jews on Manhattan's Lower East Side as a fledgling journalist in 1916, and a concept central to Catholicism: Do this in memory of me. Dorothy's respect for Jewish tradition was informed by her lifelong love and study of the Hebrew scriptures, and by her sensitivity to the plight of Jews worldwide. As early as 1933, the *Catholic Worker* paper had denounced Catholic anti-Semitism and decried the new Nazi regime in Germany. Only a few months before going to the play, in fact, Dorothy had been honored as a "woman of valor" by the Little Synagogue in Manhattan with its Baal Shem Tov Award.

As we walked up Broadway that Sunday afternoon, Dorothy looked splendid in a two-piece, pale green suit. She wore a pair of custom-made, size 9 1/2 Murray Space shoes (the gift of yet another friend), and her pace was steady but measured. The shoes were dark blue, orthopedic looking, and had two buckles at the top. She used them almost every day. (A famous photo spies her wearing them as she calmly awaits arrest with striking agriculture workers in California in 1973. At age seventy-five, she sits seemingly impervious before a phalanx of heavily armed sheriff's officers.) Making our way gradually to the theater, we were stopped by two young women who inquired whether she was Dorothy Day. (Her picture had been in a number of papers that year, when the Nixon administration attempted to shut down the Catholic Worker for alleged tax evasion; Bill Moyers had produced a film on her for public television titled *Still a Rebel;* and three of her books had been reissued as cheap paperbacks, her picture on each.) Dorothy was delighted to be recognized by these beautiful strangers. To her it meant the Catholic Worker was being taken seriously. Then it was off to the play.

Dorothy loved the Russian authors, particularly Dostoevsky, Tolstoy, and Chekhov. In December 1961, while rereading Chekhov, she had written that the question Chekhov "brings out in all his stories is: 'What is to be done? What is life for?'" His conclusion, she said, "is that we are here to work, to serve our brothers." He himself was a doctor who wrote on the side to support himself and his family. "Not to be a parasite, not to live off of others, to earn our own living by a life of service— this answered the question for him," she noted. Further, Chekhov was concerned about faith. His heroine in *Uncle Vanya,* Sonya, testifies, "I have faith, Uncle, fervent, passionate faith." And when Christ returns at the end of time, she concludes in triumph, "We shall see evil and all our pain sink away in the great compassion that shall enfold the world."

Dorothy Day had such powerful, unadulterated faith. It was not based on creedal propositions or on catechetical formulas but on a passionate relationship with the living God. It cost her. "For me, Christ was not bought for thirty pieces of silver but with my heart's blood," she wrote in 1967. "We buy not cheap in this market." She had given up friends and what she called a "life of natural happiness" with the man she loved, Forster Batterham, the father of her daughter, for it. He had refused to marry Dorothy and derided her conversion to Catholicism. Still, years later Dorothy was able to say, "It is joy that brought me to the faith, joy at the birth of my child thirty-five years ago; and that joy is constantly renewed as I receive Our Lord at Mass." As a result of her wrenching personal sacrifice, she considered the loss of faith "the greatest of disasters—the greatest unhappiness." She found daily Mass to be an antidote to apostasy, calling it the most important work of the day. "If I can just remember to do that well—as well as I am able [note her practicality]—everything else will take care of itself," she said.

When Dorothy turned seventy-two, Vivian Gornick was dispatched to interview her for the *Village Voice*. "I cannot bear the [religious] romantics," Dorothy told the writer as they sat in the small backyard of the First Street house. "I want a religious realist. I want one who prays to see things as they are and to do something about it." In her 1952 spiritual autobiography, *The Long Loneliness,* Dorothy had pointedly asked, "Why was so much done in remedying social evils instead of avoiding them in the first place? . . . Where were the saints to try to change the social order, not just to minister to slaves, but to do away with slavery?" It was very much as a realist that she had entered the Church in 1927; and in 1933, when she and Maurin started the Catholic Worker, she had not sought approval for the venture from church officials. Instead, as she recounted some years later, she relied on the advice of three priests (all editors), who told her "to launch out, but not to ask permission. It would not be given, it was implied."

In 1968, when the Catholic sociologist and peace activist Gordon Zahn (who had brought the story of Franz Jägerstätter to the attention of the English-speaking world) was having a serious crisis of faith over the institutional church, Dorothy reassured him that "as a convert, I never expected much of the bishops. In all history, popes and bishops and father abbots seem to have been blind and power-loving and greedy. I never expected leadership from them. It is the saints who keep appearing throughout history who keep things going." However, she told Zahn, "What I do expect is the bread of life and down through the ages there is that continuity"—the sacraments and tradition. "The gospel is hard," she continued. "Loving your enemies, and the worst are of your own household, is hard." Still, as she was to instruct another coworker thinking of leaving the Church, "No matter how corrupt the Church may become, it carries with it the seeds of its own regeneration. To read the lives of the saints has always helped me," she counseled.

Goodness and beauty attract. I used to go up mornings to visit with Dorothy in her room on the third floor of St. Joseph House. Often she would still be in her robe, her long hair uncombed and hanging down to her waist, her feet in slippers or bare. She would have already said the morning psalms, had her cup of coffee (both essential to starting her day), and been reading one thing or another. The conversation was unhurried and instructive: points of history, insights into theology, family stories, editorial directives, personal advice. There would be assignments ("Go hear E. F. Schumacher and report on it for the paper"), warnings ("Be sure you don't work too hard; beware of your tendency toward sentimentality"), and personal wisdom ("Don't get married until you *have* to"). There would be spiritual direction, often from scripture: You must take up your cross daily; we are to forgive seventy times seven; where there is no love, put love and you will find love; we love God as much as we love the one we love least; and pray. "As breath is to the body, prayer is to the soul," she reflected. As for faith itself, she said often, "Every act of faith increases your faith." Faith, like love, must be fervent, passionate; it is purchased only with one's heart's blood. It must be sought after, suffered for, put to the test, deepened, renewed, and taken joy in.

"You will know your vocation by the joy that it brings you," Dorothy told Kathleen and me when we were about to leave the New York Catholic Worker in 1975. She said she would pray for us to find the same sort of surety she had experienced when she first met Peter Maurin. It had been the answer to her fervent prayer: *What is to be done?* Ever since, she said, she had never doubted her vocation—in hard, numbing times as well as in more peaceable and stable ones.

*Will I find faith on earth?* Jesus asks. And clearly he is looking for the real thing: passionate, practical, thoughtful faith—the only kind worthy of the living God. Where to begin to find and nurture it? Perhaps with how we lace and unlace our shoes. And from there? Perhaps with how we bathe the feet of our brothers and sisters.

# A NEST OF CROSSES

## MOTHER MARY MACKILLOP

*Cathleen Kaveny*

Mother Mary Mackillop went to bed tired and ill on the evening of September 29, 1871. The twenty-nine-year-old foundress of the Institute of St. Joseph, a new order of sisters dedicated to teaching the poorest children in Australia, had heard rumblings about the bishop of Adelaide's disgruntlement with her fledgling community, as well as with her personally. Still, nothing could have prepared her for what happened early the next morning.

At 8:00 A.M. on September 30, Mary was summoned from her sickbed at one of the sisters' satellite houses to the convent next to the Adelaide Cathedral. Immediately upon her arrival, she asked for a blessing from Bishop Lawrence Sheil, who was waiting for her. He refused her request and ordered all the sisters into the chapel. While the others took their seats, Mary was directed to kneel alone before the bishop. Wearing his miter (symbolizing his participation in the rule of Christ) and carrying his crozier (symbolizing his participation in Christ's role as the Good Shepherd), Bishop Sheil proceeded to excommunicate Mother Mary MacKillop from the Roman Catholic Church. After castigating her for her spiritual pride and blaming her for infecting the sisters with worldly wickedness, he ordered her to leave the community immediately. Bishop Sheil went on to inform the distressed group of religious sisters that anyone who spoke up in Mary's defense would share in her fate.

One of the sisters in the chapel shrieked as if she were possessed by a demon, resisting all attempts to quiet her. Mary herself, however, was preternaturally calm. She later wrote of the experience:

> *I really felt like one in a dream. I seemed not to realize the presence of the Bishop and priests; I know I did not see them, but I felt, oh, such a love for their office, a love, a sort of reverence, for the very sentence which I knew then was being in full force passed upon me. I do not know how to describe the feeling, but I was intensely happy and felt nearer to God than I had ever felt before. The sensation of the calm beautiful presence of God I shall never forget.*

How can we make sense of the reaction of Australia's first saint to this unjust and deeply humiliating ecclesiastical action? After all, most people would have been shocked or angry, or even both simultaneously.

The key to understanding Mary, I think, lies in her selection of a religious name. When she founded the Institute of St. Joseph together with Father Julian Woods in 1867, Mary MacKillop became Mother Mary of the Cross. Mary's choice of a name was a sign of her deep desire to be united to Jesus Christ in his suffering.

That desire was fulfilled over the course of her vocation in a manner that is both ironic and revelatory. Most of the suffering that Mary was forced to endure over the years was imposed upon her by Christ's duly ordained ecclesiastical representatives in the Roman Catholic Church. Powerful Australian priests and prelates besmirched her reputation and impeded her vocation at almost every turn. The heaviest cross carried by Australia's first saint turned out to be the institutional Church that she loved and served, the Church that is meant to be the visible manifestation of the body of Christ on this earth.

Many Catholics today also experience the institutional Church as a cross they must bear in faith. In a widely publicized opinion piece in the *Chicago Tribune* entitled "Excommunicate Me, Please," Sheila O'Brien, an Illinois Appellate Court judge, shares not only her love for the Catholic Church, but also her anguish at some of its doctrines, policies, and decisions. Particularly painful, she says, has been the Church's long-standing indifference to the sexual abuse of children, coupled with its aggressive rejection of the ordination of women. O'Brien writes, "Each person must decide: Stay and fight (cutting off the money but with little hope for change) or leave. Both options are spiritually and emotionally exhausting."

I do not blame those who decide to leave. But those who try to stay, I think, can find some inspiration and sustenance in the story of Mary MacKillop. This is not to say that contemporary Catholics will accept or even understand every aspect of her approach to the challenges she faced. Nor, for that matter, would Mary have understood them; it would have been unthinkable for her to leave the Church. But venerating a saint does not mean endorsing each and every one of his or her choices. In fact, the Catholic understanding of the communion of saints permits us to ask questions of our forebears in the faith as well as to beg their intercession. It also allows us to trust that the beatific vision has expanded their empathy for us.

## THE STORY OF THE EXCOMMUNICATION

Just how did Mary MacKillop become an excommunicated saint? The problems began while Bishop Sheil was in Rome for the First Vatican Council and Mary was pursuing opportunities for the Josephites outside of Adelaide. When he returned to the city in February 1871, Bishop Sheil was confronted with a complaint against the sisters signed by a number of his priests. The charges themselves were unremarkable; the complaint alleged, for instance, that the Josephites were incompetent teachers and insubordinate to local clergy.

But the substance of the charges was not the main motivation for the letter's draftsman, Charles Horan. In fact, Horan was engaged in a twisted program of revenge. Some months earlier, the Josephites had gathered evidence that a Franciscan priest serving their school in Kapunda had committed sexual abuse. The priest was expelled from the region after the Josephites reported him to diocesan officials. When Horan, who was also a Franciscan, assumed a key administrative role in the diocese, he retaliated against the sisters for their exposure of the disgraceful behavior of his fellow friar.

Unfortunately, it was not only persons outside the Josephite community who precipitated the excommunication crisis. Insiders also acted in ways that undermined the order's standing and reputation in the diocese. Julian Woods, the co-founder with Mary of the Institute of St. Joseph, was a mercurial and self-involved man. While Mary was traveling around Australia on behalf of the order, Woods became increasingly interested in spiritualism, miracles, and arcane messages from the world beyond. He also became allied with members of the order who were unstable and malicious. For example, in 1870, the Josephites were plagued by a series of mysterious events. The Hosts vanished from their chapel, bloodstains materialized on their altar cloths, and a series of mysterious fires erupted in their convent. Although the local priests suspected that the cause was human chicanery, Woods insisted on attributing the events to supernatural causes. In this case, however, the local priests were right. Sister Angela, one of the nuns who would go on to make further trouble for Mother Mary and the Josephites, had staged the events in a pattern of deliberate deception and manipulation. Her deceit and its eventual exposure did incalculable harm to the reputation of the order in Adelaide. So did Woods's continued insistence upon the supernatural source of the events even after the fraud had been uncovered.

The bishop's strong desire to exert total control over all religious sisters within his diocese also contributed to the excommunication crisis. When asked about the situation by Bishop Matthew Quinn of Bathurst, Bishop Sheil tellingly replied:

*Their Superioress General I have expelled and excommunicated because she excited the sisters to rebel against my authority. Many of the Sisters challenge my power to alter or modify their rule which derives all its force solely from my approbation.*

But the bishop's desire to control the sisters in this way contravened fundamental aspects of their constitution. The Josephites' rule provided for common governance under a single mother superior. While Mary clearly recognized that any bishop had the right to decide whether or not he wanted the Josephites in his diocese, she adamantly maintained that he could not alter their rule once they were there in order to meet his own objectives. Needless to say, the bishop did not see the matter in the same way.

From the eternal perspective of God's abiding love, the bishop's excommunication was an impotent act. Mary was always a faithful member of the body of Christ. Moreover, from a canonical perspective, the excommunication was highly irregular. But unjust and legally defective decrees can have terrible consequences, in this life, if not in the next. The excommunication left Mary and her sisters bereft and exposed in every possible respect. Banished from the Church, Mary could not openly stay with Catholics. She found quiet refuge with Protestant friends and with Jesuits who did not accept the validity of her punishment. Expelled from their convent, some of Mary's sisters were rescued by a Jewish man who provided them with rent-free housing. The newspapers soon took notice of the colorful tensions between the bishop and the Josephites. The Church in Adelaide was divided, as some Catholics supported the sisters while others viewed them as rebellious troublemakers.

The saga ended as dramatically as it began. By December 1871, it was widely known in Adelaide that Bishop Sheil was ill; some said he had been ill since returning from Rome. A later investigation suggested that his mental capacities were so impaired that he was not able to perform the duties of his office. Rumor had it that he was suffering the consequences of addiction to drink; in any case, drink certainly made his condition worse. Father Horan had gradually come to exert almost total control over the bishop; according to one report, Horan kept him "like a little boy, in a torpid state," by regularly feeding him a mixture of brandy and water.

Almost miraculously, Bishop Sheil had a deathbed conversion. Notwithstanding his brandy consumption, Sheil's mind somehow cleared enough to recognize Horan's treachery. An observer quoted him as saying, "I am dying with a broken heart. Those whom I trusted contracted bad habits. At times I acted at their suggestions—I'm sorry. That is why I am so unhappy." On February 23, 1872, Bishop Lawrence Sheil received his last rites—and lifted the excommunication of Mother Mary MacKillop. At no point was Mary ever bitter toward Bishop Sheil. In fact, she frequently expressed sympathy for his illness.

## CONSCIENCE AMIDST A "NEST OF CROSSES"

The story of Mary's excommunication presents, in encapsulated form, many of the difficulties that she was to face again and again throughout her long ministry. Other Australian bishops would attempt to quash the sisters' autonomy in religious life. Other Josephites would behave maliciously and incompetently. And Julian Woods's eccentric and self-serving behavior would continue to undermine the new order. At one point early in their relationship, Woods had said to Mary, "I believe you will come into a nest of crosses"—not realizing, of course, that he was destined to become one of those crosses himself.

How did Mary MacKillop find the drive to continue working on behalf of the Josephite mission despite all she suffered at the hands of the institutional Church? I think she believed herself bound in conscience to do so. In our own era, we tend to think of conscience as primarily a negative barrier; it tells us what we must *not* do, as the phrase "conscientious objection" suggests. In Mary's life, however, conscience was a positive force; it was her dynamic, trusting response to God's call to build a community of solidarity in Christ with the poor of Australia.

For Mary, conscience was creative; it impelled her to discern, frame, and implement an entirely new form of religious life. No other order of Australian women was committed to solidarity with the poor in the manner of the Josephites. Conscience was also constructive; Mary could not waste time dwelling upon the obstacles to her vision but needed to strategize about how to overcome them. Most dramatically, after the Adelaide debacle, this obscure and impoverished woman from the Antipodes made her way to Rome in order to seek Vatican approval and protection for her order's constitution. She got what she needed, in the essentials, if not in every detail.

Mary's conscientious refusals—her "No's"—were not arbitrary; they were necessary to protect the integrity of all to which she had said "Yes." Furthermore, her "No's" were not matters of automatic rebellion, but were shaped by her duty of obedience and marked by prudent discernment. For example, according to its original constitution, the Institute of St. Joseph was prohibited from owning property; the purpose was to share more fully in the fate of the poor. When the Vatican refused to approve this provision, Mary acquiesced in their decision. She came to see the prudence in ensuring that the sisters who gave their lives to the mission would not be dependent upon the fickle will of bishops or wealthy Catholics in order to have a roof over their heads. In her acquiescence, however, she parted ways from Julian Woods. He would have defied Vatican directives in order to maintain the original provision. At the same time, Mary understood that conscience requires drawing the line, not total capitulation to ecclesiastical pressures. She continued to resist, sometimes unsuccessfully, local episcopal pressure to give special treatment to wealthy students. Such a step, in her view, would fatally undermine the charism of the Josephites.

How did Mary bear her cross? In ways that may seem counterintuitive to us today. It was easier for her to withstand the false and vicious attacks on her character; precisely because they were unjust, she saw them as uniting her more closely with Christ, who suffered similar attacks. It was also not difficult for her to maintain her resistance against the Australian bishops who attempted to undermine the Josephite structure of common governance. In these cases, Mary believed that it was the bishops who were disobedient, not she, since they were failing to defer to a decision about the order that came directly from the Vatican.

The most difficult challenge was enduring the consequences of imprudent or arbitrary decisions on the part of superiors that were nonetheless fully lawful. For Mary, these decisions constituted a "most subtle cross." In 1885, the Vatican had replaced Mary as superior general with the more mild-mannered and deferential Mother Bernard Walsh. Doubtless, this change in leadership was a strategic move designed to mollify some of the bishops who had trouble dealing directly with Mary. Nonetheless, the administrative restructuring threatened the well-being of the order, since Mother Bernard proved to be a weak and incompetent leader. Mary struggled to give her new mother superior practical advice while avoiding undermining or usurping her authority. It was difficult to for Mary to witness Mother Bernard's managerial ineptness. But it was more painful for her to watch Mother Bernard capitulate to the bishops' periodic requests to cater to wealthy students while persistently ignoring the Josephites' mandate to care for Aboriginal children, who were the poorest of the poor.

## THE CROSS AND THE BODY (OF CHRIST): SOLIDARITY WITH MARY MACKILLOP

Mary MacKillop was a woman of her own time and place. Her emphasis on the redemptive value of suffering, so characteristic of nineteenth-century Catholic spirituality, is not widely appreciated or even understood today. Nonetheless, I think her story can be helpful to us. Borrowing from David Tracy, we can say that the lives of the saints are "classics" that reveal some universally applicable insight in and through the particularities of their times, place, and circumstances.

How can the life of Saint Mary of the Cross help us grapple with our own crosses in our own time and place? First, I think she helps us see the connection between suffering and embodiment. Crucifixion was the most terrible punishment inflicted by the Roman Empire; in fact, *cruciare* is the Latin word for torture. When people are experiencing significant pain, it can seem to them as if they are being betrayed by their own bodies. Severe pain does not remain localized in its effects; rather, it precipitates a sort of civil war by breaking down the psychosomatic unity of the person who suffers it. As Elaine Scary has pointed out in *The Body in Pain: The Making and Unmaking of the World,* one of the objectives of torture is to bring about just such a breakdown. The power of a torturer is to turn my own self against myself. For example, if the pain from cigarette burns prompts me to yield a precious secret, it can seem as if my mind and heart have been betrayed by the weakness of my own skin.

When embodied human beings are tortured—when they are crucified—they are betrayed by their own selves and torn apart by warring elements of their own bodies and minds. I think the same can be said of the Body of Christ on earth, which is the Church. For Mary, sharing in the cross of Christ, sharing in his torture, ultimately meant suffering betrayal at the hands of other members of Christ's body. While her sensibility toward suffering may be characteristic of nineteenth-century spirituality, her experience of the Church is also firmly acknowledged in some of the more sober reflections of Second Vatican Council. In *Lumen Gentium* (Dogmatic Constitution on the Church), the council recognized that "until there shall be new heavens and a new earth in which justice dwells . . . the pilgrim Church in her sacraments and institutions . . . dwells among creatures who groan and travail in pain."

The question that many Catholics are asking now is how to endure the pain inflicted upon our hearts and souls by other members of the Body of Christ. We need to recall that we are members of the Body of Christ, crucified. Yet the crucified Christ has also risen from the dead. The work of redemption has definitively begun. Catholics who are trying to participate wholeheartedly in that work while struggling to carry the cross of the body of Christ have a friend and advocate in Mary MacKillop.

My account of the history is taken from the authorized biography, Paul Gardiner, S.J., *Mary MacKillop: An Extraordinary Australian* (Alexandria, Australia: E. J. Dwyer, 1994).

# "I PRAY I MAY
# BE READY WITH
# MY WITNESS"

## JOHN BERRYMAN

*Paul Mariani*

O N THE MORNING of January 7, 1972, at the close of the third year of the presidency of Richard Milhous Nixon, with the Jabberwocky's war to end all wars still marching into those mind-numbing fetid marshes, Professor John Berryman, once showered with Pulitzers and other signs of recognition for his brilliant, game-changing poems, now bearded and stoop-shouldered, trudged across the campus of the University of Minnesota in gelid Minneapolis before halting on the cement pedestrian walkway which crosses the upper Mississippi.

From this vertiginous vantage, the mighty Mississippi looks dwarfish, and there's a malebolge-like coal strip sidling up to its banks hundreds of feet below. It was here that Professor Berryman, as his hero Hart Crane had balanced on the stern rail of the S.S. *Orizaba* forty years earlier, likewise balanced on the high metal rail as students rushed to their classes that morning. Like Crane before him, he appeared to wave to those around him before he pushed forward to plunge through the unforgiving air.

He was fifty-seven, had been in AA and dry for the past eleven months, and then had courted a bottle of whiskey before downing a many few.

Two days earlier he had scribbled out one last poem, fittingly a Dream Song with a missing final line, in which he explained in his best witty and manic mode how he meant to escape what he saw now was in the cards—that the lectures he had prided himself on would fall short of his own expectations, which meant students

*dropping the course,*
*the Administration hearing*
*& offering me either a medical leave of absence*
*or resignation—Kitticat, they can't fire me.*

He had a better plan on how to keep the cops and his wife and everyone else off his back. All it took to make a man would be a simple tilt forward, sans knife blade to the throat, and then he was gone.

So how is it that this apostate, this renegade, this brilliant American poet who had lived through the Oklahoma prairie's summers and winters and the Florida Bust and his failed banker father's suicide and the Depression and New York City and Columbia and Cambridge University and his mother's betrayals, followed by World War II and the long Cold War and the McCarthy hearings and the Cuban Missile Crisis and Khrushchev ("We will bury you!") and the race riots and the long, desperate protests against the war in Vietnam and Laos and Cambodia . . . how is it that this philanderer who made charts of his conquests, a man who married three times and sorely tried all three wives, this binger, this brilliant, blasphemous naysayer, should somehow make it into the hallowed pages of this present company?

The trouble seems to have begun—and ended—with the death of the father when Berryman was just eleven. He and his younger brother, Robert, were living (if that is the word) with their parents then—John Allyn and Martha Smith—in an apartment down on Clearwater Island in Tampa Bay. Before long, Berryman's mother began carrying on an affair with the janitor, while his suicidal father found accommodations elsewhere. There were arguments, scenes, recriminations, accusations, and shouts out in the hall beyond the boys' closed bedroom door. Then, early on the morning of Friday, June 26, 1926, he heard his mother's footsteps in the hall before she came into the room to tell them that their father was dead. He had apparently killed himself with a bullet to the chest and lay spread-eagled now in the alley behind the apartment. Afterward, Martha and the janitor, twenty years her senior, whose name was John Berryman, married and moved to an apartment in Queens, New York, where John and Robert were informed that their last name was no longer Smith but Berryman.

In time Martha would tell the old geezer that it was time to move out while she remade herself, telling her son to inform his friends that she was not his mother, actually, but his older (and single) sister.

In time too Berryman, going over the evidence that he could gather about the death of his father, wondered if indeed his mother and stepfather hadn't killed his father and left the gun near his body. No wonder Berryman would later obsess over *Hamlet*'s play within the play, when Hamlet's father's death is rehearsed on stage before the usurper king and Hamlet's mother. Once, in fact, Berryman went so far as to invite his mother to hear him lecture on *Hamlet* while he was teaching at Princeton, hoping to finally out his mother with the scene verbally reenacted for her further edification. But she coolly avoided that well-laid trap as well, leaving Berryman to pick up the shattered pieces of himself.

The obsession about the father followed him all his life, before, during, and after he composed his brilliant four-hundred-plus Dream Songs. No wonder the last but one of Berryman's published *Dream Songs* should begin this way:

> *The marker slants, flowerless, day's almost done,*
> *I stand above my father's grave with rage . . .*
> *I spit upon this dreadful banker's grave*
> *Who shot his heart out in a Florida dawn*
> *O ho alas alas*
>
> *When will indifference come, I moan & rave. . . .*

Which brought to a tentative end what the first Song had begun:

> *Huffy Henry hid      the day*
> *unappeasable Henry sulked.*

There's the gap, then, on the very first page of Berryman's nightmare creation: the day he'd tried for so many years to simply hide, when everything changed forever and a departure came, so that, from then on, nothing ever "fell out as it might or ought."

As a boy back in Oklahoma, he had served each morning at the early Mass with Father Boniface, the two of them up there by the small pre–Vatican II altar, intoning the Latin together—*Introibo ad altare Dei*—while half a dozen blue-hairs knelt in the pews behind them. And he had been happy. Happy.

Well, that phase was over now. With the death of his father, his other Father had gone too, confined it seemed forever to the shadows, or at least to the irrelevancies of classic literature, by which he would make his living. God had abandoned him, and he in turn was leaving God behind, to make good in any way he could.

Sex, adulteries, booze, high talk among his intellectual peers about the state of the world and the present perilous state of God. He would read. Read everything: the classics and the Bible as literature and his worthy contemporaries, and—after a year in England, affect a quasi-British accent spiced with American jazz talk for the rest of his days. If he had to pay homage, let him pay it to the greats who deserved it, or at least half-deserved it, considering he would do his damnedest to outshine them all: Gerard Manley Hopkins, A. E. Housman, W. B. Yeats, T. S. Eliot, Ezra Pound, W. H. Auden, and later his friend Saul Bellow and Ralph Ellison and Dylan Thomas and Robert Lowell and Adrienne Rich, making elaborate lists of the living poets just to see how he and they were faring with the passage of time.

The trouble was that he was not indifferent to the torments of others. "Hard on the land wears the strong sea"—the first Dream Song ends, recalling the beach where his father would swim out and feign his disappearance, thus shaking his son's heart to its core—"and empty grows every bed." It's a line from Bessie Smith's "Empty Bed Blues," and it reminds us of what only a black woman also named Smith could sing: that sooner or later every bed indeed grows empty.

"I am obliged to perform in complete darkness," he wrote in one Dream Song, "operations of great delicacy." The real trouble was that he had to perform these operations on himself. And then write them down for others to see what he had discovered in his heart and brain to the place where—thanks to Freudian analysis and his memories of confession—his poetry had led him.

It's a funny quip, as funny as e. e. cummings's on the demise of Buffalo Bill—"and what I want to know is / how do you like your blueeyed boy / Mister Death." Funny, that is, until you see it tattooed on the chest of a young soldier returned from Afghanistan, dead by his own hand.

For Berryman another name for Mr. Death was God. As in lines he wrote approaching his fifty-second birthday. "Why did we come at all," he asks in this Dream Song, and why are we even here,

> *consonant to whose bidding? Perhaps God is a slob,*
> *playful, vast, rough-hewn.*

*Perhaps God resembles one of the last etchings of Goya . . .*
*Something disturbed,*
*ill-pleased, & with a touch of paranoia*

*who calls for this thud of love from his creatures-O.*
*Perhaps God ought to be curbed.*

But here's the rub. Even when he goes after God most violently, he knows he still owes a tremendous debt to those for whom the same God was not less than everything. If Berryman's poems, early and late, are difficult, he sees, they are difficult in the same way that biblical passages and even their glosses are difficult. In the same way, he noted, that Saint Jerome, having "had difficulties with his biblical commentary," went on to quote from a commentary on the fathers of the church to the effect that, if a passage was obscure (*vide* Saint John and Berryman) it was "due to the enormity of the task, the teacher's lack of skills, & the indifference of his listeners." So on he wrote, rabbi and exegeticist, in the shadow of the Bible.

And then, as he says, there came a change, a change that was nothing less than a metanoia.

It happened when he was hospitalized for extreme intoxication as a danger to himself and others. This time he found himself in St. Mary's, a Catholic hospital in the city in the late spring of 1970, where he was informed by Jim Zosel, an Episcopal priest in charge of the group's welfare that, no, he could not take a taxi over to his classes and teach, because every time he did, he would cajole or command the driver to stop at one of the local bars afterward so he could refresh himself with half a dozen drinks before returning for rehab at the hospital. But because Berryman was teaching the Bible as literature that term, the priest volunteered to take over his classes while he worked to recover.

That was when something deep within him gave way. That someone could actually care enough about this unworthy soul to do such a thing.

And so his recovery began. He joined AA, acted as a sponsor to others, stayed off the booze "each damned day," and began attending weekly Mass, though he remained an acute critical observer of the stylistic shortcomings and content of the priest's homilies in these too-easy, post-Vatican days. Berryman had been assembling new poems in a post–*Dream Song* mode, many of them unrhymed quatrains that owed as much to that eternal questioner, Emily Dickinson, as they did to that witty, irreverent French *poete maudit,* Tristan Corbière, who had died of consumption at twenty-nine, like Dickinson unknown to the larger literary world beyond.

Well, Mr. Berryman was certainly known. In fact, he was in demand everywhere, he knew, showered with awards and prizes and rave notices in magazines like *Time* and *Life*. Likewise, from his college days on, he had had his share of love, Eros, if that was what one called it. *Love & Fame* he meant to call the new volume, and he was pleased—as pleased as hell—with what he had already wrought.

And then came the turn that puzzled, amused, and disturbed the literary critics as well as his fellow poets. It began abruptly with Berryman's "Eleven Addresses to the Lord," which turned the book Saint Augustine–like completely on its head. If God was that "slob" he'd complained of four years earlier, the locked ward he now found himself in told him in no uncertain terms who the real slob was.

"Master of beauty," the sequence begins, like Father Hopkins celebrating the all-mastering God as the true Artist:

*Craftsman of the snowflake,*
*inimitable contriver,*
*endower of Earth so gorgeous & different from the boring*
    *Moon,*
*thank you for such as it is my gift.*

Prayers of praise, then, prayers of thanksgiving. Like the Lord's Prayer. Like the psalms. But with their own wry sense of humor. Gallows humor, trench humor, perhaps, but funny and vulnerable, those photos of the unforgiving desert landscape of the moon's surface showing him the condition of his own soul. Nothing for it then but to beg for rescue from the prison of himself, rescue by a God who really seemed to care. "You have come to my rescue again & again," he sang now, "in my impassible, sometimes despairing years."

Oh, he still had questions, as that wily elder Robert Frost who had chided him up at Bread Loaf always had. Given the human condition, he understood now that he would still have questions half an hour after he was dead. Who, for example, could really claim to know the Mystery of God? And—by logical extension—how could one actually come to love the Unknowable?

Did we live again after death? It didn't "seem likely / from either the scientific or the philosophical point of view." But who was he to say? One thing was clear: he was surer now than ever that "all things are possible to you." He also understood that he was ready now to move on with "gratitude &

awe," hoping "to stand until death forever at attention / for any your least instruction or enlightenment." Somehow he knew that the Ineffable would assist him again and again.

A honeymoon phase between him and God, no doubt: the cry of a brilliant, intense, broken man who had come to admit that he——he——was in need of some deep consolation. He thought of those who had gone before, like Saint Germanicus, the Roman officer still in his prime when he had been condemned to face the lions in the arena for his faith and had thrown himself instead on a raging lion, "wishing to pass quickly from a lawless life."

Or Saint Polycarp, John the Evangelist's disciple, who had been given the stark choice by the Roman authorities of denying Christ or being burned alive, only to answer thus:

> *Eighty & six years have I been his servant,*
> *and he has done me no harm.*
> *How can I blaspheme my King who saved me?*

Berryman ended his remarkable sequence with yet another prayer, a plea this time, that this same God would somehow make him acceptable too at the end:

> *Which then Thou wilt award.*
> *Cancer, senility, mania,*
> *I pray I may be ready with my witness.*

And life——such as it was——went on. In the winter of 1971 he was still at it with yet another set of poems, this time his own version of the Divine Office. It is the "Opus Dei" sequence that opens his final, posthumous volume of poems, *Delusions*. He quoted from five different sources by way of entry into the book—among them Matthew 11:17, Chaucer, and Tolstoy's "The Devil," in which Berryman reminded his readers that if Tolstoy's protagonist (for which read himself) "was mentally deranged, everyone is in the same case," the most mentally deranged being those "who see in others indications of insanity they do not notice in themselves."

"With the human exhausted," Professor Helen Vendler of Harvard once mocked, "Berryman solicited the divine." But the poems he wrote in this new vein, especially in his "Opus Dei" sequence, she insisted, were just no good. If Mr. Berryman had discovered a "newly simple heart" and new visions into the workings of his God,

> *whatever temporary calm they gave his soul, gave no new life to his poetry, and the last two poems, particularly, ["Vespers" and "Compline"] are intolerable to read. . . . When he became the redeemed child of God, his shamefaced vocabulary drooped useless, and no poet can be expected to invent, all at once and at the end of his life, a convincing new stance, a new style in architecture along with his change of heart. Berryman's suicide threw all finally into question—Henry's sly resourcefulness as much as Berryman's abject faith. In the end, it seems, neither was enough to get through the day on, and even though a voice divine the storm allayed and a light propitious shone, this castaway could not avoid another rising of the gulf to overwhelm him.*

But Vendler, when it comes to the religious sensibility, seems to turn a stone ear on her subject. The truth is that Berryman wrote out of what he knew, a radically broken man using all the resources he still had at his command. One thing was sure: he was not going to wax ironic and detached in the best modern or postmodern mode. Or at least, knowing himself too well, he was going to try his damnedest not to. He had tried this approach in that purgatorial cell with the other inmates who had hit rock bottom and—having heard it all before—they had detected at once the buzzing lies and false reconstructions and obfuscations and all the other—call it what it was—verbal merde.

*You, hypocrite lecteur, mon semblable, mon frère.* Thus T. S. Eliot, speaking through the voice of Baudelaire in perhaps the central poem of the twentieth century, "The Waste Land," which stands like a steel crossbar behind Berryman's late religious poems, poetic fragments shored up against his own ruins.

Where was he when he wrote these fragments, then? Where was the world? And where in all that hell was God? "Adorns my crossbar Your high frenzied Son," he wrote, much as Saint Paul had written to his people in Sin City Corinth nineteen hundred years earlier, having sworn—after his failure to convince the Stoics and Cynics at Athens, the Sorbonne and Cambridge of their day—to preach the heart of that strange, shattering mystery: Christ crucified, the divine Word that had remained "mute over catcalls."

"Gunfire & riot" were fanning "thro' new Detroit" even as he sweated over his final sequence. Protesters were being tried, imprisoned, and fined, while others—college students—were being gunned down for refusing to participate any longer in the madness of Vietnam. The homeless were still homeless and the hungry went on being hungry. And, yes, his own body was failing and, yes, he had made mistakes and, yes, he was a human wreck, but he would bear witness in a terrible time as best he could. He hoped and prayed that that heretic Origen was right after all and that hell was "empty / Or will be at apocatastasis," that is, at the end of time. Human failure—sin—seemed inevitable, given who and what we were. And, yes, no doubt we would suffer for it "now & later / but not forever, dear friends & brothers!"

I like to think of John Berryman as the patron saint of purgatory, shoulders hunched, still climbing on all fours the steep inclines of those mountains toward that distant summit shimmering in light, relieved to know he can sin no more. He's walking beside Hart Crane, and they are both listening to Hart Crane's distant "sapphire flutings," which Berryman recalls in the closing lines of his evening prayer just before he lays his weary head down.

He is in Minneapolis as he writes these lines, and it is midwinter and he and his family and all the citizens of this earthly city are journeying on. And in this winter landscape he recalls a moment when the sky shone red. Just now, he knows, there are "no fair bells in this city," and, in truth, his house is as cold and fireless as himself.

Still, he will try and manage to ask his Father that, even if he should fall from some terrifying height as Hart Crane did, that in his infinite mercy he will send his angels to save him even then. In the meantime, here in this wintry nick, he will have to content himself like John of the Cross and Hopkins and God's own Son himself and lie down at the Father's disposal as he waits out his own dark night.

# A PASTORAL, PERSON-ORIENTED THEOLOGY WORTHY OF VATICAN II

### EDWARD SCHILLEBEECKX

*Robert McClory*

S OME FORTY YEARS AGO I met Edward Schillebeeckx when he was visiting the Chicago Theological Union, and I later read a book-length interview with him by a Dutch journalist. I was both impressed and puzzled because so much of what Schillebeeckx said challenged what I believed as a Catholic at the time. I could not easily integrate his views with the neoscholastic philosophy and theology I had been immersed in as a student. But a lot has happened since then. I have been removing some of my old convictions, as one might throw unneeded baggage off a train, and I have updated or repacked some others. So when I visited the Netherlands in 2007 to research a story for the *National Catholic Reporter,* I was ready for Schillebeeckx. And when I returned to the United States, I began seriously to read his books and articles. This proved to be a somewhat challenging commitment because, as Robert Schreiter observed in his English translation of *The Schillebeeckx Reader,* "He is given to long, meandering sentences which are regularly interspersed with parenthetical remarks, allusive references to other authors or periods of history, and a liberal use of qualifiers and emphases. . . . And then when it seems a conclusion is about to be reached, another element or issue is brought in, which prompts a lengthy excursus." Nevertheless, I found that persistence uncovers the gold at the foundation of his heart and mind. And I believe that if Catholic theologians and bishops of the world had listened to this wise and holy man, the Church would be undergoing far less tension and turmoil than it is experiencing in the early twenty-first century.

Edward Schillebeeckx was born in Belgium and entered the Dominican order in 1934. His studies brought him to the Dominican study center, the Saulchoir, near Paris, where he was influenced by Marie-Dominic Chenu and Yves Congar, advocates of the New Theology. He also studied the works of Protestant theologians like Karl Barth, becoming convinced of the need for a more pastoral, personal approach to theology, one that would give consideration to the experiences of real people rather than basing conclusions solely on abstract, intellectual concepts. In 1958 he was appointed to the theology faculty at Radboud University at Nijmegen, the Netherlands;

that would remain the base of his research, study, teaching, and activism for the rest of his life.

His first book, *Christ the Sacrament of the Encounter with God,* published in English in 1963, became a near-best-seller. In it he attempted to alter the concept of sacraments as principally conveyors of a supernatural product known as sanctifying grace. Rather, he argued, they should be seen as interactions between the believer and the living Jesus Christ. This emphasis on the personal and experiential would animate much of his analysis of theology and Christian history in the more than four hundred books and articles, published in fourteen languages, that he produced.

## VATICAN II AND THE DUTCH FOLLOW-UP

When plans were proposed for the Second Vatican Council in the late 1950s, Schillebeeckx began a fruitful collaboration with Cardinal Bernard Alfrink, archbishop of Utrecht and leader of the Dutch hierarchy. At the cardinal's invitation, he co-wrote a statement, eventually endorsed by all seven of the Dutch bishops, that anticipated most of the progressive ideas that were approved at the council. The topics included liturgy, ecumenism, relations with non-Christian religions, lay initiatives, and a call for a more collegial, cooperative relationship between bishops and pope. The Dogmatic Constitution on the Church, considered one of the two most influential documents of the council and often identified by its Latin title *Lumen Gentium,* reflected many Schillebeeckxian convictions, especially the role of the bishops as successors of the apostles and leaders in their own right rather than as mere branch managers of an institution headed by one supreme executive. However, the effect here, as in other council documents, was somewhat diluted by conservative council members who insisted on inserting mentions of papal supremacy into the texts, whether relevant or not. Although not appointed a *peritus* (expert) for the council, Schillebeeckx in fact functioned as such due to Alfrink's reliance on him for ideas and critique. During the latter stages of the council, Schillebeeckx joined with Karl Rahner, Hans Küng, and Yves Congar in founding the theological journal *Concilium*. His open spirit and personalist approach also marked the *New Dutch Catechism,* which became a worldwide best-seller even before the Vatican Council completed its work.

In the years immediately after Vatican II, the Netherlands became the most powerful force in the world for implementing council decrees and fostering the council spirit. Schillebeeckx, often front and center, remained an active facilitator in all these initiatives. One of the most ambitious, one that nearly became a reality, was the Dutch Pastoral Council. It was conceived to be a permanent body, with fifty-six members, some clergy and some laity, all elected by diocesan pastoral councils throughout the country; it would also have another twenty-eight members to be chosen by the council itself. Enthusiasm for the creation of such a participative body and for other changes in Church governance was extremely high in the 1960s and early 1970s, as chronicled by author John Coleman in his book, *The Evolution of Dutch Catholicism, 1958–1974.* Polls taken after Vatican II indicated upward of 75 percent of Dutch Catholics in favor of the council and supportive of optional celibacy for priests and expanded lay participation in the selection of bishops. In many dioceses provisions were established requiring bishops to act collegially with their priests and giving laity a voice in Church decisions.

## THE VATICAN PUSH-BACK

But the higher the spirits, the louder grew the opposition from a range of entrenched, traditional Catholic organizations. Among the most strident, the *Confortatie* group took careful note of all that was happening and besieged Rome to take action against the Dutch progressives lest the wave of reform break through Holland's frail dikes and engulf the whole country in a sea of liberalism. And Rome did respond, expressing disagreement with the new initiatives, especially the proposed pastoral council. After several years of discussion, the Vatican's Congregation for the Clergy ruled in 1972 that all members of a national pastoral council must be appointed by the bishops and not elected, that it should not present itself in any way as speaking for the body of believers, and that it should not attempt to have a permanent character or presence in the country. By way of consolation, the congregation added, "All believers have the right and duty to take an active part in the mission given to the church . . . but they do not have either the right or duty to give advice to the hierarchy in their exercise of their pastoral task."

The reversal of Dutch Church reform was underway. The bishops who had fostered Vatican II, including Alfrink, retired, although he and others continued to support reform ideas and structures. They were replaced by men eager above all to please the Vatican. The pastoral council was dissolved without ever having a meeting. The *New Dutch Catechism* continued to have influence until Rome persuaded bishops to deny permission for new translations, suggesting that much of its content was unacceptable. Liberal lay leaders throughout the country were dismissed. So sweeping was the putdown that Dutch Catholics were hit with a kind of depression from which, forty years later, they have not recovered. Mass attendance (the lowest of any country in Europe) is reportedly under 7 percent in most dioceses, some of which have not had a priest ordained in fifteen years.

### A PROLIFIC SCHOLAR AND WRITER

Meanwhile, Professor Schillebeeckx continued to teach, write, and research with energy and enthusiasm, as if anticipating the coming of a better day. Despite the crackdown, he refused to proceed more cautiously or try to align his conclusions with the Vatican-imposed interpretations of doctrine. His works were always stimulating and controversial but generally respected, even by many who disagreed with him, because of the exhaustive theological and historical research Schillebeeckx invariably provided to bolster his positions. On several occasions, however, he was summoned to Rome, for instance, in 1984 for the doubtful orthodoxy of his book, *Jesus: An Experiment in Christology;* in 1985 regarding his teaching on the resurrection of Jesus; and in 1986 for his analysis of ministry in the early Church. Particularly upsetting to Church authorities was his recommendation that Catholics should "do what needs to be done," and if that meant breaking Church regulations on occasion or contradicting official interpretations, so be it.

That he was never censured or silenced remains a mystery. According to some observers, it may be that Rome backed off due to the outspoken public support accorded Schillebeeckx by Catholic theologians and schools of theology every time he was called in. Others have speculated that Vatican prosecutors were so baffled by the Dutch language and Schillebeeckx's penchant for piling sentences on top of one another in grand profusion that they were unable to create a credible indictment. One wag suggested he was spared because his critics could not spell, much less pronounce, his name.

It is impossible to communicate in a short essay the essential ideas of the man because he has written on such a wide variety of subjects and in such great depth. But here are a few samples of his positions on crucial issues, from his book, *The Language of Faith: Essays on Jesus, Theology and the Church:*

> *On evil:* "If we cannot justify evil and the unfathomable mass of innocent suffering or explain it as the unavoidable other side of God's fundamental plan in his will for good, then the only meaningful reaction to this history of suffering is in fact to offer resistance, to act in a way meant to turn history to good effect. This is urgently necessary. . . . For one can refuse to allow evil the right to exist, on the basis that it has no justification for existence."

> *On Jesus's death as sacrifice:* "The Christian should not claim that God himself required the death of Jesus as compensation for what we make of our history. This

sadistic mysticism of suffering is certainly alien to the
most authentic tendencies of the great Christian tradition.
According to theologian Jurgen Moltmann, Jesus shows
solidarity with publicans and sinners, with the outcasts
and with those who are everywhere excluded. But God
himself then casts Jesus out as a sacrifice for our sins?
The difficulty in this conception is that it has God doing
to Jesus what was actually done to Jesus by the history of
human injustice."

*On liberation and reconciliation:* "The crucifixion of
Jesus shows that any attempt at liberating action that is
concerned with humanity is valid in and of itself and
not subsequently as a result of any success which may
follow. What counts is not success. . . . The important
thing is loving service. We are shown the true face of God
and man in the *vain* love of Jesus which knows that its
value does not lie in success but in its very being as radical love."

*On what the Eucharist does:* "The sacramental bread and
wine are therefore not only the sign which makes Christ's
presence real to us but also the sign bringing about the
real presence of the church to him. The Eucharistic
meal thus signifies both Christ's gift of himself and the
church's responding gift of herself."

*On women in the Church:* "The 1976 papal document
*Ordinatio Sacerdotalis* sets out to make a contribution to
women's liberation. However as long as women are left
completely outside all decision-making authority in the

church, there can be no question of real women's liberation. . . . All the arguments [against women's ordination]
converge on the insight that this is a purely historically
conditioned, cultural pattern. All the arguments in favor
of 'another attractive task' for women in the church on
the basis of 'her own feminine' characteristics and intu-
itions, may sound fine, but they do not provide any support for the exclusion of women from leadership in the
church."

## A CALL FOR "ALTERNATIVE POSSIBILITIES"

The issue I was investigating when I went to the Netherlands in 2007 was a recently released booklet titled *Church
and Ministry,* which was sent to every Catholic parish in the
country by the Dutch Dominican province. Because of the
acute priest shortage and other profound changes in Church
and world, it stated that the time has come for every parish
to select someone, man or woman, married or single, straight
or gay, to preside regularly at the Eucharist. Their selection
by the community amounts to "ordination from below," said
the booklet, and should appropriately be followed up by the
local bishop coming to the parish and ordaining the person
"from above." If the bishop should refuse, wrote the Dominicans, parishes may move forward without the bishop's participation, confident "that they are able to celebrate a real and
genuine Eucharist."

Understandably, this Dominican initiative aroused international attention and a spurt of public approval and condemnation. Schillebeeckx was not the author, but his fingerprints

were all over the booklet, and the Dominican priests who wrote it readily acknowledged when I met with them that the theology was straight out of his 1980 book, *Ministry: Leadership in the Community of Jesus Christ*. The book is a thoroughly documented combination of history, theology, and common sense that explains how our present practice of Eucharist came about through a series of evolutionary changes over a millennium and beyond.

In the early Church, Schillebeeckx explains, the three key ministries (bishop or leader, presbyter or helper, and deacon or server) were so closely linked with community that it was considered essential that these ministers always be selected by the local community, never imposed from outside. He cites Cyprian of Carthage's declaration in the third century: "A bishop should never be given to a people who do not want him." And even in the fifth century, the connection between leader and local community was still so essential that the Ecumenical Council of Carthage warned that should a bishop ordain someone who has not been nominated by a particular community, the ordination is not only illegal, it is invalid. Furthermore, Schillebeeckx contends in *Ministry* that it was virtually unheard of for the leader to be moved to a different community; and if for personal reasons a minister did cease to be the presider at the community Eucharist, he ipso facto returned to being a layman in the strict sense.

But times changed, the Church grew, and everything became more complicated. Schillebeeckx shows how this early bottom-up ordering of relations gave way to an imposed top-down practice or order (with hierarchs and clerics, all stamped permanently by the sacred seal of ordination) becoming the norm in all areas of Church practice. Now, he argues, times have changed again, and some practices from that earlier era, including a resuscitation of former bottom-up approaches, are necessary if the Church is to thrive again, let alone survive. Here, from *Ministry,* are three crucial paragraphs that sum up what he is attempting to say:

1. "Against the background of the existing Church order then, new and sometimes urgently required alternative possibilities must be seen through the medium of what is bound to be regarded as *illegal,* at least temporarily. This is not a new phenomenon in the Church—it has always been the case. I am bound to say that an alternative praxis of critical Christian communities is both dogmatically and apostolically possible. It is, in my opinion, a legitimate Christian possibility which is demanded by our present needs. Given the existing canonical order of the Church, this alternative praxis is not even *contra* (against) the present order but *praeter* (alongside) the order, that is, it is not in accordance with the letter of the church's order, but it is in accordance with what (in earlier situations) that church order really wanted to safeguard."

2. "It would be wrong in my opinion to place all the blame (for the outmoded sacred image of the priest) on Rome. Leadership or authority can only be exercised meaningfully and appear in changed forms if both the people and their office bearers (including the bishops) have reached a sufficient level of conscious-

ness. It is not possible to ask the highest authority in a world church to change the prevailing order in that church if the change does not meet with the approval of the majority of Christian communities."

3. "If in changed circumstances there is a threat that a community may be without priests, and if this situation becomes increasingly widespread, then criteria which are not intrinsically necessary to the nature of this ministry and are also a cause of the shortage of priests, must give way to the original New Testament right of the community to leaders."

The immediate media flurry aroused by the booklet was followed by silence. Then several months later, leaders of the initiative were ordered to Rome and chided for not submitting *Church and Ministry* for Vatican clearance before sending it out. They refused to apologize for the province's audacity but were not disciplined.

### "ALWAYS THE OPTIMIST"

While in Nijmegen, my wife and I met with Schillebeeckx at the small cottage where he lived in retirement, attended by a Dominican sister and preparing for publication a compilation of his sermons. He was fully aware of the direction in which the institutional Church is moving, as he stated so accurately in a 1990 interview:

*My concern is that the further we move away in history from Vatican II, the more some people begin to interpret unity as uniformity. They seem to want to go back to the monolithic church which must form a bulwark . . . against the Western liberal consumer society. I think that above all in the West, with its pluralist society, such an ideal of a monolith church is out of date and runs into a blind alley. And there is the danger that in that case, people with that ideal before their eyes will begin to force the church in the direction of a ghetto church, a church of the little flock, the holy remnant. But though the church is not of this world, it is of men and women. Men and women who are believing subjects of the church.*

Though in failing health, Schillebeeckx seemed at peace and personally untroubled by this ongoing ghettoization of the Church. "I am optimistic," he said, "always optimistic. I believe in God and in Jesus Christ."

He died two years later at the age of ninety-five. It is my hope and prayer that the immense work of this fearless, far-seeing prophet will be brought forth, celebrated and put to practical use on the day the Church regains its bearings and begins to seek out mentors and guides. May that day be closer than we think.

# WHAT ABOUT
# THE POOR?

## FATHER HORACE MCKENNA, S.J.

*Alice McDermott*

In 1968, CARDINAL PATRICK O'BOYLE of the Washington archdiocese responded to Father Horace McKenna's
very public stand against *Humanae Vitae* by banning the
Jesuit from the confessional. It was a particularly insidious
punishment. Father McKenna and forty other area priests
had signed a dissenting "Statement of Conscience" in response to the pope's encyclical, arguing that the decision to
use birth control should be left to the individual. O'Boyle,
who was personally generous and had been a vigorous op-
ponent of segregation, nevertheless took a hard line against
these priests. He sent a ten-page letter to each and then called
them in one by one to demand a retraction. When he asked
Father McKenna on what authority he opposed his bishop

and his Church, McKenna answered, "Forty years in the confessional."

Common Catholic usage refers to priests who "hear confessions," but Father McKenna, it seemed, actually listened to them.

"I found in my experience," he said,

> *that there were what I called "martyrs to matrimony." One lady told me that she had had four children in four years. A man said, "I am driven out of the house. My wife won't look at me after having five children." What can I tell these people? I can't tell them that they can't engage in intercourse without a haunting fear of being driven out of the house or being hopelessly burdened. So I felt that these people, in these situations, were free to do what they thought right and best.*
>
> *Cardinal O'Boyle kept cautioning me about pride and self-will and everything like that, but I said, "This is one of the main decisions of my life. I don't want to go against the Pope. I don't want to endanger my salvation. I don't want to lead anybody in the wrong direction, but this is what I think conscience has to say." I didn't know the historical character of the question as being the old question of freedom of conscience. I thought it was the old question of being told to do something you couldn't possibly do and that authority shouldn't command the impossible.*

When Horace McKenna died in 1982, his parishioners decorated the simple confessional he had used—the "peace box" as he came to call it—with daisies. According to his biographer, John S. Monagan, it was as a minister of the sacrament of penance that Horace McKenna "most completely fulfilled the pastoral role. . . . He had the ability to reduce difficulties to basic terms, to convey a sense of compassion and love, and to strengthen the penitent with memorable, sound and simple advice."[*]

In 1968, when that memorable, sound, and simple advice betrayed the paucity of compassion and love in Pope Paul VI's encyclical, Cardinal O'Boyle's solution was to ban Father McKenna from the confessional, the logic being, perhaps, that if you do not hear you cannot listen.

The ban lasted two and a half years. Father McKenna somewhat famously said of it, "That's what you get for trying to argue sex with an Irishman."

Nearly half a century later, it's easy enough to let the reasonableness, and the good humor, of Father McKenna's resistance to *Humanae Vitae* dilute our understanding of what was at stake for him at the time. Self-righteousness can blind the liberal as well the conservative, and those of us who feel certain about the practical, much less the moral, failure of Paul VI's decree might easily miss the depth of courage it took for this aging priest to make his stand against it. For Father McKenna, his very salvation was on the line. "It was no matter of theory for him," Monagan writes, "but of eternal judgment, and, as he said himself, he 'didn't know which side Our Lord was going to come down on.'"

The controversy over *Humanae Vitae* was not the first time Horace McKenna annoyed and irritated the hierarchy of the Catholic Church. In the 1930s and '40s, as pastor of St. Peter

---

[*]*Horace, Priest of the Poor.* John S. Monagan (Washington, D.C.: Rose Hill Books, 1985).

Claver parish in rural Ridge, Maryland, he challenged the accommodations the Church made to the racism of the era. Working incrementally at first—he insisted that black altar boys serve at a tercentenary Mass, promoted the vocation and education of black nuns, established a cooperative for black farmers—he later grew adamant. He threatened to close his all-black parish school rather than to continue to implement the Church's policy of segregation. "I'm no longer going to be a bandage on the Mystical Body of Christ," he told the chancellor of the archdiocese. "I'm going to let the wound cure by itself."

While his white parishioners at Ridge recognized the saintliness of Father McKenna's efforts for the poor and the disenfranchised—efforts that began to gain him a reputation in the larger world: a profile in *Commonweal* about his co-operative, a thinly disguised appearance as a character in a popular novel—they also hoped, as Monagan reports, that he would come to his senses and stop "going with those dirty colored people."

In April 1951, when Father McKenna allowed black school children and white school children to celebrate Mass together, the white population of Ridge had enough. At a meeting at the firehouse a few days later, "the lid," as Father McKenna later put it, "blew off the interracial situation." Violence was avoided only through McKenna's continual use of the "soft answer," although one witness said that the treatment Father McKenna received at the hands of his white parishioners was nothing less than "a crucifixion."

Shortly thereafter, Father McKenna was transferred to St. Aloysius Church in Washington, D.C., just eight blocks from the Capitol. He was made assistant pastor, no longer director of his own parish, and placed in a community of twenty-five fellow Jesuits, many of whom were involved in running Gonzaga High School, next door. The neighborhood at the time was struggling to maintain its gentility. The parish was about two-thirds Irish and German American, one-third black, but the parish school remained all white, despite Cardinal O'Boyle's desegregation order of a few years before. Immediately McKenna campaigned to integrate the school. Citing failing (white) enrollment and rising costs, parish authorities chose to close it instead.

As he had done in Ridge, Father McKenna at St. Al's took his ministry to the people, going out into the streets, inviting the poor and the derelict to come to the rectory for financial aid and spiritual counseling. In 1956, he wrote to his Jesuit superiors, "The poor are the critique of this generation . . . and I think that the parishes are where the waves of the poor break at our feet and come to us like a daily mission from the Creator, with a built-in mandate." Acting on this mandate, Father McKenna soon drew long lines of supplicants to the rectory, often disrupting normal parish business. Eventually, the pastor at St. Al's began to restrict Father McKenna's generosity with parish time and space and money. After five years of locking horns with his superior, McKenna was transferred to an inner-city parish in Philadelphia, one that was rapidly becoming all black and thus, perhaps, better suited to Father McKenna's indecorous activism. He was there in August 1963, when his request to attend the March on Washington where Martin Luther King Jr. gave his "I Have a Dream" speech was denied by the chancery of Cardinal John Krol. A sure sign that Father McKenna's status as troublemaker had been duly noted.

By the time Horace McKenna returned to St. Al's in 1964 for his "second hitch" in Washington, white flight had left the parish both predominately black and predominately poor. Urban renewal land development had decimated the residential neighborhoods around the church. With his characteristic single-mindedness, McKenna joined forces with the Community for Creative Nonviolence, the Luther Place Memorial Church, and the Church of What's Happening Now to make homelessness a national issue. He founded Sursum Corda (in English, Lift Up Your Hearts), a development of townhouse-style single-family homes for the poor, and SOME (So Others Might Eat) a food assistance program (he did not like the term "soup kitchen"). He supported the development of the House of Ruth, a shelter for women, and Martha's Table, which brought food to hungry children. He walked the streets of his parish, got to know the needs and the concerns of his people.

Once, after watching a group of teenage mothers with their babies, he approached to ask whether they needed advice about parenting. (One of the girls recalled her reaction: "How's this little old man going to teach us about parenting?") He invited them to come to the church the following day, where he showed a filmstrip about baby care and had a nurse on hand to answer their questions. When he visited neighborhood families, he left money "on the shelf, on the kitchen sink, everywhere." McKenna's "line"—the queue of homeless men who waited for him outside the church—became a familiar sight on North Capitol Street. He drove, badly, a beat-up Renault, and among the many stories of his generosity is the tale of the man who once listed his address as "the backseat of Father McKenna's car."

Father McKenna spoke out against the Vietnam War and regretted that his fellow Jesuits "were more cautious than he might have hoped" in this regard. He admired the Quakers who held vigil outside the White House throughout the war. His pacifism was simple and direct and grew out of his conviction that every human being was a revelation of God's love. "We should strive not to kill or hurt anyone," he said. The same kind of memorable, sound, and simple advice he offered the Catholic penitent in the confessional—except for those two and a half years when he was forbidden to do so.

Although I moved to the Washington area in 1989, seven years after his death, I quickly became aware of Father McKenna's work. If you were any kind of practicing Catholic in the area, it couldn't be helped. Neighborhoods in various parishes regularly took turns funding meals at SOME. The McKenna Center, the men's homeless shelter established in his honor in the basement of St. Al's, was well known as a recipient of poor box collections and in memoriam contributions, as well as the many volunteer hours of the high school boys next door. Catholic school kids made sandwiches for McKenna's Wagon, a food truck that served the district's poor. Sursum Corda, which had become by the late '80s a labyrinth of decay and drug violence, was often cited by my more conservative friends as terrible evidence of good intentions gone wrong.

But for those of us of a more liberal Catholic persuasion, Horace McKenna's biography hit all the right notes: civil rights, responsibility for the poor, unapologetic pacifism. Father McKenna welcomed the changes of Vatican II, approved the ordination of women (Monagan writes, "Mary was the first priest," he told a fellow Jesuit, "Who else but she could lift Jesus?") and sought a general opening up of the Church. In the 1970s he supported the goals of liberation theology. ("Now in a swarming world," he wrote, "united and disunited, her (the Church's) witness to Word and Sacrament is through her works of Mercy.") Shortly before his death at eighty-four, he attended a workshop regarding ministry to the gay community.

When my sons attended Gonzaga High School, I began to meet people who had known and worked with Father McKenna at St. Al's. They described him as charming, a small man with thick white hair, a stammering New York accent and a ready wit, stubborn, yes, challenging, no doubt. Whatever was in his pocket was yours. Whoever came to his door was taken care of. He was narcoleptic and would fall asleep at community meetings only to wake suddenly to shout out, "But what about the poor?" Saintly, yes, no question, but not likely ever to be canonized, it was agreed, due to his stand against the Church on *Humanae Vitae*.

Time, and the real-world ineffectiveness of the ban among so many Catholics, has no doubt muted the drama of Father McKenna's confrontation with his bishop in 1968. It must be remembered, then, that Horace McKenna was born in 1899, the sixth of seven children in a large, upper-middle-class Catholic family on New York's West Side. He attended Fordham Prep and entered the Jesuit Novitiate in Pough-keepsie at seventeen. He taught in the Philippines and at Jesuit prep schools in Boston and Philadelphia. He was ordained a Jesuit in 1929. In St. Peter's Church in Maryland, and again at St. Al's, he slept in a bedroom that gave him easy access to the altar, so that he could visit the Blessed Sacrament at will, at any hour of the day or night. He loved "the Sacrament of Peace" that was confession. He was devoted to the Blessed Mother. While many of the forty-one priests who signed the Statement of Conscience eventually left the priesthood, there is no evidence that Father McKenna ever entertained such a notion. He was thoroughly faithful, a thoroughly old-fashioned Catholic, if you will. And if, in the way of saints, he was often annoying to the powers that be, he was also thoroughly obedient. Except in the matter of *Humanae Vitae*.

Father McKenna believed in the Resurrection and the Life. His description of the end of time should be read as a prayer:

> *Then, in my dream of the Last Day,*
> *Our Lord will come back and reward us for having,*
>    *by his grace,*
> *straightened the world out,*
> *and having the poor competent,*
> *and the rich thoughtful,*
> *and the well-protected kindly and generous and involved,*
> *and the educated enthralled with the kingdom of God,*
> *and the spiritual able to perceive him in such a way as to*
>    *make him visible to us.*

Of his own death, Father McKenna said, "When God lets me into heaven, I think I'll ask to go off in a corner somewhere for half an hour and sit down and cry because the strain is off, the work is done, and I haven't been unfaithful or disloyal, all these needs that I have known are in the hands of Providence and I don't have to worry any longer who's at the door, whose breadbox is empty, whose baby is sick, whose house is shaken and discouraged, and whose children can't read."

In 1968, not knowing "which side our Lord would come down on," Father McKenna put the vision of that reward, the prospect of that final peace, at risk. He stood against his bishop and the pope, put in jeopardy his immortal soul, in order to take the side, in love and compassion, of the poor. The woman who could not endure another pregnancy, the man who felt driven from his house. The Catholic couples who, as he said, had promised each other something more than "affection by time clock."

Horace McKenna's activism, his orneriness, his wit, his selflessness, and his common sense may endear him to progressive Catholics of a more liberal persuasion, but it is to his orthodoxy, his thorough and unwavering faith in Christ's promise of eternal life that we should look, conservative and liberal alike, in order to understand the depth of his love. He put his very soul at risk in the defense of those who suffer.

Not long ago, I was at a beltway cocktail party when Father McKenna's name came up, as it often does in social circles here. When Father McKenna died in Georgetown Hospital, I was told by a man who had been there, the odor of sanctity filled the room.

Indication, perhaps, for those of us who believe, of whose side Our Lord has chosen after all.

# THE WORTHLESS
# SERVANT

CHARLES STROBEL

*Ann Patchett*

IN THE MIDDLE OF JUNE in Nashville, a few days before the summer became unendurably hot, I was in the
car with Charlie Strobel, driving out towards the river. To
grow up Catholic in Nashville is to know at least some of
the members of the Strobel family, and long before Charlie
and I became friends, I knew the stories of what he had accomplished, and what he had lost. We were on our way to the
Stadium Inn to visit some homeless men who were about to
get their own apartment, and while he drove, Charlie told me
a story about Father Dan Richardson. Father Dan was the
priest at Assumption, the North Nashville parish in the poor
neighborhood where Charlie grew up. It was not too far from
where we were headed now.

"Father Dan was a father figure to me," Charlie said, his

own father having died when he was four. "We lived down the street from the church, and by the time I was in the third or fourth grade, I was an acolyte."

Assumption was a parish with an older congregation, and Charlie remembered the funerals coming one after the other. For every funeral, Father Dan gave the exact same homily. "We knew it word for word. We could mouth it along behind him," Charlie said, and though he is sixty-nine now, a good distance from his altar boy self, he begins the recitation:

"Father Dan would say, 'We're on this earth to get ready to die. And when we die, God's not going to say, "Charlie [Ann, Sally, John, fill-in-the-blank], what did you do for a living? How much money did you make? How many houses did you have?" ' God is only going to ask us two questions: 'Did you love me?' and, 'Did you love your neighbor?' And we can imagine that Charlie [Ann, Sally, John, fill-in-the-blank] will answer truthfully, saying, 'Yes, Lord, You know I loved you. You know I loved my neighbor.' And then God will say, 'Well done, good and faithful servant. Now enter into the kingdom of heaven.' "

Charlie smiled at the thought of it. "He nailed it *every single time*. He had this soft voice, and his cadence was perfect. Even though I knew exactly what was coming, it never failed to grab me. It was sad, especially if I knew the person who had died, but I never heard it as anything but a positive and hopeful message. We come from God, we return to God, so death was never frightening."

Charlie realized then that he had missed his exit. Neither one of us had been paying attention to the interstate, and neither of us was sorry. It gave him time to finish the story.

"Even after I grew up and became a priest, I could never call him Dan. It was always Father Dan. I'd always say to him, 'What are you going to get me for Christmas this year?' And he'd say, 'A bridge,' because the homeless lived under bridges." Father Dan, who was Irish, was always one for a joke.

"When I went to see him for the last time before he died, we had a personal talk, a father-son talk, and I told him how much I loved him. Then I said, 'Now I'm going to be your priest,' and I did his whole routine—'We are on this earth to get ready to die, and when we die, God's not going to ask, "Dan, how much money did you make?" He's going to ask two questions: "Did you love me?" and, "Did you love your neighbor?" And I know you'll say, "Yes, Lord, you know I loved you. You know I loved my neighbor." And God will say, "Enter, good and faithful servant." '

I was struck by how often the lessons we learn when we're young, the things we could never imagine needing, make it possible to meet what life will ask of us later. "I've grown to be who I am," Charlie said, "because of those life experiences each of us has."

In its finest hour, the Stadium Inn must have been a cheap motel where fans of the opposing teams could spend the night after a football game. But any football fan who booked a room there now would be able to realize the error of his ways without ever getting out of the car. When we pulled up to the front, Charlie stopped and looked at the men sitting on the steps, then he looked at me. "I'll leave the car running," he said, trying to calculate how long he might be inside. "You lock the doors and wait."

When I told him I was happy to go with him, he gave me an enormous smile. "Oh, that's wonderful," he said. He reached in the backseat and pulled out a two-burner hot plate. The Stadium Inn was what my policeman father would call a flophouse, a pay-by-the-week motel of the lowest possible order. Charlie greeted every man and woman who leaned by the door or sprawled in the lobby. He announced our plans to visit Ron and Sid to the woman at the front desk, who claimed to have no idea who they were. Then he told her he was Charlie Strobel and that he was expected. "Oh," she said, smiling and nodding. She gave us the room number and directed us to the elevator. Ron and Sid would soon be moving into their own apartment, an apartment that had no stove. They would need a hot plate. We took the one we had upstairs.

Every human catastrophe the carpet in the hallway had endured over the years had been solved with a splash of bleach, which rendered it a long, abstract painting. Beneath the low yellow light, the row of closed doors each thumped out a distinct musical beat, including the door we were standing in front of. I saw an eye study us at the peephole and then pull away. I stepped to the side, certain that I must look like a parole officer. "Sid," Charlie called out in the tone of a cheerful and persistent relative who had dropped in for a visit. "It's Charlie. Open up the door." He waited, and then he knocked again.

It was a long wait, but finally the door cracked open and a single dark eye peered out of a cloud of cigarette smoke, then the door opened wider. "Father!" the man said, and gave Charlie a hug. (Charlie can do without the title, as he thinks it creates a distance between people. Still, if the word *Father* makes anyone feel better, he accepts it.)

Sid and Ron are salt and pepper shakers, Sid with dark brown hair and a heavy brown beard, Ron with faded red hair and a greying beard going halfway down his chest. Both men wore loose jeans, tank tops, baseball caps. Neither could have weighed more than a hundred pounds, their upper arms no bigger than their wrists. Introductions were made and they shook my hand. For all their reticence about opening the door, they were clearly pleased we had come. There were two unmade beds in the room with a heaping ashtray between them, a console television playing the country music station. A shopping cart was parked against the wall, neatly packed, its contents tarped over and tied. "We're ready to go," Ron said, giving the cart a pat. "We've got somebody coming tomorrow to help us move."

"Are you staying sober?" Charlie asked, his voice making it clear that he will be proud of them if they are, and love them still if they are not.

"We are, Father," Sid said.

"Four days, Father," Ron said.

Charlie tried to lead them in a conversation about how much better it was to be clean, and though they clearly wished to please him, their hearts weren't in it. They planned to find jobs once they settled, maybe dishwashing. Ron took off his baseball cap and pushed back his hair to reveal a long scar running across his forehead. "I don't know though," he said. "I don't think so clear since I got hit."

Charlie gave them the hot plate and they marveled at the newness of the thing, still in the box. They talked about the move, and Charlie promised to get them bus passes. When we were finally ready to leave, both men hugged him again and promised good behavior for the future. They told us about a man five doors down the hall, someone who wasn't doing as well at staying out of trouble, and so we went and knocked on that door for a long time, but despite the music blaring from the other side, no amount of calling could draw anyone out.

"That's the best I've seen them look in a long time," Charlie said cheerfully as the shuddering elevator dropped to the first floor. "Their eyes looked good, didn't you think?"

I hadn't seen their eyes before, but I was struck by the sweetness of both men, and how more than anything they looked tired. Homelessness is an exhausting and dangerous state of being.

Charlie has a good story that he likes to bring out for fundraisers—that his career with the homeless can all be traced back to a single peanut butter and jelly sandwich he made for a man who knocked on the rectory door when he was a young priest at Holy Name. The next step came soon after that, as he explained in a lecture he gave at the local Unitarian church:

*They were in the church parking lot, sleeping under my window, and the temperature that evening was dropping below freezing. I didn't think too long about it, probably because I knew I would talk myself out of it. As a pastor, I knew the consequences of such a decision were far greater than simply giving a dozen men one night's lodging. What do you do tomorrow night when they return? And the next night and*

*the next night and on and on? One simple decision could
be parlayed into a lifetime commitment. What would the
parishioners say? Or the bishop? Or the neighbors? For the
moment, I decided that it was the thing to do. Like Scarlett
O'Hara, I found myself saying, "I'll worry about that tomorrow." So I invited them to spend the night, and they've been
with me ever since.*

It was while he was trying to meet those immediate needs
that Doy Abbott arrived.

"He was my terrorist," Charlie said. "Every morning he
woke me up to demand breakfast. He was a regular back at
Holy Name. He kicked in the screen door. We had to have
that door replaced three times. He cussed out everyone in
the parish. He expected everything to be done for him. My
mother used to say to me, 'Doy is your ticket to heaven.' And
I'd tell her, if he's my ticket to heaven I don't want to go.
Everyone in the parish was afraid of him."

Everyone except Mary Hopwood. She was the house-
keeper and the secretary and the bookkeeper for the parish. She'd come to work at the age of fifty-five, after raising
twelve children of her own. With Doy her tone was always
quiet and respectful, and he was respectful in return. They
listened to one another.

"About that time I read something Dorothy Day had said.
She said what she wanted to do was love the poor, not ana-
lyze them, not rehabilitate them. When I read that it was like
a light clicking on. I thought about Mrs. Hopwood. I realized
that Doy was not my problem to solve but my brother to love.
I decided on the spot that I was going to love him and not

expect anything from him, and overnight he changed. He stopped the cussing, stopped the violence. I feel we became brothers. I was his servant and he was my master. I was there with him when he died."

Charles Strobel founded the Room In the Inn and its Campus for Human Development in 1986 as a center of learning, respite, shelter, and relief for the homeless. Like the homeless, he can pretty much be found there seven days a week. Originally, it was formed as an organization of local parishes of all denominations that welcomed the homeless in for a meal and to spend the night once the cold set in. The first building they had was traditionally dismal, with some classrooms for AA meetings and art projects, showers, clothing, and a place to pray. Charlie's primary gift may be his ability to serve to poor, but he possesses the equally necessary gifts of being able to work with a board, the local government, the police, religious organizations of every stripe, and the people who have the money to underwrite his vision. His radical idea was that the homeless need not be served in low, dark places, and that people with nothing should be able to stand beside people with everything and hold up their heads. The building that now comprises the campus is new and looks it, as stylishly modern in its glass and steel construction as the expensive condominiums that sprawl through Nashville a few short blocks away. The dignity with which Charlie had always treated the homeless was finally reflected in their surroundings. The mission statement of the campus reads, *Emphasizing the scriptural ideals of love and community through service to the homeless, our Campus provides faithful people of Nashville an opportunity to respond directly to the*

*broken and the disenfranchised among us. The fellowship with*
*the poor is at the heart of our purpose.*

Which basically means that *I* am the person the campus is
serving. This center is there to give me the chance to experience what has been the enormous joy of Charlie's life—the
opportunity to respond directly to the broken and disenfranchised among us.

"All you have to do," he tells me, "is give a little bit of understanding to the possibility that life might not have been
fair."

The trouble with good fortune is that people tend to
equate it with personal goodness, so that if things are going
well for us and less well for others, we think they must have
done something to have brought it on themselves. We speak
of ourselves as being blessed, but what can that mean except
that others are not blessed, and that God has picked out a
few of us to love more? It is our responsibility to care for one
another, to create fairness in the face of unfairness, and find
equality where none may have existed in the past. Despite
his own dealings with unfairness, this is what Charlie has
accomplished.

When Charlie's father died of a heart attack at the age of
forty-six, he left behind four children between the ages of
eight years and four months. Afterwards, Charlie's mother,
Mary Catherine Strobel, who had lost her own mother in a
house fire when she was an infant and her much-loved father
when she was sixteen, took a job working as a clerk for the
fire department for $185 a month. There were also two great-
aunts that she took care of, Mollie, who was eighty-one at
the time, and Kate, who was seventy-eight. The way Mary

Catherine interpreted her husband's death and their subsequent hardships was that none of it was God's fault. God, along with their father, would be right there watching over them.

And while God, in the newfound company of Martin Strobel, watched the children from heaven, Aunt Kate and Aunt Mollie watched them during the day while Mary Catherine worked. "They were the reason it was so easy for me to believe Jesus's words, 'I am among you as one who serves,'" he said of his aunts. "And that led me to the next step in logic, to believe that God loves us and provides for all our needs—just as any devoted servant would—because I had experienced it so lovingly from Aunt Mollie and Aunt Kate."

He told me a story from Luke 17, in which the servant who does everything that is asked of him and then, joyfully, does more, is called a "worthless servant" (or an "unprofitable servant," or "a servant who deserves no credit," depending on the translation). It is a state of loving service so deep, so all-encompassing, that the servant loses himself, so that the worthlessness becomes a kind of transcendence. "They were worthless servants," Charlie said, remembering his aunts, his mother. "They wanted nothing more than to serve us, which means that we were their masters. They did everything they could for us. They never disciplined us. I never remember their asking me to help them around the house." Charlie asked whether I was following him, because the concept of the achievement to be found in worthlessness can be a murky one. It is not the stuff of Sunday sermons. Certainly, I could think of many instances in which people who had been served were not then inspired to go and serve others, but if being profoundly loved enabled us to love profoundly then, yes, I understood.

"Wouldn't that be a wonderful thing to have on your tombstone?" he said to me. "Worthless Servant?"

I told him I wasn't there yet, but that I could see it as something to aspire to.

"I hesitate to say this," he said, and then he gave such a long pause that I wondered if he did in fact plan to proceed, "so many people have struggles with their faith, but God has never been a struggle for me. *I've* been a struggle for me, but I could never honestly believe in the nonexistence of God."

It was the only thing he hesitated to tell me for the entire day. He felt it might be cavalier to admit that something that was so difficult for so many had come to him, and stayed with him, without effort.

In the main lobby of the Room In the Inn there is a sculpture of a tree on the wall with more than 650 leaves. Every leaf bears the name of a homeless man or woman who has died in Nashville, and the presence of God did not waver any time a new leaf was added. It did not waver in December 1986, when Charlie's mother, Mary Catherine Strobel, then seventy-four, was kidnapped from the parking lot of Sears in Nashville and murdered by an escaped convict from Michigan, the first victim in a spree that ultimately took six lives.

But the way the story was remembered over the years was that she had been working at the Room In the Inn at the time, and that she was killed by a homeless man. People said that Mary Catherine had started the Room In the Inn, and that Charlie took up her work as a penance. By making her murder a consequence of her own associations, people could safely distance themselves from such a random act of violence. Charlie was often asked if he would continue his work after his mother's death. "If it was worth doing before," he said, "why wouldn't it be worth doing now?"

"Many have said that she did not deserve to die the way that she did," her son said at the funeral mass. "Yet for years, we have heard it said that 'God did not spare his only Son but delivered him up, and the Son emptied himself and humbled himself, obediently accepting even death, death on a cross.' In Mama's death, our family believes that the viciousness inflicted on such gentleness and kindness, as was her way, brings about a great *communion* with Jesus. So, how can we question its course? It seems to run true to the form of Jesus's own death. And why speak of anger and revenge? Those words are not compatible with the very thought of our mother."

"Of course her death changed all of us," he told me that afternoon after we had left Ron and Sid, while we were on our way to visit a formerly homeless woman in the hospital who was struggling to care for her grandchildren as her health declined sharply. "But maybe not the way people thought it did. Our mother's death helped me focus on what was important. After that I became more single-minded about what I should be doing with my life."

There is throughout the course of life a long line of fathers and sons, parents and children, servants and masters, forgiven and forgivers, and at different moments we are called on to take up one role and then the other. When we do it right, we are bearing the example of Christ in mind. When we finally made it back to the Room In the Inn, it was past

8:00 in the evening and still light out, the longest day of the year. The achievement of Charlie's life surrounded us, not the dazzling building or the flowers stretching out in front of the property, but the crowd of people spreading out in every direction. This was the place they had come to feel safe, to feel loved. These are the people he serves.

# A BEAUTIFUL AND DIFFICULT TRUTH

## OSCAR ROMERO

*Jim Shepard*

O**N A RETREAT IN MEXICO** in 1971, Oscar Romero, looking back over his nearly completed first full year as a bishop and twenty-nine years of service as a priest, made a list of his faults as he understood them: a tendency to avoid social relations and a more intimate knowledge of people; an excessive sensitivity to criticism; a disorder in his work; a lack of austerity; and a lack of courage when it came to speaking out in defense of his positions.

That last concern might have been the principal reason he was chosen in 1977 to be archbishop of the Diocese of San Salvador, El Salvador's largest city. At a time when the attempt to modify even slightly the traditional agrarian structures had instigated yet another bloody wave of repression, the government had pressured the Vatican to select a candidate

dedicated to keeping the peace, someone conservative and/
or "apolitical" who would not defend the small farmers and
the poor as his predecessor had. Romero seemed the safe bet:
thought to be cautious, scholastic, and inclined toward the
preservation of order. Six years earlier he'd replaced a fire-
brand as editor of a diocesan newspaper and had converted it
mostly to blandness: a Jesuit magazine had published a study
of his editorship and had noted that his version of the paper
criticized injustice in the abstract but projects for liberation
in the concrete, directing itself at a public "satisfied with the
present situation." In his homilies and pastoral letters, as well,
he voiced a concern for justice but suggested no solutions beyond wishing that his country's landowners weren't so selfish
and corrupt.

It was an even more forlorn wish in El Salvador than in
most countries. Since its liberation from Spain in 1821, the
country's wealth, mostly in the form of coffee plantations,
had been so successfully transferred by force from the many
to the few that by the early twentieth century an oligarchy of
fourteen families ruled the country, controlling the government and the military, and an uprising by the peasants or
*campesinos* in 1932 had been so brutally suppressed that more
than *thirty thousand* had been killed.

Three years after the world's Catholic bishops had gathered
for Vatican II, which John XXIII had convened in his attempt
to help the modern Church better understand the world to
which it offered salvation, the Latin American bishops as-
sembled in Medellín in Colombia and acknowledged that the
socioeconomic conditions of the majority of the 300 million
people over whom they presided were dramatically worsening.

The Church, they proclaimed, could no longer acquiesce in that situation, since injustice was not God's will. Any identification with the afflictions and aspirations of the people, especially the dispossessed, made the Church, then, inherently subversive in a social order founded on exploitation.

So for the first time repression in El Salvador targeted the Church. The week Romero was installed as archbishop, two priests, an American and a Belgian, were expelled for their work in the barrios, and the archdiocesan printing press, bookshop, and the Central American University, run by Jesuits, had all already been bombed.

Aware of the clergy's unhappiness with his appointment, he began to win hearts by immediately requesting everyone's support *and* advice. And for three weeks after his installation, Archbishop Romero reacted with sympathy but also with caution to the events unfolding around him, including a priest arrested and tortured, and somewhere between eight and sixty people killed when Salvadoran security forces fired on demonstrators protesting the fraudulent presidential elections. In reaction to the latter, Romero authored a letter with his fellow bishops lamenting the violence, but he then fretted that it shouldn't be read at the Masses, since it might be seen as "untimely" or "partial."

Then in what's presented by many of his chroniclers as a damascene conversion, everything changed for Archbishop Romero on March 12, 1977, when Father Rutilio Grande, a Jesuit, was shot out of his Jeep along with an old man and a boy of fifteen who happened to be riding with him. Grande had been a close friend of Romero's and master of ceremonies at his ordination as bishop, and Romero found himself making the first of what would seem a never-ending series of trips to the sides of priests and/or Christians who'd been murdered for having acted on their beliefs. As many have noted, it was as if with his friend's death he began his way of the cross. "It is my lot to gather up the trampled, the dead, and all that the persecution of the Church leaves behind," he said later, noting how long he walked the roads "gathering up dead friends, listening to widows and orphans, and trying to spread hope."

At fifty-nine years of age and for the final three years of his life he became the very model of a Vatican II bishop immersed in the joys and sufferings of his people, with a compassion and selflessness as close to Christ's as you're likely to find in the twentieth century. He wrote the country's president demanding justice, and the president responded that such murders had possibly been staged by outside agitators to disrupt the peace. Two months later a lawyer Romero had hired to follow the case reported "an embarrassing and clear indifference" on the state's part toward the investigation. The bodies of the murdered had been buried unexamined and not exhumed, and a suspect ordered arrested by one judge still lounged at home, unconcerned.

The bishops formulated a strongly worded protest that they discovered was only read in the churches because no newspaper would publish it, so at a meeting of the clergy Romero asked for initiatives and implemented three that emerged with wide support: the closing of Catholic schools for a week; the elimination of all Masses save one at the cathedral the following Sunday, to memorialize the dead; and a refusal to participate in civil functions until the situation was resolved.

All three were viewed as outrageous provocations. Romero spent the days following in meetings, berated by everyone from the national businessmen's association—which wanted the archdiocesan radio station to stop broadcasting anything but classical music but otherwise had no other suggestions— to the papal nuncio, who accused him of irresponsibility and imprudence after having not bothered to attend the meeting in which the initiatives had been discussed. The decision not to take part in state functions was seen as particularly provocative and dangerous, but Romero held firm. The mass went ahead as planned, drawing a hundred thousand attendees to the cathedral plaza and making it the largest demonstration within memory, with pastors reporting countless parishioners returning to the Church after long estrangements.

Faced with such an extraordinary situation, Romero was willing to let his God be always the God of change encountered in Genesis —"Go from your country and your kindred and your father's house to the land that I will show you" (Gen. 12.1)—and confronted each new catastrophe as it arose. There were no guidebooks. It's a measure of the instability with which he had to deal that in his three-year tenure he negotiated with four different governments, none of which was able to prevent the country's ghastly spiral into civil war, or more precisely, into its war against its own people. By the time the killing had mostly ended, in 1991, seventy-five thousand were dead, a million refugees had been created, and the country's economic apparatus had been demolished.

The government that assumed power in July 1977 had abandoned even the pretense of reformist intent, and after a foreign minister was killed by guerrillas, security forces murdered another priest, Alfonso Navarro, in reprisal, making clear that they now identified as one of their principal political enemies members of the Church. A week later in the town of Aguilares, thirty-eight *campesinos* were massacred and the tabernacle with the Blessed Sacrament desecrated. At the Mass in which Romero installed the new pastor, there weren't enough communion hosts for all who wanted to receive, and afterward the crowd accompanied the restored Blessed Sacrament around the central plaza in a procession. As they passed the town hall, National Guardsmen emerged with automatic weapons and watched them go by.

Breaking with his national tradition and in the face of relentless civic pressure, Archbishop Romero refused to attend the new president's inauguration, sending a signal that not even the presence of the papal nuncio could disguise. The media in response vilified the archbishop, the clergy, and any of those who encouraged grassroots Christian communities and/or land reform or legal accountability on the part of the security forces. But when it came to the media, Romero was no naïf; his twenty-three years as a diocesan secretary had schooled him nicely on the usefulness of the printing press and the radio station, and the Sunday broadcasts of his sermons converted them to national events in which the mainstream media's determination to ignore or distort the country's agonies was successfully resisted. Homilies lasted more than an hour, beginning with the Gospel and proceeding to the news, and were heard everywhere on the streets, from cafés to taxi radios. When the station transmitter was blown up, Romero urged his congregation to themselves become microphones of God.

There was a lot to resist. At times the government's cover stories were so transparently spurious as to suggest an overweening and mocking arrogance. Toward the end of Romero's tenure, his friend Apolinario Serrano and three other organizers were killed, and the official story in the media was that the four of them armed with two pistols had charged an army post of three hundred heavily armed men.

In the late '70s I was muddling through graduate school, having fallen away from the Church four or five years earlier. I was sympathetic to liberation theology, though in a mostly unfocused way, and so I first heard about Oscar Romero when he was murdered. At first his killing seemed like what it was, in secular terms—just another one of those political outrages our country was aiding and abetting in Central America, under the banner of supporting anyone who claimed to be pro-business and anti-communist—but as I learned more I found myself hugely moved by hearing in his words my own unarticulated hopes for what the Church could be. In each of his four pastoral letters—the fruit of his discussions with theologians and people from all levels of the social strata—he laid out the logic of liberation theology: that a belief in God as the source of justice, love, and truth compels us to understand that if the individual represents God's glory, then the love of the afflicted preached in the gospel mandates that Church members not divorce faith from life and submit themselves to the demands of the Sermon on the Mount. Christ called everyone to his side but continually stressed the need to cherish the most disadvantaged—"Just as you did it to one of the least of these who are members of my family, you did it to me" (Matt. 25:40)—and so should his Church. As the theologian Jon Sobrino put it, sin was an offense against God *because* it was an offense against people.

So what in that makes Romero a candidate for this collection? The previous assertions would seem to most of us pretty orthodox. But it was in his move from orthodoxy to orthopraxy—from *thinking* the right thing to *doing* the right thing—that he strayed so surprisingly far from the institutional mainstream. He came to believe that in the face of widespread suffering his ministry couldn't be adequately fulfilled by simply proclaiming the faith, and that for the community to take charge of its own salvation in such a situation there would need to be a conversion of hearts *and* of social structures. As he wrote in his second pastoral letter, "The love of Christ urges us on (2 Cor. 5:14), a clear demand before the brother or sister in need (1 John 3:17)." He went on to note that the Church is praised and allowed its privileges "so long as it preaches eternal salvation and does not involve itself in the real problems of our world," but when it's faithful to its mission of denouncing oppression and "proclaims its hope for a more just, humane world, then it is persecuted and calumniated," and branded subversive.

I was moved by Oscar Romero as well because he loved his country and denounced all that disgraced it. He believed that persecution afflicted Christ because it afflicted his followers— "Saul, Saul, why do you persecute me?" (Acts 9:4)—and despite the transparent risk to his life he never found prudent reasons for silence. At a time when it was much safer to claim that everyone shared equal blame for his country's distress, he publically affirmed that the ruling class's economic self-interest was the main cause of state violence and that its security forces' primary agenda was to suppress protest. He denounced selfishness as a sin that dehumanized, and he exhorted the rich to take on as their own the problem of the poor. He called, in other words, for what Hans Küng has termed "civic courage," from the Latin *civilis,* "for the common good." Küng quotes Paul, who claimed to have opposed to his face his fellow apostle Peter for not having lived by the truth of the gospel, and notes that that account, from the second chapter of Paul's Letter to the Galatians, was not until Vatican II read aloud in the liturgy, since "Paul's courage could have infected the episcopate and indeed the Vatican."

Oscar Romero seems to most of us a hero of conscience, but four of his five fellow Salvadoran bishops and his papal nuncio regarded his commitment as theologically wrong and politically ignorant, if not criminal. He continually had to cope with that rift, along with everything else, and was more than once recalled to Rome to justify himself. It's heartbreaking to read in his letters and diaries how he suffered from his brother bishops' hostility. And hostility it was: in 1979 they sent to Rome an attack on Romero claiming him to be a wily and politicized Marxist who gave his blessing to terrorists, and reconfiguring each of the murdered priests as either having been killed by their own leftist associates or having died in armed struggle with the forces of order. One bishop responded to the torture of a priest in his diocese by explaining that the priest had acted in the area of politics and had therefore suffered the consequences. Another whose priest was murdered immediately recalled his delegates from a national forum hosted by the president, making clear he understood who was responsible. But later, he announced in a homily that other priests in his diocese were associated with leftist groups and that he wouldn't be able to do anything to save them. Romero registered with horror in his diary that this seemed to be excusing, if not inviting, further murders.

In November 1977 the government instituted the Law of Defense and Guarantee of Public Order, legitimizing arbitrary imprisonment and torture and suppressing the right to hold meetings, and gradually worked to enthrone national security as the primary value that justified any and all excesses. (If that sounds familiar to you, as an American today, it should.) By 1979 two massacres involving the machine gunning of demonstrators received worldwide coverage after having been filmed by foreign TV crews. In June of that year, after another priest, Rafael Palacios, was shot down in the street, Romero asked at the funeral, "Where is our nation's justice? Where is the Supreme Court? Where is our democracy's honor?" When the papal nuncio notified him of the president's concern for his safety, he responded that it was difficult to accept protection while his people remained unprotected. By the time he made his annual retreat in 1980 his confessor saw it as his Gethsemane. The week before he had said of the oligarchy: "Let them share what they are and have. Let them not keep silencing with violence the voice of those of us who offer this invitation," and then revealed that he had been informed he was on a list of those to be eliminated. A month later he called on security forces not to obey instructions to kill. The next day he was shot as he raised the host at Mass.

Two hundred and fifty thousand people attended the funeral. The mourners were bombed and machine gunned, and at least forty were killed. His murderers, though identified, were never brought to justice.

"Do this in remembrance of me" (Luke 22:19), Jesus instructed at the Last Supper, and as the chasm between haves and have-nots continues to widen and the former annexes more and more of the world's resources as its right, elevating the embrace of privilege into a principle, we will all need to recall what Oscar Romero, in his address at the University of Louvain, explained that following Jesus in such times will mean: "Here neutrality is impossible. Either we serve the life of Salvadorans or we are accomplices in their death." "I am a shepherd who, with his people," he said, "has begun to learn a beautiful and difficult truth: our Christian faith requires that we submerge ourselves in this world." "It would be sad," he claimed, "if in a country where murder is being committed so horribly, we were not to find priests also among its victims. They are the testimony of a church incarnated in the problems of its people." He opened his sermon at the funeral for Father Navarro with the story of a caravan that, desperate with thirst, sought water in mirages, despite its guide's passionate protests, until finally in exasperation they shot the guide, who stretched out his hand in his agony, so that he died still pointing the way.

---

The author would like to cite his indebtedness in particular to the following sources: Archbishop Oscar Romero, *Voice of the Voiceless: The Four Pastoral Letters and Other Statements* (Maryknoll, New York: Orbis Books, 1985) and James R. Brockman, *Romero: A Life* (Maryknoll, New York: Orbis Books, 1989)

# REFORMING THE STIGMATA

## MARTIN LUTHER

*Martha E. Stortz*

### I

I think about bodies a lot.

I watch my own body succumb to age and gravity. "Everything heads south," my late husband joked.

I think about his body, which headed south too soon, ravaged by cancer.

I think about the body politic, scarred by bitter partisanship.

I think about the bodies of "crucified peoples" from the killing fields of Cambodia, El Salvador, Auschwitz, the Horn of Africa.

I think about the body of this planet, beset by weather not part of its natural rhythms.

I think about the body of Christ, pinned to a cross, pierced and broken.

All of these bodies are marked.

II

Incarnation forces Christians to think about bodies: God had one. Creation is God's body; Christ, the revelation of God in human form. Ignoring the body violates incarnation, suggesting that belief can be disembodied in ways that Christ himself was not. Further, ignoring the body deprives us of resources we need for a Church that needs to be "always in the process of reforming" (*semper reformanda*).

The phrase belongs to Martin Luther (1483–1546), one of many late medieval voices for reform. He saw his contribution as a movement for the gospel within the Church, except for Luther "gospel" was a person, not a bundle of theological propositions. The manger at Bethlehem held a baby, not a book. That child had a body.

As a biblical scholar, Luther attended to the bodies that animated the texts. Writing on Genesis, Luther described the first inhabitant of the Garden of Eden as "intoxicated with rejoicing." Adam frolics before the Fall. Full-body delight, not some passive beatitude, is our natural state.

But then, Luther had a body himself, and that body was marked. In addition to the physical ailments that plagued late medieval people, he suffered from kidney stones and constipation his entire life. He knew how acute pain cripples a natural capacity for delight. Suffering shrinks the world to its source.

Perhaps that's why Luther was drawn to the apostle Paul. Paul too had a marked body. To the Church at Galatia, the apostle writes, "I carry the marks of Jesus branded on my body" (Gal. 6:17), and he complains to the Corinthians of a "thorn . . . in the flesh" (2 Cor. 12:7). Commenting on Paul's Letter to the Romans, Luther described sin as "the heart turned in on itself." The image is no abstraction: think how a thorn, a kidney stone, an ingrown toenail focuses the mind. Luther and Paul before him drew their best theological insights straight out of the body.

Bodies matter—and Christ's body matters most. A Christian spirituality that addresses age and death, genocide and environmental catastrophe begins with bodies.

### III

I'll start with mine, as I pedaled furiously to the lecture a prominent professor was giving at the University of Tübingen. It was cold; I was late. A car passed too close on my left, and I overcompensated, smashing my right knee into the door handle of a parked car. When I stopped to survey the damage, my thick winter tights had not been broken. I cycled on.

Returning home a few hours later, I peeled the tights off and found myself peering into a textbook view of a knee's inner workings. Tights masked a deep puncture wound. Hours later, I emerged from the surgeon's office in a walking cast up to my hip. Today, a six-inch scar snakes up my right knee. I'm marked.

Aren't we all?

IV

So it is with God. Think about Christ's body, not abstractly, as some mystical Body that believers past and present call "Church." Think rather about Christ's physical body, the one that trod the dusty streets of ancient Jerusalem. His feet cracked and collected dirt, and he welcomed anyone who would oil them (Luke 7:37; John 12:3). Think of Christ's physical body, the one that endured the blows of Romans, the sting of a crown of thorns, the spit of centurions, the slow asphyxiation of crucifixion.

Think about Christ's body the way Fra Angelico (d. 1455) did, as he decorated the convent of San Marco. He painted his way into that marked body. In one fresco, Christ is blind-folded and tied to a column. Around him, hanging in the air, the artist hung instruments of his torture: a leather strap coiled to strike, a mace swung back for a direct hit, a stick braced for beating, two pursed lips on a face with no body, spit flying from them. Because he cannot see, Christ knows neither the origin nor the agency behind these weapons. He simply registers each blow deeply in the body.

Encountering the scene, so do we.

V

The shock of these images unmasks our reluctance to believe that God has a body. We're still closet Gnostics, eager to embrace God's divinity, anxious about God's humanity. I might like to have cosmetic surgery on my knee and erase that ugly scar. But it's dangerous to do cosmetic surgery on the body of

Christ and erase those wounds. Without the wounds, we lose the God who experienced the full range of human experience: birth, suffering, torture, and finally, death. This God knows the killing fields, because this God has been there.

Consider the apostle Thomas, not as *doubting,* but as *believing* Thomas. He knew that God had a body—and he knew that body would be marked. Convinced that even the resurrected body of Christ bore marks of his torture and execution, Thomas demanded to see and touch them. He got living proof.

Thomas died a martyr in India. Pierced and burned alive, he died with the consolation that his suffering had been shared. Christ had been there first: he'd seen proof.


VI


Beset by plague, war, and political instability, late medieval Christians needed similar consolation. Religious art registers their yearning. Medieval historian Ewert Cousins observes, "As the Middle Ages progressed, the passion of Christ permeated more deeply the religious psyche of Western Christendom." A single icon captured the cult of suffering: Francis of Assisi receiving the wounds of Christ, the *stigmata,* into his own body. They came to him on retreat at a mountain outside the city of Assisi in September 1224. Aroused from prayer, he saw that his body was marked.

The stigmatization captured the imagination of medieval Christians, both lay and religious. At the highest levels of churchly power, Francis evoked reverence and fear. His holiness was undeniable: he bore it in his flesh. Yet, his commitment to poverty challenged a Church that had accumulated great wealth—and wanted to hang on to it. Within two years of his death, Francis was canonized. Such speedy beatification signaled caution to the rank and file: saints were extraordinary and outside the reach of ordinary Christians.

No one took the hint. Outside the skittish circles of papal power, Francis's story ignited popular piety. His asceticism galvanized movements of apostolic poverty; his stigmatization animated brushes of artists. Giotto painted Francis receiving the stigmata onto the walls of cathedrals in Florence, Pisa, and Assisi. Jan van Eyck made Francis Flemish in feature and set the scene in a northern European landscape. Countless other artists, local and unknown, gave the saint a face from their streets and a place in their familiar.

VII

These images could not have escaped Martin Luther as the young monk made his way to Rome in 1510. Five years earlier, he'd ditched a career in law to enter the house of the Augustinian Eremites in Erfurt. A thunderstorm threatened bodily harm, and the young scholar vowed to Saint Anne that if he survived, he'd become a monk. Becoming an Augustinian fulfilled his vow.

The order had itself developed in 1256 out of the Franciscan impulse toward apostolic poverty. By Luther's time, the German houses divided over how strictly they should interpret "poverty." Did poverty mean the spiritual desert of contemplation? Or did it also embrace actual physical denial? The superiors sent Luther and another companion to Rome to seek papal counsel. In short, the dispute that put Luther on that ancient pilgrimage route to the Holy City involved bodies—and how poverty should mark them.

On the ancient pilgrimage route to the Holy City, Luther saw image after image of Francis receiving the stigmata. Those images registered. They persisted throughout the years of struggle with Rome: the posting of his "Ninety-Five Theses" on the doors of the Castle Church at Wittenberg in 1517; his official excommunication from the Roman Church by Pope Leo X and subsequent sojourn at the Wartburg Castle in 1521; his exit from monastic life in 1524; his marriage to Katharina von Bora, a former nun, in 1525. Throughout, Luther continued to teach at the University of Wittenberg.

In 1535, as he prepared for lectures on the apostle Paul's Letter to the Galatians, Luther brought four marked bodies together: Christ, Paul, Francis—and the bodies of all believers. Treating Galatians 6:17, the passage where Paul admits that he bears "the marks of Jesus branded on my body," Luther summoned the image of Francis: "Even if Francis did bear the stigmata on his body, *as he is portrayed* . . ." (emphasis mine). He mentioned Francis, because he had to. Everyone connected the stigmata with the saint—and with saintliness.

Luther challenged that connection. He wondered whether Francis received the stigmata "on account of Christ." He worried that the Franciscan movement restricted to a spiritual elite the "universal gospel" that rightly belonged to all Christians. He argued that all Christians encounter the crucified Christ—and not in some seraphic vision, but in the living Word. He knew that encounter marked them. Finally, Luther concluded, all Christians receive the stigmata.

Consider again Giotto's image of Francis receiving the stigmata. Block out the image of the saint, and in his place, put the communion of saints, living and dead. Put all the people you worshiped with last Sunday. Put all the people you've ever worshiped with across the years and around the world. All of us receive "the marks of Jesus branded on our bodies": we are all marked.

## VIII

Four years later, in 1539, in a treatise "On the Councils and the Church," Luther returned to the Church, the marked body of Christ in the world. Here he identified the Church, not as place or papacy, but as people: "the Christian holy people." How can "a poor confused person tell where such Christian holy people are in the world?"

Quite simply: by their marks. Luther didn't expect contemporary Christians to be any different than the apostle Thomas. Just as Thomas needed concrete, bodily proof that he was in the presence of his Lord, so Christians then and now need physical evidence. That evidence comes in the form of seven deeply embodied practices that mark the Body of Christ in the world. Luther laid them out like a chant:

> *Where you find people preaching and hearing the Word,*
> *there you find the Church.*
> *Where you find people baptizing members into the body*
> *of Christ,*
> *there you find the Church.*

*Where you find people breaking bread together in memory*
   *of Jesus,*
  *there you find the Church.*
*Where you find people forgiving one another,*
  *there you find the Church.*
*Where you find people calling out leaders,*
  *there you find the Church.*
*Where you find people praying to God, praising God, and*
   *teaching their children,*
  *there you find the Church.*
*Where you find people walking in the way of the cross,*
  *there you find the church.*

Gifts of the Spirit, these seven practices mark all believers—not just saints. They are Luther's version of the stigmata, now borne by all Christians. Luther drew the Church back to the body, literally, re-forming faithful bodies into the Body of Christ in the world.

IX

I see a similar hunger for reform in the churches today—and I wonder if spiritual practices point a way forward. Let's look at some physical evidence.

First, notice tattoos and piercings. I observed the dizzying display parading up and down Telegraph Avenue in Berkeley, California. The epicenter of the free speech movement of the 1960s morphed into the marked body movement of the new millennium. Were these exercises in exhibitionism?

Or efforts to stake out turf in a world that seemed to be crumbling?

Certainly the institutions charged with the care of these marked bodies had failed them: sex abuse scandals and episcopal cover-up in the Church, homophobia in the Scouts, shootings in high schools, shopping malls, and movie theaters, a vicious, incantational politics in public life. Could anything in the body politic be trusted? If they couldn't belong to anything else, these young people could belong to their own bodies. They inscribed them as the last remaining "still point of the turning world" (T. S. Eliot, "Burnt Norton," *The Four Quartets*).

Second, consider the woman who came up to me after a lecture and said, "I like your approach; I just wish you didn't have to be so Christian about it all." We talked further, and she regularly practiced an eclectic mixture of yoga, centering prayer, Zen meditation, and journaling. She described herself as a recovering Christian, "spiritual, but not religious."

She's not alone. Whether betrayed—or simply bored—by the churches of their childhood, seekers refuse affiliation with organized religion but hold tight to a sense of mystery and meaning. For them, being "religious" means intellectual assent to outdated confessions and creeds. Religion is a head trip; it leaves the body behind.

In contrast, being "spiritual" invites the body to mentor the soul. Practices invite the body's wisdom to point the way to mystery and meaning.

Third, be with someone suffering. When my husband was dying, I wanted to enter that pain. I considered gulping down his meds, just to experience their impact on his body. Love took me where I wouldn't have gone otherwise.

Then I realized: this is the love Luther had for his daughter Magdalena, who died four years before he did, leaving in her absence the sadness which haunted his last years. This is the love that fueled Francis's vision of the crucified Christ, as he prayed all night on Mount La Verna. This is the love Paul had for his "Christ Jesus," the model for his hymn to love in 1 Corinthians 13. This is the love that moved God to become human in the first place.

It was an enormous consolation to know that whatever suffering we experience, someone else went there first—and not just anyone, but the One "in whom we live and move and have our being" (Acts 17:28).

Finally, find the body of Christ in the world today. An arresting Stations of the Cross series hangs on the walls of the chapel at the Jesuit University of Central America in San Salvador. These fourteen black-and-white etchings do not depict the traditional sequences of events in the passion of Christ, but rather the torture of the Salvadoran people during their civil war. Bruises, beatings, barbed wire, and bullets mark their bodies along with rape, beating, mutilation. These are "the crucified people," as Father Jon Sobrino puts it. Their bodies are marked.

Reform in the Church today begins with the body—and Christ's body matters most.

# SEND MY ROOTS RAIN

## GERARD MANLEY HOPKINS

*Colm Toibin*

THERE IS SOMETHING oddly miserable about Dublin. It has to do perhaps with the lowness of the buildings, the length of the winter, and the uncertainty of the weather, but it also becomes apparent in the strange intensity of bar life in the city, as though drinking large quantities of alcohol in public were a celebration of the very thing from which the drinkers were seeking to escape. There is also something beaten down and watchful about even the most affluent-looking person moving along the street in Dublin. James Joyce noticed this and called the city "the center of paralysis"; he sought to use a tone of "scrupulous meanness" in most of the stories in his book *Dubliners*. So mean indeed was the style and so broken the characters that he attempted to make up for this in the last story, "The Dead," which is, among other things, a celebration of Dublin's hospitality.

But maybe I am talking about a particular stretch of Dublin where I have lived for twenty-five years—the area around Lower Leeson Street, Hatch Street, Earlsfort Terrace, and the side of St. Stephen's Green that runs between Leeson Street and Harcourt Street. Perhaps because few people live in these streets, they seem damp and desolate at night. One of the buildings on St. Stephen's Green, called Newman House, was formerly the Catholic University of Ireland, which was opened in 1854 with John Henry Newman as rector until 1858. In 1880, it became University College Dublin. James Joyce studied here from 1898 to 1902. In this same building the poet Gerard Manley Hopkins came to live in 1884 and died in 1889. There is a plaque outside now to all three: Newman, Hopkins, and Joyce.

It was in this building that Hopkins wrote the late sonnets that dealt with darkness and something close to despair. They were written in small handwriting on paper normally used for the writing of sermons. Hopkins was probably referring to these poems when he wrote to his friend, the poet Robert Bridges, on September 1, 1885: "I shall shortly have some sonnets to send you, five or more. Four of these came like inspirations and against my will. And in the life I lead now, which is one of a continually jaded and harassed mind, if in any leisure I try to do anything I make no way—nor with my work, alas!, but so it must be."

While the building on St. Stephen's Green looks grand and imposing—and the downstairs rooms are large and high ceilinged—the upper rooms of the house, the rooms that Hopkins inhabited, have a strange dinginess even to this day. Also, the building was in bad repair in the years when Hopkins lived there. In March 1884 he wrote to Robert

Bridges, "The House we are in, the College, is a sort of ruin and for purposes of study very nearly naked. . . . I have been warmly welcomed and kindly treated. But Dublin is a joyless place."

Hopkins suffered in Dublin. He disliked Ireland and felt exiled. In his Retreat Notes of January 1, 1889, he wrote, "What is my wretched life? Five wasted years almost have passed in Ireland. I am ashamed of the little I have done, of my waste of time, although my helplessness and weakness is such that I could scarcely do otherwise. . . . All my undertakings miscarry: I am like a straining eunuch. I wish then for death: yet if I died now I should die imperfect, no master of myself, and that is the worst failure of all. O my God, look down on me."

In one of the sonnets, addressed to his family who did not share his Catholic faith, Hopkins wrote about the alien place where he would end his days: "I am in Ireland now; now I am at a third remove." He found himself overworked at the university as a professor of Greek, having to mark as many as 1,795 examination papers in 1887. In July 1885 he wrote to his mother, "I am now working at examination papers all day and this work began last month and will outlast this one. It is great, very great drudgery. I can not of course say it is wholly useless, but I believe that most of it is and that I bear a burden which crushes me and does little to help any good end."

The sonnets he wrote in Dublin move beyond the personal by allowing the voice of the speaker, or the writer, a diction that is stilled, severe, and magisterial and then filled with weakness and an imploring sound. There is a sense in them that their composition arose from the deepest and most urgent need. They have the tone of desperate prayer, of a cry from the depths, but it is clear also that they were made by one man in one place and in one time, and they arose from a very specific and sharp set of feelings and precise experiences. How Hopkins came to such a state of despair in Dublin is a complex story to do with his own unique personality. It is also a story that has to do with faith and religion and the tension that exists between the two.

If Hopkins was a heretic—and his move toward despair in the Dublin sonnets and some of the letters and notes he wrote is close to heresy—then his first heresy was to find the Church of England unequal to his needs; his second heresy came when he sought a home in a Catholic Church and found the Church and its rules ready to embrace him and comfort him but also ready to silence him and destroy him. His knowledge of what he had lost was total; sometimes he was unsure what he had gained. He charted his elaborate personal journey in all its pain in letters and poems but much of the time he suffered in silence. His desire to strike out alone was countered by his need for friendship and support. The gap between his rich system of belief and how he felt on given days made its way into the very core of the poems he wrote in a dingy upper room in a city where he did not want to be.

In theory he loved the Catholic Church and its rituals. In practice, he felt an immense desolation. Out of the struggle between the theory and the practice came the poems.

Gerard Manley Hopkins was born in Stratford, Essex, which is now part of Greater London, in 1844. He was the first in a large family. His father wrote poems and reviewed books of poetry; his mother was interested in music. Both his parents were deeply religious High Church Anglicans. His father described Hopkins's mother's faith as "woven in with her very being." Among the extended family were a number of painters. Hopkins throughout his life showed talent as a visual artist. He also composed music. The family moved to Hampstead in London in 1852. Between 1863 and 1867 Hopkins studied classics at Balliol College Oxford. There he was taught by Walter Pater, who became a friend; he also formed a friendship with a fellow student Robert Bridges, later the poet laureate, and they maintained a close relationship throughout Hopkins's life. It was Bridges who rescued his poems for posterity.

While Hopkins was studying, a specter haunted Oxford. It was the specter of Catholicism. In the wake of John Henry Newman's conversion in 1845, many religious young men felt tempted to move away from the Anglican Church. Newman's example mattered. He had been an academic at Oxford; he was a formidable intellectual and an Anglican priest who set the agenda in religious debate. Thus, once he converted, the Catholic Church could now be associated with a man of large intelligence and charisma rather than the hordes of uneducated Irish emigrants who flocked to the churches, for example, or the old English recusant families who had kept the faith through dark times. Newman, by the force of his personality, made conversion to the Church a route that could be followed by those who were dissatisfied with their spiritual lives as Anglicans.

The feelings of young men who wished to move from the Anglican faith to the Catholic faith were complicated by the matter of sexuality. If they wished to become Anglican priests, they could marry; were they to become Catholic priests, they could not. Many of them, including Newman himself it seems, had no great interest in marrying. In the case of Hopkins and some of his associates at Oxford, it is possible to go further and say that their interest in spirituality became entwined with a homosexuality that they could not name and did not deal with directly.

This is not a simple matter. In the case of Hopkins's refined and fragile sensibility it cannot be said that he loved Catholic ritual and began to believe in Catholic dogma as a result of his sexuality. It would also be too easy to say that his sexual discontent gave rise to a spiritual discontent. However, his religious dilemma and his sexual inclinations nonetheless circled each other and mirrored each other. While his deep feelings for Catholic ritual cannot be precisely connected with his sexual feelings, nonetheless it is hard to imagine what shape his spiritual disquiet might have taken were it not accompanied by a sexual identity that was perplexing for him and shameful.

During his time at Oxford, Hopkins came to some realization of his true nature, both sexual and religious. While it was clear that his sexual nature would have to be denied, he began to have the courage to express his religious feelings and felt a need to have them recognized. While his sexuality moved into the realm of pure privacy, almost as a way of compensating, his spiritual feelings became open and were fearlessly declared. On August 28, 1866, he wrote to John Henry Newman, "I address you with great hesitation knowing that you are in the midst of yr. own engagements and because you must be exposed to applications on all sides. I am anxious to become a Catholic, and I thought that you might possibly be able to see me for a short time when I pass through Birmingham in a few days, I believe on Friday."

His problem in converting was how to deal with his family, to whom such an action would be simply inexplicable. The letter explaining his decision reached his parents on October 13, 1866. Two days later he wrote to Newman, "I have been up at Oxford just long enough to have heard fr. my father and mother in return for my letter announcing my conversion. Their answers are terrible. I cannot read them twice." His parents were worried about what his conversions would do to his career prospects, among other things. Hopkins's tone in response to them was resolute, almost cold and somewhat pompous. "The Church," he wrote, "strictly forbids all communion in sacred things with non-Catholics." His parents were also concerned that they had not been consulted in advance: "Have you not dealt hardly," his father wrote in the draft of a letter that has survived, "may I not say unfairly by us in leaving us in absolute ignorance of all till your decision was finally taken? Were you not on the point of being received into the Church of Rome without even warning us?" In this same draft there is a sentence that was written by his mother: "O Gerard my darling boy are you indeed gone from me?"

One of Hopkins's great influences at Oxford was the theologian Henry Parry Liddon, whose sermons were considered spellbinding. As he made his mind up to convert to Rome, Hopkins studiously avoided Liddon, who had to be told by a colleague that not only Hopkins but four other of Liddon's other protégés, including William Addis, who was one of

Hopkins's closest friends, were converting to Catholicism within a few days of each other. Liddon wrote to Hopkins, "If you could examine your own thought fully, you would probably find that love & sympathy for Addis is the strongest motive that is taking you to Rome." Hopkins's father wrote to Liddon, seeking his support. Liddon wrote two more letters to Hopkins, not having received a reply to his first. When Hopkins finally replied it was to say that he had not been converted by "personal illumination which dispenses with the need of thought or knowledge on the points at issue." He concluded coldly, "Do not trouble yourself to write again: this needs no answer and I know how precious your time is."

Hopkins graduated with a double first from Oxford, which would almost automatically have prepared the way for an academic career, with a fellowship at one of the Oxford colleges. Because of his conversion, however, such routes would not be open to him. It was now unclear what he would do and how he would live. Becoming a Catholic in England in 1866 was an act of heresy; doors would be shut accordingly.

Two years later, at the age of twenty-four, Hopkins joined the Jesuits. He would have to do nine years of training because Jesuits were not ordained until the age of thirty-three, the age of Christ at the time of the crucifixion. He would have to learn blind obedience. One of his friends later said, "Humanly speaking he made a grievous mistake in joining the Jesuits for on further acquaintance his whole soul must have revolted against a system which has killed many and many a noble soul. . . . To get on with the Jesuits you must become on many grave points a machine, without will, without conscience, and that to his nature was an impossibility." Nevertheless, Hopkins forced his will to bend to that of the organization, to which he remained loyal for the rest of his life, obedient in matters both large and small.

When he took a bath, for example, he would have to use a "modesty powder" provided by his superiors to make the water opaque. (Since novices were only allowed one bath every month, this powder may not have been entirely necessary.) Beside their concern that the novices would not see their own genitalia, the Jesuits also were known in the years when Hopkins joined them for their open and deliberate philistinism; following this would prove very difficult for a young man who relished beauty.

In 1975 the Jesuit magazine *The Month* would write:

> *There is no convincing evidence that the Society was an enemy to his genius. His fellow-Jesuits were also fellow Victorians. . . . They neither helped nor hindered him much. The dark side of his own temperament was a greater enemy. The real trouble was duller, but, in a sense, worse. It was the low valuation set on Art by the Society after its restoration, and by no means consistent with its own more ancient and grander tradition. It had become, at least in England, and more generally elsewhere, philistine, puritanical. Art, except in banal, popular forms, was regarded as irrelevant, a distraction from the main business of preaching the Gospel. And its preaching see-sawed between the coldly rational and the sickly sentimental.*

In other words, as a result of his conversion and his joining the Jesuits, Hopkins lost not only his family, none of whom came to his ordination in 1877, and many of his friends, and the chance to follow a brilliant academic career, but he now moved in a harsh world that had no interest in the things that interested him—poetry, for example, or other forms of beauty in art and nature.

The tension among the body, the mind, and the soul was always there in him. While it made him unhappy, he was also resolute and dedicated. The tension surfaced in the privacy of his prayer; it also emerged in his poetry when he began to write again.

But it did not emerge easily. He destroyed his poetry on becoming a novice. As a poet thereafter he was silent for long periods. Some of the images he wrote in his journals made their way into subsequent poems. However, it is his very silence and the feeling that the writing of poetry was not part of his vocation that give the poems their immediacy. Their sense of hard-won language chiseled onto the page, their gnarled and clotted tone, arise from a feeling that poetry for a Jesuit novice or a Jesuit priest was almost a form of temptation.

His first major poem as a Jesuit was a long poem, "The Wreck of the Deutschland," written as a response to the death of five Franciscan nuns on the ship when it sank in December 1875. When he offered it to the Jesuit magazine for publication, it was not accepted by Father Coleridge, the editor. When another priest read it he responded that "the only result was to give me a very bad headache, and to lead me to hand the poem back to Fr Coleridge with the remark that it was indeed unreadable."

Hopkins's poetry came from a source that was close to the surface and yet almost unconsciously so. His poems were unmediated by irony or by caution. Thus the sexual imagery in "The Wreck of the Deutschland" allowed expression to something that Hopkins managed to repress in every other moment of his life but could not repress now:

> *The dense and the driven Passion, and frightful sweat:*
> *Thence the discharge of it, there its swelling to be,*
> *Though felt before, though in high flood yet—*
> *What none would have known of it, only the heart, being*
>   *hard at bay.*

From the silence came clotted and strangely charged utterance. But since Hopkins had more freedom to think about poetry than to write poems, he also could formulate what he thought poetry could and should do. The two terms associated with him are "inscape" and "sprung rhythm." These terms are both complicated and simple. *Inscape* is complicated because Hopkins's own sense of it was open to change. In general, he meant that the act of looking was essentially dynamic, and that things in nature or people could radiate a presence that was utterly unique. This could also mean that things, even when we do not look at them, have an inner spirit, an inner meaning, an inner form that is utterly individual. Any attempt then to write about nature, or even to look at the world, requires a full recognition of this idea, but also of what flows from each thing seen.

*Sprung rhythm* is a bit easier since it is technical rather than metaphysical. "To speak shortly," Hopkins wrote, "it consists in scanning by accents or stresses alone, without any account of the number of syllables, so that a foot may be one strong syllable or it may be many light and one strong." Hopkins liked it, he wrote to Bridges, because "that is the native and natural rhythm of speech, the least forced, the most rhetorical and emphatic of all possible rhythms."

Although Hopkins had been a brilliant undergraduate, he did not shine as a Jesuit novice or as a Jesuit priest. "Hopkins," one of his colleagues noted, "was a man who in his shyness felt enormously awkward when he had to perform any public task. His mind and his hand seemed to freeze; he begins to worry and fuss, and nervousness seems to consume him before even the most routine public utterance." His sermons were literate, elaborate, and badly delivered. In 1877, as he delivered a sermon to fellow Jesuits on the miracle of the loaves and the fishes, his congregation began to laugh. "People laughed at it prodigiously," he wrote. "I saw some of them roll on their chairs with laughter." On another occasion, as he preached to a female congregation, he compared the Church to a cow and with the sacraments as seven teats through which grace flowed.

In another sermon he spoke of how much he looked forward to seeing Christ in the flesh and imagined him "moderately tall, well-built and tender in frame, his features straight and beautiful, his hair inclining to auburn, parted in the middle, curling and clustering about the ears and neck as the leaves of a filbert, so they speak, upon the nut."

Hopkins's circumstances affected his poetry deeply but he had no control over his circumstances. In August 1874 he wrote to his father from the Jesuit house of St. Beuno's at St. Asaph in North Wales, "I came here yesterday, to begin my studies in theology. . . . The house stands on a steep hillside, it commands the long-drawn valley of the Clwyd to the sea, a vast prospect, and opposite is Snowdon and its range, just now it being bright visible but coming and going with the weather." It was this landscape that inspired his best nature poetry. "God's Grandeur" was written in February 1877; "The Windhover" three months later; "Pied Beauty" soon after that:

> Glory be to God for dappled things—
> For skies of couple-colour as a brinded cow;
> For rose-moles all in the stipple upon trout that swim;
> Fresh-firecoal chestnut-falls; finches's wings;
> Landscape plotted and pieced—fold, fallow, and plough;
> And all trades, their gear and tackle and trim.

By 1878 he was moved from Wales. He did some teaching and returned to Oxford for a year. Then the Jesuits moved him to two industrial parishes in the north of England, one outside Manchester and the other in Liverpool. It was now that his muse, as he wrote, turned "sullen." He was not made for parish work among the city poor. He disliked the city, writing to Bridges later, "As I went up Brunswick Road (or any street) in Liverpool on a frosty morning it used to disgust me to see the pavement regularly starred with the spit of the workmen going to their work; and they do not turn aside, but spit straight before them as you approach." Despite his dislike for his work in the parishes, he managed one of his great poems in Liverpool, "Felix Randal," about the death of one of his ordinary parishioners:

*This seeing the sick endears them to us, us too it endears.*
*My tongue had taught thee comfort, touch had quenched*
*    thy tears,*
*Thy tears that touched my heart, child, Felix, poor Felix*
*    Randal.*


At the end of 1883, as they wondered what to do with Hopkins, the Jesuits considered for the first time sending him to Dublin to teach Greek. One of his superiors wrote, "I also feel that University work would be more in his line than anything else. Sometimes what we in the Community deem oddities are the very qualities which outside are appreciated as original & valuable." In February 1884 Hopkins began his work in a country that was in a state of political ferment, due to the leadership of Charles Stewart Parnell. Even among the Catholic clergy, there was a dislike of English outsiders. It is clear from Hopkins's letters that he supported the British Empire and disliked Irish nationalism, at times vehemently so. In a letter to his sister Kate, he even mocked the Irish accent ("Im intoirely ashamed o meself. Sure its a wonder I could lave you iligant corspondance so long onanswered"). He did not get on well with the students. "I do not object to their being rude to me personally," he said to the poet Katharine Tynan, "but I do object to their being rude to a professor and a priest."

There is one reference in his letters to his reading of Irish legends, just as when he was in Wales he had briefly studied the Welsh language. But there is no sense that he took any advantage of his time in Ireland. There are a few references to the life he might have had if his poems had been published. With Katharine Tynan, he went to the studio of the painter John Butler Yeats, the father of the poet W. B. Yeats. Soon he met the young poet himself. But they saw Hopkins as a priest in a foreign country rather than as one of the most innovative poets of his age.

On May 3, 1889, he wrote to his father to say he was ill. Two days later he wrote to his mother. They came to Dublin and were at his bedside when he died of typhoid fever on June 8. He was buried in the Jesuit plot in Glasnevin cemetery in Dublin, the same cemetery where James Joyce would bury the fictional Paddy Dignam in his novel *Ulysses*.

The sonnets written by Hopkins in Dublin do not doubt the existence of God but rather meditate with dark foreboding on the heresy that God has no comfort to offer the poet. The sorrow, the darkness within him, belongs to him alone. There will be no relief. One of the sonnets ends:

> *I see*
> *The lost are like this, and their scourge to be*
> *As I am mine, their sweating selves; but worse.*

In other sonnets, however, Hopkins uses the language of prayer as a way of desperately imploring the Deity who has abandoned him:

> *[B]irds build—but not I build; no, but strain,*
> *Time's eunuch, and not breed one work that wakes.*
> *Mine, O thou lord of life, send my roots rain.*

Less than three years before Hopkins died, he wrote to Robert Bridges about the meaning of fame: "What are works of art for? To educate, to be standards. Education is meant for the many, standards are for public use. To produce them is of little use unless what we produce is known, if known widely known, the wider known the better. . . . A great work by an Englishman is like a great battle won by England. It is an unfading bay tree." In 1913 Bridges became poet laureate. Five years later he published the first edition of Hopkins's poems, thus winning the fame for him that he had shied away from while he lived or that had been forbidden him because of his priestly vows.

# THE MAN WHO
# SAID NO

## FRANZ JÄGERSTÄTTER

*Tobias Wolff*

I

"The most important thing one human being can do for another is to bar the door to his spiritual ease." So wrote James Baldwin. If that is true, then I owe thanks to an Austrian farmer named Franz Jägerstätter for the profound discomfort he has caused me.

His story is still not well known outside Austria and Germany, and was hardly known at all until 1964, when the American sociologist Gordon Zahn published his book *In Solitary Witness,** the first full account of Jägerstätter's life and

---

*Gordon Zahn, *In Solitary Witness: The Life and Death of Franz Jägerstätter* (Springfield, IL: Templegate Publishers, 1964).

death. Zahn himself had learned about Jägerstätter only by accident, while writing another book, *German Catholics and Hitler's Wars*. In the course of his research he came across a cryptic reference to Jägerstätter in an account of the execution of an Austrian priest, Franz Reinisch, for his refusal to take the compulsory military vow of fealty to Adolf Hitler. The author, a former prison chaplain named Heinrich Kreuzberg, had briefly noted another execution for the same offense, of a man he identified only as Franz II. Zahn visited Father Kreuzberg and, having learned Jägerstätter's identity, went on to meet with his widow and parish priest. Eventually he spent months in Jägerstätter's village in northwest Austria, St. Radegund, interviewing his family, neighbors, fellow parishioners, and friends, anyone who could add to the portrait of this remarkable man.

The story, in brief: Franz Jägerstätter was born out of wedlock in 1907. His father was killed in the Great War when Franz was eight, and two years later his mother married a prosperous local farmer, Heinrich Jägerstätter, who adopted her son. Franz attended school for only eight years, until 1921, and shared one teacher in one room with all the other elementary grades. He was clearly something of an autodidact; his religious meditations and letters from prison show impressive rhetorical gifts, an incisive, relentless logic, and a moral clarity humbling for the reader who knows what it demanded of the writer and what he finally paid for it.

Jägerstätter was by all accounts a rakish youth, drinking and fighting with the lads, tearing about on the only motorcycle in the village. Repeating the pattern set by his father, he had a child out of wedlock, a daughter, Hildegard.

Jägerstätter did not flee his responsibility. He grew close to Hildegard, steadfastly supported her, and offered to adopt her when he married Franziska Schwaninger in 1936. Her mother refused the offer.

Franziska was a notably pious young woman. In the years to come other villagers would blame her for Franz's deepening religious commitment, which they saw as somewhat unmanly and a distraction from matters more proper to his sphere—working the farm he'd inherited from his stepfather and seeing to the needs of his growing family; within four years he and Franziska had three daughters of their own. In fact Franziska was not to "blame" for her husband's sense of vocation. She certainly encouraged him, but he had grown deeply in his faith well before they married, to the point of considering life in a monastery. Franziska was to feel her neighbors' suspicion of her influence even more sharply when Jägerstätter, out of that same consuming devotion, accepted what he saw as the necessary consequence of his faith and took the steps that would cost him his home, his family, his freedom, and finally his life.

The precipitating event was Hitler's annexation of Austria—the *Anschluss* of March 1938. Jägerstätter was well aware of what had been going on in Germany since Hitler came to power there in 1933: the state's orchestration of violence against its own citizens; the militarization of the country, accompanied by ominous threats against its neighbors; indoctrination of the young in racism, pagan tribalism, and the glorification of war; forcible euthanasia of the helpless and infirm, and increasing restrictions on the Christian churches. Jägerstätter had developed an intense detestation of Nazism, and he was encouraged in this attitude by leaders of the Catholic Church in Austria. His own bishop, Johannes Maria Gföllner of Linz, had condemned Nazi ideology as heathen materialism and declared that no true believer in this movement could also be a Christian.

Such teachings by the Catholic hierarchy were widespread in Austria before the Anschluss, as they had been in Germany before Hitler essentially bought the Church off with an agreement to recognize its institutional autonomy and freedom to teach the faith in return for renouncing opposition to Nazi policies, including persecution of the Jews, and refraining from political and charitable activities. From the time this treaty, or Concordat, took effect in 1933 Catholic resistance to Nazism was left entirely to the individual believer, God help him; and Hitler, emboldened by the Church's surrender of its effective moral power, gave no more respect to this treaty than to any other. The gag he had persuaded the Church in Germany to tie around its own mouth became, in Austria, a noose. In return for its cooperation after the Anschluss, and its support for ratification in the plebiscite, he canceled Church publications, restricted its schedule of services, imprisoned priests, and all but prohibited religious education of the young. Like the Church, he wanted more than a man's sullen obedience; he wanted his soul, and in that competition he was emerging as the clear winner.

Jägerstätter made no secret of his opposition to the Anschluss. He later expressed a sense of anger and disgrace that his countrymen had with such docility, even enthusiasm, submitted to what had in fact been a military invasion and coup. In April, a month after the German army occupied their country, the Austrian people were asked to register their approval in a national plebiscite. The vote was overwhelmingly in favor of the annexation. Jägerstätter was the only man in St. Radegund to vote against it. His adamant opposition to Nazism—when greeted with a *Heil Hitler!* he always replied *Pfui Hitler!*—put him increasingly at odds with his neighbors.

Jägerstätter was called up for military service in 1940, trained as a driver, then released in April 1941 to continue his work as a farmer until the army had further need of him, as it certainly would. Hitler had by then invaded Czechoslovakia, Poland, France, Norway, Denmark, Luxembourg, the Netherlands, and Belgium; his appetite only whetted, he was preparing to set his armies loose on Russia and, weather permitting, England. War on such a scale could not be sustained without a steady flow of men—*warm bodies,* in the cynical military parlance of my day—to the front. Jägerstätter knew that he would be summoned to bear arms for Hitler. His orders finally came in February 1943.

By then he had hardened in his determination to refuse that summons, even though refusal carried the death penalty. He was not, strictly speaking, a pacifist; he expressed admiration for those who were defending their countries against German aggression, just as he had felt shamed by Austria's failure to do so. Jägerstätter could not see Hitler's war of conquest as anything but unnecessary, unjust, *unholy,* and the Führer and his circle as evil men of malignant purpose. Confirmed as he was in that view, how could he take the oath of unconditional loyalty to Hitler? To do so might save his life but cost him his immortal soul, and "immortal soul" wasn't just an expression to Jägerstätter. He believed that he had a soul, and that it would live forever with the consequences of what he did here. As he was later to write, "Why do we give so little thought to eternity? Why is it so hard to make sacrifices for heaven?"

Jägerstätter was not one to shrink from argument; he made these thoughts known. They met with scant sympathy in St. Radegund. Most of the eligible village men were already in uniform; before the war ended fifty-seven of them would be killed. Jägerstätter was not encouraged to refuse a burden so many of his neighbors had accepted. Besides, he had a wife and children. The government subsidy for families deprived of their men would be withheld from them, and the family of a shirker could hardly look to others in St. Radegund to help with the farm. How could he do that to them? It seemed to many of his neighbors evidence of self-indulgent, hysterical religiosity. Some blamed Franziska; others thought him mentally unbalanced. People in the village still spoke critically of his refusal twenty years after the war.

Before receiving his orders, Jägerstätter had discussed his position with the parish priest, who tried to talk him out of refusing, even suggesting that it might be a form of suicide. Jägerstätter's conscience was not satisfied with this argument. He spoke to another priest, and then to the bishop of Linz, Joseph Fliesser, who had replaced the outspoken anti-Nazi Bishop Gföllner. All these men tried to give Jägerstätter acceptable reasons for avoiding certain death: that his first responsibility was to his family, who would suffer for his refusal; that it was his duty to defend the fatherland; to render unto Caesar what was Caesar's, and let the sin, if sin there was, fall on Caesar's head. Jägerstätter did not believe that the fact of having a family excused him from the conscientious exercise of his free will, nor could he be persuaded that the evil of submitting to Hitler would be put on Hitler's account.

Jägerstätter had hoped that in consulting religious authorities he would find a satisfactory way out. He did not. When the call to arms came he endured a painful parting from Franziska, the two of them unable to break their embrace until his train began to move. Upon arriving at the base in Enns he declared his refusal. He was arrested on March 1, 1943, and taken to the military prison in Linz. Franziska did not try to change his mind, but in her letters asked him to keep trying to find a way to reconcile his convictions with military service. In fact he was doing just that; he was willing to volunteer for the medical corps, where he "could do good and exercise Christian love of neighbor in concrete ways." If he actually made this offer it was not accepted, and in May he was transferred to the prison at Tegel, outside Berlin, to await trial.

Tegel was a place of misery. The prisoners were kept solitary in small cells, subject to brutal treatment, sometimes crying out in their loneliness and despair—"A foretaste of purgatory and hell" according to Father Reinisch, the executed priest in whose footsteps Jägerstätter was following, though he did not then know of him. Jägerstätter was tried by a military court on July 6, 1943. The officers sitting in judgment respected his courage and integrity and would have spared him had he been willing to relent, as, his attorney later said, they *pleaded* with him to do. He would not. That left no room for leniency: to refuse military service was a capital offense. He was sentenced to death and led away in handcuffs.

He could still have saved his life by agreeing to serve. At his lawyer's urging, Franziska came to Tegel with the priest from St. Radegund three days after the trial to make one last attempt to change his mind. Jägerstätter was not there when they arrived, but from the windows of the waiting room she saw him being driven into the prison courtyard in the back of a truck. He was in chains. As Gordon Zahn described the scene from her account, "Some soldiers jumped out and formed a circle. Then Jägerstätter was pushed out so roughly that he fell to the ground, a sight which caused her to scream his name from the window. Hearing her voice, he jumped to his feet and looked wildly about him—as if, she added, he thought her voice had come from another world. He had not known they were coming to see him."

This vivid glimpse of Franz and Franziska, caught in the agony of their separation, their helplessness, their knowledge of greater pain still to come, stabs us with an apprehension of what they had been living through hour by hour, moment by moment, since the day Jägerstätter left for Enns. We see, in his wildly searching eyes, in her anguished cry, the price of his convictions, to Franziska as well as himself, and the almost unimaginable strength of those convictions, given that he could walk out of that prison simply by signing his name. Both Franziska and the priest tried to convince him to do just this, but finally he could not be persuaded that serving Hitler would not mean his damnation. Their meeting was attended by armed guards. She tried to give him some food she had brought; he was not allowed to take it. After twenty minutes the visit was ended. They never in this world saw each other again. In his letters home he consistently affirmed his faith that in God's love he would be restored to his family forever. May it be so. On August 9, 1943, Franz Jägerstätter was taken to the guillotine and beheaded.

## II

When I was young, and just beginning to read about Nazi Germany's wars of conquest, I used to wonder why the ordinary men of that country had agreed to serve in such an evil enterprise. Over the years the question changed: Would *I* have agreed, had I been alive in that place and time?

I have my answer.

At eighteen, short of a high school diploma and with no prospects in sight, I enlisted in the U.S. Army. This was in the spring of 1964, before the Tonkin Gulf episode, when the U.S. military presence in Vietnam was limited almost entirely to advisers and special forces. We had lost very few men in that struggle, which was represented as the attempt of a communist dictatorship to take over a young democracy. By the time I got my orders in the spring of 1967, we were at war. Tens of thousands of American soldiers had been killed, hundreds of thousands wounded, and the Vietnamese had suffered even greater losses.

Having spent a year studying Vietnamese at the Defense Language Institute in Washington, D.C., I knew enough about the country and its history to make me uneasy with official explanations for our being there. Though I dutifully argued with my brother and civilian friends who opposed the war, my answers began to sound hollow even to me. The more I learned, the more uneasy I became. We were dying and killing for a corrupt government that did not have the support of its own people, whom we were also killing when they got in the way. It did not meet the test of a just and necessary war, or even one we were likely to win.

But I stifled my doubts, because I was going, and doubt would do me no good there. I didn't want to go, and was afraid to go, but I was even more afraid not to go. I couldn't imagine spending years in prison for desertion or seeking asylum in Canada. When the slightest thought of refusing came to mind, I shook it off. I was a highly trained officer by then, a paratrooper, a linguist. I felt honor bound to the men I had served with and would serve with. How could I leave the line they were holding? And how could I live with this in the years to come? Would I lose my self-respect? I would always be suspected of cowardice, and worse, I would suspect myself of cowardice, made more shameful by hiding it behind professions of principle. And, frankly, I was curious. What would it be like? War is interesting to young men— even to those who oppose it.

So I went, I suppose for the same reasons as the great majority of German and Austrian men who obeyed their orders though they were not ardent Nazis and surely harbored doubts of their own. But they had even less room than I for contemplating refusal. There was no large community of war resisters to embrace them, no public debate to give intellectual and historical substance to their misgivings, no Church to encourage opposition to Nazi violence with clear and openly expressed moral teachings, no Canada to take them in. They couldn't even hope for prison—they would be executed, and their families made to suffer.

The wonder is not that so few refused, but that any did. And that makes Franz Jägerstätter not only a heroic figure, but a troubling one. The reasons that were persuasive enough for almost all his countrymen, and later for me, did not convince him. And his steadfast, articulate refusal to accept those reasons throws a hard light on the evasions, special pleadings, tricks of logic, and deliberate deafness and blindness by which we resign ourselves to the pull of circumstances we should resist.

Even when we question it, we tend to think of authority as a power residing in government, the police, the courts, in the hierarchy of whatever church we might belong to—privileged conduits of God's will. But the most influential forces are within us, especially those we don't recognize. Jägerstätter was born and raised in St. Radegund. He made the village his own family's home, farmed there, served as sexton of the local church. Everyone knew everyone else. Everyone was Catholic except for a cousin of Jägerstätter who had become a Jehovah's Witness—a deviation from the norm that only shows how monolithic the norm was. Such a community becomes a sort of organism; to be in it but not of it, to offend its common understandings and expectations, is to risk being seen as a kind of cancer, and severed from its ancient, nourishing bonds. The sense of identity and belonging such a community confers, the habit of consensus, the corollary fear of being judged by your neighbors, all these grow instinctive over the years, and as such can become a decisively coercive force without one's being aware of it.

How did Franz Jägerstätter, a cherished son of his village, find the resolve to defy its collective will, first by voting against the Anschluss, then by continually, dangerously, criticizing its deference to Nazi rule, and finally by refusing to serve? How did he overcome the authority of the village speaking within him, expose himself to censure and his family to ostracism? How lonely it must have been. And lonelier still when the Church he loved treated with the enemy and remained silent in the face of crimes and criminal war, leaving him to speak the truth on his own, with his very life. Thus this loyal Catholic found himself in the position of having to reject the counsel of a succession of priests, even his own bishop, in order to follow his conscience. He knew they were trying to save his life, and he did not blame them, but we can sense the depth of Jägerstätter's isolation in his relief when the prison chaplain told him about the priest who had given his life for the same principles. The chaplain wrote to Franziska, "I have seen no more fortunate man in prison than your husband after my few words about Franz Reinisch."

Imprisoned, alone, without support from his village or Church, where did he find strength to persist? In the knowledge of his wife's love and respect, certainly; though she urged Franz to seek a way to reconcile his conscience with military service, she accepted that he could not, and never reproached him nor withheld her love and support. But beyond that, as in the affirmation Jägerstätter took from Father Reinisch's refusal, we can discern his vision of the Church as having a life and authority beyond the momentary, expedient policies of its hierarchy. The "communion of saints" is a phrase, like "immortal soul," that can roll off the tongue without our giving much thought to what it might mean for us. To Jägerstätter, who continually read and meditated on the lives of saints, it came to mean an actual community— a *living* community in which he could find encouragement, brave example, faith lived out clearly and at any cost, and, finally, as the consequence of his refusal loomed ever nearer, the company in which he hoped to take his place—and, by belated official reckoning, *did* find his place: he was beatified in 2007. This was where he found his true Church, having been left on his own by the compromises and silence of the clerical establishment.

Such faith is both heartening and troubling to those, like me, accustomed to living with ambiguity, distrust of absolutes, the habit of skepticism and doubt. I have taught for some forty years now, and if there has been any one thread running through my teaching, it has been the hope that my students would find value in ideas and arguments that challenge the assumptions they bring to the classroom. From the divinely charged, sacramental world of Flannery O'Connor, discomfiting to the strict secularists among us, we might move to James Baldwin, who gives an account of his youthful religious fervor as rooted not in hope and love but in loneliness and fear, then goes on to mount a relentless critique of the way religion has been used to stifle reason, divide people, console the powerful, and anaesthetize the conscience. Many of my students chafe at these apparently contradictory narratives, even take one or the other of them as a personal affront.

But I hope that they listen, and think, and in time come to recognize possibilities of truth in contesting visions of our condition.

Yet I sometimes wonder whether, in asking students to test their certainties against all comers, I have trespassed; helped to foster not critical thinking and open-mindedness but an excuse for hedging and standing by. How much of this judicious weighing of idea against idea, claim against claim, belief against belief, can we take without losing our capacity for deep faith and courageous action? In short, I worry whether Franz Jägerstätter could have survived a series of teachers like me with enough confidence to be the man I so deeply admire, who put his very life on the line for what he believed—no, *knew*—to be true. Without that knowing he couldn't have done what he did. Would the effect of my teaching, and that of most of my colleagues, prove subversive of such certainty? But I don't know another way to teach, and even in my awe of Jägerstätter's heroism my wariness of absolutism abides. And perhaps I flatter myself; he might well have laughed at my precious ambiguities and gone on his way even more secure in his faith.

Franz Jägerstätter makes me uncomfortable. He made his friends and neighbors uncomfortable. He made priests and bishops uncomfortable, and he would make most Catholics uncomfortable today. He was insistently pious in discourse, even with priests. In his writings he speaks of Adam and Eve as if they were real people, and of heaven as if it were an actual place; no metaphorical readings of scripture for him. He was emphatically opposed to contraception and considered abortion murder. At the same time, though not really a pacifist, he was adamant in his opposition to wars of choice, and we can be sure he'd have plenty to say on the subjects of torture and capital punishment. No one faction can claim him or domesticate him to its own purposes. Taken as he is, with no wishful blurring of the portrait, he will make us all uncomfortable. He wouldn't have minded.

A brief note of acknowledgment: Zahn's book has since been supplemented by several others, most notably *Franz Jägerstätter: Letters and Writings from Prison,* edited by Erna Putz and translated by Robert A. Krieg, with an excellent introduction by Jim Forest.

# SHORT BIOGRAPHIES OF AUTHORS

TOM BEAUDOIN is the associate professor of theology in the Graduate School of Religion and Religious Education at Fordham University, where he teaches and writes about the relationship between religion and culture in practice. His latest book is *Witness to Dispossession: The Vocation of a Postmodern Theologian.*

LISA SOWLE CAHILL is the Monan Professor of Theology at Boston College. Her many articles and books address the Bible and ethics: sex and gender; bioethics; and Catholic ethics and social teaching. Her most recent book is *Global Justice, Christology, and Christian Ethics* (Cambridge University Press, to appear in 2013).

BO CALDWELL is the author of the novels *The Distant Land of My Father* and *City of Tranquil Light.* Her essays and short stories have appeared in *America, The Washington Post Magazine,* and literary journals. She was a Stegner Fellow at Stanford University and the recipient of a National Endowment of the Arts Fellowship.

JAMES CARROLL is the author of six works of nonfiction, including *American Requiem, Constantine's Sword,* and *Prac-*

*ticing Catholic,* and eleven novels, including the forthcoming *Warburg in Rome.* A *Boston Globe* columnist, and Distinguished Scholar-in-Residence at Suffolk University, he lives in Boston with his wife, the novelist Alexandra Marshall.

JOAN CHITTISTER, O.S.B., is a Benedictine nun, the co-chair of the Global Peace Initiative for Women, and the founder of Benetvision. She is a regular contributor to the *Huffington Post* and the *National Catholic Reporter* and the author of forty-five books, the most recent being *Following the Path to Passion, to Purpose, and to Joy.*

PAUL J. CONTINO is the Seaver Professor of Humanities at Pepperdine University and co-editor of *Christianity and Literature.* He has published a number of essays on Dostoevsky, as well as other writers such as Zhuangzi, Dante, and Andre Dubus. He has contributed to *Commonweal, America,* and other magazines and has received the Catholic Press Association Award.

JOHN CORNWELL is a journalist and fellow at Jesus College, Cambridge University, as well as the director of the Science and Human Dimension Project. His many books include *A Thief in the Night, Hitler's Pope,* and most recently, *Newman's Unquiet Grave: The Reluctant Saint.*

CHARLES E. CURRAN is a Catholic priest and the Scurlock University Professor at Southern Methodist University. A distinguished moral theologian, he has presided over three national academic societies. His numerous books include

*Catholic Moral Theology in the United States: A History* and *Loyal Dissent: Memoir of a Catholic Theologian.*

PAUL ELIE, for many years a senior editor with Farrar, Straus and Giroux, is now a senior fellow with Georgetown University's Berkley Center for Religion, Peace, and World Affairs. He is the author of *The Life You Save May Be Your Own: An American Pilgrimage* and *Reinventing Bach*. He edited the anthology *A Tremor of Bliss: Contemporary Writers on the Saints.*

ROBERT ELLSBERG is the publisher of Orbis Books. He has edited three books on Dorothy Day, including *All the Way to Heaven: Selected Letters of Dorothy Day,* as well as anthologies of writings by Gandhi, Flannery O'Connor, Thich Nhat Hanh, and Charles de Foucauld. His own books include *All Saints: Daily Reflections on Saints, Prophets, and Witnesses for Our Time, Blessed Among All Women,* and *The Saints' Guide to Happiness.*

MARY GORDON is the author of seven novels, two story collections, two memoirs, and two works of nonfiction: *Reading Jesus* and *Joan of Arc*. Among her honors are a Guggenheim Fellowship, a Literature Award from the American Academy of Arts and Letters and the Story Prize. She is the McIntosh Professor of English at Barnard College.

PATRICIA HAMPL is the Regents Professor at the University of Minnesota. Her books include the memoirs *Virgin Time* and

*The Florist's Daughter* and the essay collection *I Could Tell You Stories*. Her writing has appeared in many publications, including *The New Yorker,* the *New York Times,* the *Los Angeles Times, Best American Short Stories,* and *Best American Essays.*

RON HANSEN has published eight novels, including *Mariette in Ecstasy, Exiles,* and *A Wild Surge of Guilty Passion;* and he is the author, too, of *A Stay Against Confusion: Essays on Faith and Fiction.* His most recent book is *She Loves Me Not: New and Selected Stories.* He is the Gerard Manley Hopkins, S.J., Professor in the Arts and Humanities at Santa Clara University.

KATHRYN HARRISON is the author of *St. Thérèse of Lisieux;* a collection of personal essays, *Seeking Rapture;* three memoirs, including *The Kiss;* and seven novels. Her essays and reviews have appeared in *The New Yorker, Harper's,* the *New York Times Book Review,* and other publications. She is currently writing a biography about Joan of Arc.

MELINDA HENNEBERGER is a political writer for the *Washington Post* and edits the paper's "She the People" blog, a forum for women writers. Previously, she was editor-in-chief of *Politics Daily* and a Washington correspondent and Rome bureau chief for the *New York Times.*

PAULA HUSTON is the author of seven books, as well as the co-editor and contributing essayist for the collection *Signatures of Grace.* Her work has been honored by Best American Short Stories and anthologized in *Best Spiritual Writing.* She teaches in Seattle Pacific University's MFA program and is a Camaldolese Benedictine oblate.

PATRICK JORDAN was associated with Dorothy Day for the last thirteen years of her life. He and his wife Kathleen met and married at the New York Catholic Worker. He is a former managing editor of the *Catholic Worker* newspaper and of *Commonweal* magazine and edited *Dorothy Day: Writings from Commonweal.*

CATHLEEN KAVENY is the Murphy Foundation Professor of Law and professor of theology at the University of Notre Dame. She has published widely in theology and law journals on issues of law, religion, and morality and serves as a regular columnist for *Commonweal* magazine.

PAUL MARIANI is the University Professor at Boston College. He has received many awards for his poetry and scholarship, including NEA, NEH, and Guggenheim fellowships. He is the author of seventeen books, including *Epitaphs for the Journey: New, Selected & Revised Poems* and *Gerard Manley Hopkins: A Life.*

ROBERT MCCLORY, the emeritus professor of journalism at Northwestern University, is a former Catholic priest, a regular contributor to the *National Catholic Reporter,* and the author of seven books, including *Faithful Dissenters,* and most recently, *Radical Disciple: Father Pfleger, St. Sabina Church, and the Fight for Social Justice.*

ALICE MCDERMOTT, the Macksey Professor at Johns Hopkins University, is the author of six novels, including *Charming Billy,* which received the National Book Award, and her latest, *After This,* a finalist for the 2006 Pulitzer Prize. Her articles, stories, and reviews have appeared in the *New York Times,* the *Atlantic Monthly,* and elsewhere.

ANN PATCHETT is the author of six novels, including *State of Wonder* and *Bel Canto,* which won the PEN/Faulkner Award, and two works of nonfiction, *Truth & Beauty* and *What Now?* Patchett has written for many publications, including the *Atlantic Monthly, Harper's,* the *New York Times, Vogue,* and *The Washington Post.*

JIM SHEPARD is the author of six novels, including most recently *Project X,* and four story collections, including most recently *Like You'd Understand, Anyway* and *You Think That's Bad.* His stories have been included in the Best American, PEN/O. Henry, and Pushcart Prize anthologies. He teaches at Williams College.

MARTHA E. STORTZ is the Christensen Professor at Augsburg College. She studies the practice of pilgrimage, hikes medieval pilgrimage routes, and ponders her travels in a blog, the postmodern version of a pilgrim chronicle. Her many books include *A World According to God* and *Blessed to Follow: The Beatitudes as a Compass for Discipleship.*

COLM TOIBIN's novels include *The Master, Brooklyn,* and *The Testament of Mary.* He is the Irene and Sidney B. Silverberg Professor in the Humanities at Columbia University and a contributing editor at the *London Review of Books*.

TOBIAS WOLFF is the Woods Professor of English at Stanford University and a fellow of the American Academy of Arts and Sciences. He is the author of several collections of short stories, as well as the memoirs *This Boy's Life* and *In Pharaoh's Army,* and the novels *Old School* and *The Barracks Thief.*

# SHORT BIOGRAPHIES OF SUBJECTS

HENRY BARTEL was born in 1873 in Russian Poland and immigrated with his Mennonite family to Hillsboro, Kansas, as a child. He left home in 1899 and married Nellie Schmidt the following year. In November of 1901 they traveled to the interior of China to serve as missionaries, and in 1905 they founded in Tsaohsien the first Mennonite mission in China, which in 1913 became the China Mennonite Mission Society. Dedicated to spreading the gospel in China, the Bartels lived and worked in Tsaohsien for thirty-six years before moving to northwest China, where they helped to establish two additional Mennonite missions. The couple raised five children, all of whom served as missionaries in Asia. In 1952, after fifty years of service in China, Henry Bartel left China under pressure from the communist government. He returned to his childhood home in Kansas and died there in 1965.

JOHN BERRYMAN was born in Oklahoma in 1914. His mother was a schoolteacher; his father a banker who, after two years of failed land speculation, killed himself in 1926. In 1939, after attending Columbia and Cambridge, Berryman moved to Detroit, where he taught at Wayne State University and worked as poetry editor for *The Nation*. He taught and lectured at several universities, including the Iowa Writers' Workshop, Harvard, Princeton, Brown, and the University of Minnesota.

His significant literary contribution was in the field of confessional poetry. His many notable books include 77 *Dream Songs* (which won the 1965 Pulitzer Prize) and *Berryman's Sonnets*, for which he received awards from the Academy of American Poets and the National Endowment for the Arts. *His Toy, His Dream, His Rest* won the National Book Award and the Bollingen Prize. Berryman's last book was the autobiographical *Recovery,* an account of his struggle with alcoholism. Berryman died in 1972.

MICHELANGELO MERISI DI CARAVAGGIO was born in 1571 in northern Italy. His revolutionary artistic genius earned acclaim from his early debut in Rome to his later wanderings through Sicily, Malta, and elsewhere. Caravaggio's use of *chiaroscuro* involved a rich contrast between dark and light and inspired a following of artists and patrons. He painted both the profane and the sacred: *The Musicians* and *The Fortune Teller* on the one hand, *The Conversion of Paul* and *The Calling of St. Matthew* on the other. His religious scenes reveal a radiant spirituality found in the gritty reality of sixteenth-century Rome and its inhabitants.

Despite the religious fervor that infuses so many of his paintings, Caravaggio's personal life was that of the demimonde; he drank and brawled and was involved in a murder, for which he was exiled. He died under mysterious circumstances in 1610.

BARTOLOMÉ DE LAS CASAS was born c. 1484 to a noble Basque family in Seville. Las Casas traveled to South America to pursue his fortune. In Hispaniola, he owned a large hacienda and a number of indentured servants. However, he became troubled by the brutal treatment of the Native people by the Spaniards, and in 1514, he gave up his land and slaves. He became a Dominican priest and devoted himself to the cause of fair treatment for the Natives of the Spanish colonialized territories. In 1543, Las Casas became bishop of impoverished Chiapas, although opposition to his efforts to prevent the enslavement and mistreatment of the Native people eventually forced him to return to Spain.

Las Casas authored *A Short Account of the Destruction of the Indies, Apologetic History of the Indies,* and *History of the Indies.* He died in Madrid in 1566.

DOROTHY DAY was born in Brooklyn in 1897. She spent part of her childhood in Chicago, where she was baptized an Episcopalian. She gave up all religion as a young woman, but after much searching and the birth of her daughter, converted to Catholicism in 1927. A journalist by profession, she was also a pacifist and activist who worked all her life for societal change and for the poor. During the Great Depression, she and Peter Maurin founded the Catholic Worker movement in New York City. Her account of her personal journey is the classic *The Long Loneliness.*

There are now more than two hundred Catholic Worker houses of hospitality in the United States and abroad—in both inner-city and rural locations. Day traveled widely throughout her life, speaking, writing, and demonstrating. Her last arrest was in California for supporting the cause of striking farmworkers (she was seventy-five). She died in New York in 1980. Her canonization process was introduced in Rome in 2000.

BEDE GRIFFITHS was born Alan Richard Griffiths at Walton-on-Thames in 1906. He converted to Catholicism in 1931; less than a year later, he entered the Benedictines as a novice and took the name Bede ("prayer.")

Beginning in 1955, Griffiths spent three years at Kengeri, Bangalore. There he founded the Kurisumala Ashram (Mountain of the Cross Monastery) and established himself as a proponent of major Catholic doctrinal reform. He advocated interfaith communities and Christian–Hindu contextualism as well as Christian theological reform that addressed gender and sexual orientation in a more enlightened fashion. He stressed that the Christian faith had much to learn from Eastern mysticism and modern science and that the Catholic Church should be more concerned with love than sin.

Griffiths published numerous books of spirituality and traveled the world offering his teachings and lectures, meeting with the Dalai Lama in Australia. In India, he was known as Swami Dayananda ("bliss of compassion"). Griffiths died in 1993.

BERNARD HÄRING was born in 1912 in Böttingen, Germany. He entered the seminary at twelve and was ordained as a Redemptorist priest in 1939. Häring was conscripted by the Nazis during World War II and served as a medic. He received his doctorate in theology from Tübingen University, taught at the Redemptorist theologate in Gars, and in the 1950s was assigned to teach moral theology at Alphonsian Academy in Rome, where he taught for thirty years. Häring was an influential advisor at the Second Vatican Council, contributing especially to the document on The Church in the Modern World.

In 1954, Häring published *The Law of Christ,* considered a landmark work in Catholic moral theology, along with his later three-volume *Free and Faithful in Christ.* After the publication of *Humanae Vitae,* Häring was a vocal advocate for removing the prohibition on artificial contraception and was later investigated by the Vatican for his views on medical ethics. He remained throughout his career a loving critic of the Church. Häring died in 1998.

ISAAC HECKER was born in 1819 to German immigrants in New York City. He was briefly a member of the Brook Farm collective before being baptized into the Catholic Church in 1844.

He later entered the Redemptorist order, and became a priest in 1849.

In 1857, Hecker visited Rome to propose a self-governed order of missionaries to America that would emphasize service to the community and individual freedom. In 1858, the Missionary Society of St. Paul the Apostle was founded in New York City. Hecker made a point of utilizing the popular media of the day: he established a journal, *The Catholic World,* and what is now the book publisher Paulist Press.

Hecker served as a theologian during the First Vatican

Council from 1869 to 1870. His emphasis on the importance of the Holy Spirit and individual faith was to come to fruition at Vatican II. He returned to New York, hoping to continue his work, but was invalided until his death in 1888.

HILDEGARD VON BINGEN, born in 1098 in Bermersheim, Germany, was raised by the anchoress Jutta von Spanheim from the age of eight, joining her convent while in her teens. Hildegard lived her first thirty years in near-total isolation as an anchoress and cloistered nun and was elected on Jutta's death to become abbess of the convent. In 1147, with a growing band of disciples, she established her own independent women's community. She was fearless in the face of the most powerful men of her day, criticizing Church officials (including the pope), kings, and emperors.

Hildegard was an extraordinary polymath, and one of the foremost female mystics of the Catholic Church. Though she attributed her work and skill to divine intervention and visions, her work in every field, from music to mathematics, is that of a disciplined, refined intellect. Hildegard, who died in 1179, is honored as a saint by the Catholic, Episcopal, and Anglican Churches.

GERARD MANLEY HOPKINS, born to a devout High Anglican family in Stratford, Essex, in 1844, was educated at Oxford University. Having converted to Catholicism, Hopkins entered the Jesuit order and eventually taught Greek and Latin at University College, Dublin. His life would be marked by profound conflicts between his prodigious intellect and his attraction to ascetic and self-denying religious practices. Indeed he experienced considerable anxiety over the spiritual implications of poetry writing, at one point burning all his works.

He began writing again in 1875, with his poem "The Wreck of the Deutschland," an account of a shipwreck in which five Franciscan nuns were drowned. In this poem, Hopkins introduced "sprung rhythm," one of the techniques he espoused to enliven poetic language. Hopkins suffered from depression and died of typhoid fever in 1889. His work was published posthumously by his lifelong friend and patron, the poet Robert Bridges.

IGNATIUS OF LOYOLA, baptized Íñigo, was born in 1491 to a noble Basque family. After being seriously wounded in battle, he underwent a profound conversion experience. During his subsequent studies in Paris, he formed a small society dedicated to poverty, chastity, and the Spiritual Exercises he had developed during his time of public ministry in Spain.

This small group of fellow students was to become the Society of Jesus, known also as the Jesuits, noted for their missionary outreach, their intellectual rigor, the schools and universities they founded, and, more recently, their influence on the liberation theology movement in Latin America. Ignatius was a key figure of the Counter-Reformation: his work in founding the Jesuits and composing the Spiritual Exercises, still practiced widely today, establishes him as a pivotal figure in bringing the Catholic Church into the modern age. Ignatius died in 1556 and was canonized in 1622.

FRANZ JÄGERSTÄTTER was born in Upper Austria in 1907. His mother, Rosalia Huber, bore him out of wedlock; his father was killed in World War I. In 1917, she married Heinrich Jägerstätter, who adopted Franz. Franz worked as a farmhand and miner in Eisenerz until 1933, when he inherited his adoptive father's land; three years later he married Franziska Schwaninger, with whom he had three daughters.

During the Anschluss, Jägerstätter was the only member of his village to vote against Nazi occupation. When conscripted for military service, he found the order incompatible with his political and religious views and persisted in his conscientious objections despite the efforts of his family and various clergymen to convince him to serve. He wrote from prison: "Our bond with God must be stronger than our love of our family and relatives." Jägerstätter was beheaded in 1943, and beatified in 2007.

JOAN OF ARC was born in 1412 and grew up in the village of Domrémy, in Lorraine. The Hundred Years War had devastated France; everything north of the Loire, including Paris, was occupied by the English. Joan was twelve when she first received what she described as "a voice from God to help her and guide her" to accomplish what they told her was God's will: she was to lead her people to victory and restore the throne to its rightful heir.

Assisted by her heavenly counsel, at seventeen, Joan led the French army to military victories remarkable for a seasoned general, let alone an ignorant peasant girl. Most notably, she raised the siege of Orléans, allowing Charles VII to proceed to Reims, where he was crowned king.

A year later, Joan was captured and sold to the English. Condemned as a heretic, she was sentenced to die if she refused to admit her accomplishments were the result of sorcery, and was twice escorted to the stake. The first time, afraid of the fire, she confessed she had been deceived by demonic forces, but within a week she recanted, realizing she had damned her soul to save her body. On May 30, 1431, Joan of Arc was burned to death, a relapsed heretic. She was canonized in 1920, soon after the rediscovery of her trial records proved her innocence.

CORITA KENT was born in Iowa in 1918. After high school, she entered the Sisters of the Immaculate Heart of Mary. She studied studio art, and also received a master's degree in art history from the University of Southern California in 1951. She taught at Immaculate Heart College and lived as a sister until she left the order in 1968, during a time when the sisters were heavily censured by the Church hierarchy for enacting the reforms called for by the Second Vatican Council.

Corita's images were lively, brightly colored, full of images from popular culture. They were the expression of an untrammeled joy in life and of an essentially free spirit. She was the author or co-author of several books documenting her work, such as *Learning by Heart: Teachings to Free the Creative Spirit*. Corita lived in Boston during the last years of her life and died there in 1986.

MARTIN LUTHER was born in 1483 in Eisleben, Germany. Luther studied law briefly at the University of Erfurt, before entering the order of the Augustinian Eremites in 1505.

In 1517, he sent his "Ninety-Five Theses" to Archbishop Albrecht of Mainz and Magdeburg, complaining about the local sales of indulgences. Luther's theology also challenged Church doctrine: salvation could not be earned by good works or charity and was only given by God. All Christians had the same relationship with God, rather than priests holding a more privileged position than laypeople.

Luther rejected papal authority, and after his public burning of a papal bull and refusal to recant at the Diet of Worms, Luther was declared an outlaw and heretic. While in hiding, he translated the Latin Bible into the German vernacular, a revolutionary act that underscored his egalitarian religious views. The religious controversy became political as Luther gained popular support and powerful allies, plunging Europe into the wars of the Protestant Reformation. Luther died in 1546.

MOTHER MARY MACKILLOP was born in Victoria, Australia, in 1842. She founded the order of Sisters of Saint Joseph of the Sacred Heart, which despite a series of conflicts with Church authorities in Australia was approved as a canonical congregation by Pope Leo XIII in 1888. The sisters built and maintained numerous schools and establishments for the poor throughout Australia, New South Wales, and New Zealand.

Along with her sisters, Mother MacKillop protested the sexual abuse of children by a local priest and as a result was excommunicated in 1871 by her local bishop for insubordination. He died not long after, revoking the punishment on his deathbed. Mother MacKillop continued her work among the poor until she died, still mother superior-general of her order, in 1909. The first Australian saint, she was canonized in 2010.

MARY MAGDALENE, or Mary of Magdala, occupies a uniquely powerful place in both canonical and noncanonical gospels: a loyal disciple of Jesus and recipient of his healing powers (cured of "seven demons," Luke 8:2). She was present at the crucifixion and burial in the Gospels of Matthew, Mark, and John; she is also identified as the primary witness to the resurrection in Matthew, John, and the appendix to the Gospel of Mark.

In noncanonical gospels, Mary is identified as a spiritual leader and Jesus's best-loved and wisest disciple. These texts identifying the special power and wisdom of Mary Magdalene were eventually proclaimed not only apocryphal but heretical. In 591, Pope Gregory introduced the view that Mary was a converted prostitute, though there is no textual basis to support this claim. In addition, she was conflated with an unnamed sinner in Luke and with Mary of Bethany, with the resulting minimization of her role in Jesus's life and teachings.

FATHER HORACE MCKENNA, S.J., was born into a large family in New York City in 1899 and entered the seminary at St. Andrew-on-the-Hudson in 1916. He taught in the Philippine missions, then at Boston College High School, before his ordination as a Jesuit priest in 1929. In 1931, he began twenty-five years of service as pastor of St. Peter Claver Church in Ridge, Maryland, during which time he worked tirelessly to integrate the parish. He was appointed in 1953 to the position of assistant pastor of St. Aloysius Church in Washington, D.C. From 1968 to 1969, subsequent to *Humanae Vitae,* McKenna was forbidden to hear confession because of his belief that the use of artificial contraception should be a matter of individual conscience.

McKenna's work with the impoverished people of southern Maryland and inner-city Washington, D.C., took on a life of its own in 1977. This was the year that McKenna founded the charitable organization So Others Might Eat (SOME). SOME began as a simple soup kitchen but was methodically expanded to provide medical and counseling services. McKenna also worked to provide low-income housing, such as the Sursum Corda housing project. He died in 1982.

MICHEL MONTAIGNE, author of the *Essais,* was born in 1533, at the Château de Montaigne, and died there in 1592. In addition to a tragic family life, Montaigne's stint in the Catholic army fighting the French Wars of Religion left him with a horror of violence and a sensitivity to the suffering of others.

As mayor of Bordeaux, he worked to end the Wars of Religion, moderating between the kings and aristocratic houses. He did not consider his Catholic faith an obstacle to reconciling with Protestants, preferring to work for peace over ideological purity. On the assassination of King Henri III in 1589, Montaigne helped to keep Bordeaux loyal to Henry of Navarre, later King Henri IV.

Montaigne's heart is preserved in the parish church of Saint-Michel-de-Montaigne.

OSCAR ROMERO, born in El Salvador in 1917, was ordained a priest in Rome. He returned to his homeland in 1943 to spend twenty years working in the province of San Miguel. Around him, political turmoil raged; the strain of Honduran refugees, a serious oil crisis, and general economic inequality were seriously threatening the government's stability.

Romero became a bishop in 1977 and saw the effects of the civil war immediately. Within his first week, his friend Rutilio Grande, S.J., was murdered, and Romero became personally involved in the struggles of his people. He first urged the United States to withdraw troops and funding, a request that went unanswered, and finally turned to the El Salvadoran army, calling on them to resist orders and stop terrorizing and massacring the population. A week later, on March 24, 1980, he was shot by an assassin, in the heart, as he was consecrating the host during Mass.

MAX SCHELER was born in 1874 to a Lutheran father and Orthodox Jewish mother and converted to Catholicism as a teenager. He was educated at the University of Jena, where he stayed to teach before moving on to Munich and Göttingen. As a philosopher, Scheler developed the phenomenology of Husserl and emphasized process over unchangeable universal concepts. His vision of a Catholic renaissance in Europe anticipated the Second Vatican Council. His work continues to influence Catholic thinkers; Pope John Paul II (then Karol Wojtyla) wrote his doctoral thesis on Scheler in 1954.

Scheler's major works include *Man's Place in Nature, Problems of a Sociology of Knowledge,* and *The Nature of Sympathy.* In 1921, Scheler cut ties with the Catholic Church, publicly dissociating himself from the Judeo-Christian concept of God. He died in 1928.

EDWARD SCHILLEBEECKX was born in Antwerp in 1914. After brief military service, he was ordained a Dominican priest. He studied at the University of the Louvain and joined the theological faculty at the Catholic University of Nijmegen in 1958, where he taught until his death in 2009. Schillebeeckx served as an advisor to the Dutch bishops, playing a key role in the development of the documents of the Second Vatican Council, such as The Dogmatic Constitution on the Church, as well as the *New Dutch Catechism,* published in 1966.

Schillebeeckx was a prolific author: among his influential books are *Jesus: An Experiment in Christology* and *The Language of Faith: Essays on Jesus, Theology, and the Church.* From 1968 to 1981, he was investigated by the Vatican three times for heresy, with inconclusive results. Schillebeeckx retired from Nijmegen in 1982, the year he received the Erasmus Prize. He died in 2009.

MONSIGNOR JOHN V. SHERIDAN was born in 1915, in County Longford, Ireland. He suffered from poor health and nearly died of tuberculosis in 1934. A few years later, still in a frail condition, he moved to Southern California and entered the inaugural class at St. John's Seminary in Camarillo, graduating in 1943.

Once ordained, Sheridan began his pastoral work in the Catholic Archdiocese of Los Angeles. He became a figure in the Catholic media in the 1950s, hosting a radio show and running a column in *The Tidings* called "Question Box." This would produce a book, *Questions and Answers on the Catholic Faith,* which he published in 1963. Over the course of his career, Sheridan wrote numerous books on faith and the Church. In 1965, he became the beloved pastor at Our Lady of Malibu, where he served until his death in 2010.

CHARLES STROBEL was born in Nashville, Tennessee, in 1943. He studied at Catholic University and was ordained a priest in 1970. After opening the Knoxville office of the National Conference of Christians and Jews, he served as a parish priest. In 1986, he founded an ecumenical ministry to the homeless, known as Room In the Inn.

In 1992, Strobel published *Room In the Inn: Ways Your Congregation Can Help Homeless People.* Today, Room In the Inn's Campus for Human Development is a religious non-profit organization, formed by the merger of three organizations: Room In the Inn, the Guest House, and FOCUS (Faith Organizations in Covenant for Understanding and Service). Each year, more than two hundred congregations working in partnership serve more than twelve hundred homeless people during the winter, with a variety of programs including respite care, veterans' outreach, education, and basic support services.

GEORGE TYRRELL was born in Dublin in 1861 and was raised an Evangelical Protestant but converted to Roman Catholicism in 1879. At nineteen he entered the Society of Jesus in London, and was ordained a priest in 1891. He first taught philosophy at Stonyhurst College in Lancashire, then moved back to London to write for the Jesuit journal *The Month*.

In his books and articles, Tyrrell called for a Church that would be more in tune with the spirit of the times, but reactionaries in the Holy See consigned the Jesuit's publications to the Index of Forbidden Books, and in a 1907 encyclical Pope Pius X condemned the "errors" of Tyrrell and other modernists. Soon after that Tyrrell was excommunicated, and in 1909 he died.

Tyrrell was denied burial in a Catholic cemetery, but his thought would be influential in the updating of the Church at the Second Vatican Council.

SIMONE WEIL was born in Paris in 1909 and quickly distinguished herself as a brilliant scholar and teacher. She wrote many essays and books, including *Gravity and Grace,* a collection of writings from her notebooks, and *The Need for Roots.* Profoundly touched by a series of mystical experiences in the late 1930s, Weil was drawn to Catholicism but ultimately did not accept baptism due to the Church's declared monopoly on the truth.

Weil was deeply moved by the suffering of others, which inspired her many extraordinary demonstrations of solidarity: with the anarchists in the Spanish Civil War, with Vietnamese and Algerian exiles living in Paris, with French laborers, and with her French compatriots threatened by the Nazis. Always frail, her exertions on their behalf took a toll on her health. While Weil was in England working for the Free French, she succumbed to tuberculosis, and died in 1943.

# ACKNOWLEDGMENTS

For all their help and encouragement I am particularly grateful to Martha Stortz, Tobias Wolff, and our daughter, M. Francis Wolff, who contributed the short subject biographies. Thanks to Amanda Urban for finding us our fine publisher, and to Jeanette Perez for teaching me how to edit a book. Thanks also to Ron Hansen, Bo Caldwell, and all the other writers who not only contributed essays but also shared their wise counsel and friendship. It is my hope that we will inspire our readers to find their companions, and their own place, in the communion of saints.